Tasting Hawai'i

VEGAN STYLE

ABOUT LILLIAN CUMIC'S FIRST BOOK, *HAWAI'I A VEGAN PARADISE*

"Cumic understands local flavors…She provides her takes on common nonmeat dishes such as chili garlic edamame, potato mac salad, vegetable tempura and haupia. But there are also vegan versions for tacos, noodles, pizza, no-bake cheesecake and even loco moco….one of the most useful aspects of the book are "foundational" recipes that keep the dishes interesting to all palates."

— Joleen Oshiro, CRAVE, *Honolulu Star-Advertiser*

"This book is full of local favorites using those trendy genius vegetable tricks that chefs are inventing nowadays. I just started cooking from this book, and so far everything has been super delicious. I'm excited to try the Spamish Musubi and the 'Ulu Croquettes. And there are vegan cakes and cocktails, too!"

—*Honolulu Magazine*, Mariko Merritt, illustrator and bookseller at Da Shop: Books + Curiosities

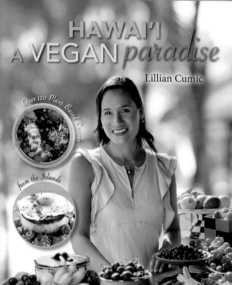

"Fresh From Hawaii. Get ready to add a Pacific twist to your cooking as Lillian Cumic treats us to three recipes with Hawaiian flavors and ingredients."

— Featured in the UK's best-selling magazine, *Vegan Food and Living*, Feb 2021 issue

"With the release of her first cookbook, world-renowned vegan chef Lillian Cumic extols what she sees as the real utopia for healthy eating: Hawai'i."

—Paige Takeya, *MidWeek*

Tasting Hawai'i
VEGAN STYLE

OVER 120 PLANT-BASED AND GLUTEN-FREE RECIPES

LILLIAN CUMIC

Mutual Publishing

ISBN: 978-1-949307-27-6
Library of Congress Control Number: 2021942142

Design by Jane Gillespie
First Printing, October 2021

Mutual Publishing, LLC
1215 Center Street, Suite 210
Honolulu, Hawai'i 96816
Ph: (808) 732-1709 / Fax: (808) 734-4094
e-mail: info@mutualpublishing.com / www.mutualpublishing.com

Printed in South Korea

DEDICATION

For Lulu,
who inspires me to
keep saving animals,
one delicious
vegan plate at a time.

CONTENTS

FOREWORD by Brian Rashid x

FOREWORD by Peter Pawling xi

ACKNOWLEDGMENTS xii

INTRODUCTION 1

The Vegan Life................................ 2

Hawaiian Food................................ 2

Vegan Food 3

Baby Steps 4

Gluten-Free 5

Farmers Markets 7

Kitchen Tools 8

Stocking Your Vegan Pantry.................. 8

Reg Flag Ingredients 10

Is Your Medication Vegan? 10

Alcohol 11

Do the Research 11

Know Your Nutrients........................ 12

How To Use This Book....................... 14

Dining Out.................................. 17

Progress Over Perfection.................... 18

The Spirit of Aloha.......................... 19

FAVORITE CONDIMENTS
GONE VEGAN ⤳ 21

Choose Your Mac Parm 23

Japanese Furikake.......................... 24

Spicy Chili Crisp........................... 25

Nutty Butter................................ 26

Oil-Free Tofu Mayo 28

Thai Basil Pesto 31

Garlic Confit 32

Hawaiian Chili Pepper Water 33

Worcestershire Sauce 34

Baked Potato Wedges.......................... 34

XO Sauce.................................... 36

Roasted XO Asparagus 37

XO Edamame 37

Spicy Cold XO Tofu 37

Vegan Honey 38

Hot Honey 38

Pineapple Ginger Honey 38

COCKTAIL HOUR PŪPŪ ⤳ 41

Bang Bang Broccoli 42

Beet These Arancini 44

Stuffed Mini Peppers 47

Phishcakes with Sweet Chili Sauce 48

Sweet Chili Sauce 49

Tater Stacks................................ 50

Miso Yaki Grilled Tofu 51

Crispy Baked Tofu.......................... 53

Choy Sum with Dengaku Sauce 54

Mushroom Walnut Pâté 55

Sun-Dried Tomato and Sun-Dried
    Tomato Cashew Butter 56

Darry & Lee's Sangria 57

Dave's Hydro Gin........................... 58

Candied Ginger............................. 59

BY THE BEACH ⤳ 61

Candied Hurricane Glaze
    Done 3 Ways 62

Candied Hurricane Popcorn
    with Pecans 62

Candied Hurricane Sweet Potato 64

Candied Hurricane Crispy Tofu.............. 65

Peanut Butter Oat Bites 66

Corn Ribs.................................. 67

Mac Parm Kale Chips 68

Vegan "Scallop" Roll 69
Carrot Smoked "Salmon" and Cashew
     Cream Cheese 71
Cashew Cream Cheese 72
Chuna Sandie 73
Lobsta Roll...................................... 74
Corn Okra Fritters 76
Oyster Bacon Chickpea Frittata............... 78

BEYOND POKE VEGAN STYLE ⮑ 81

Poke Dressing.................................. 82
Roasted Kabocha Poke 83
Beetiful Poke 84
Crispy Tofu Watercress Poke 85
Mushroom Poke 86
Edamame "'Ahi" Poke 86
Okra Natto Poke................................ 86
Watermelon Chuna Poke Bowl................ 87
Watermelon Chuna Poke 87
Cucumber Sukemono 89
Wasabi Mayo Dressing 89

THE SOUPA BOWL ⮑ 91

Almost Borscht Roasted Beet Soup 93
Cashew Cheese of Mushroom Soup 94
Creamy Charred Brussels Sprouts Soup... 96
Curry Kabocha Soup 99
Da Hawaiian Taro Spinach Soup 101
Japanese Curry Broth for Soups,
     Stews, and Noodles........................... 103
Japanese Nabe with Kombu
     Dashi Broth 104
Lemony Cream of Broccoli 106
Pea, Basil, and Mint Soup........................ 107
Rich Cauliflower Potage 108
Roasted Corn Chowder............................ 111

Roasted Eggplant and Chickpea Soup... 112

Sweet Potato and Black Bean Soup 115

Soup To Go 116

EXOTIC SALADS OF THE ISLANDS ⇝119

Paradise Salad 120

Spinach and Orange Quinoa Salad........ 122

Lomi Bell Pepper " 'Ahi" Avocado 124

Grilled Watermelon and Tofeta Salad
  with Balsamic Glaze 125

Crunchy Warm Cheese and Spinach
  Romaine Salad.................................... 127

Tea Leaf Salad 128

Kale Slaw Potato Salad.......................... 130

Tofu Egg and Corn Macaroni Salad........ 131

Island-Style Potato Salad...................... 132

A Wonderful World of Pickles................ 134

Green Avocado Pickles.......................... 134

ALL ABOUT THE SAUCE ⇝137

Bok Choy Noodles with Creamy XO
  Sauce 139

Charred Brussels with Cranberries
  and XO Sauce..................................... 140

Baked Okinawan Sweet Potato with
  Garlic Herb Butter.............................. 141

Cauliflower Steak with Cheese
  Peppercorn Sauce 142

Chinese Stir-Fry 145

Crispy Tofu Pockets with Dashi Sauce 146

Twice Frozen Tofu Skewers with Peanut
  Dipping Sauce 148

Peanut Dipping Sauce........................... 149

Bahn Mi with Sesame Ginger Tofu 150

Lemon Zucchini Pasta with Thai
  Basil Pesto 153

THIS CHEESE IS NUTS! ⇝155

Cashew Brie... 156

Cashew Mockarella................................. 158

Chocolate Chili Cheese.......................... 159

Cashew Cheese Sauce and Cheese
  Fondue 160

Sun-Dried Tomato Cheese with Furikake 162

Caprese Tartare 164

Pistachio Mac-Crusted Cheese.............. 165

Tofeta Platter 166

Tofeta In Oil.. 166

Baked Tofeta... 167

Cheesy Veggie Greatin........................... 169

Baked Mac and Cheese with Tofu
  Bacon Bits... 170

Baked Tofeta Pasta 173

FOR THE CURIOUS COOK ⇝175

Chik'n Hekka.. 176

Chik'n Nuggets...................................... 179

Crispy Oyster Chik'n.............................. 180

Bluffalo "Drumsticks" 183

Smoky Tofu Supam 185

Kalua Porky Plate with Spicy Pineapple.. 187

Porky Bean Croquettes.......................... 188

King Oyster "Ribs" 191

Moxtail Stew... 192

Cavender's Seasoning 196

George's Vegnog.................................... 197

Conpoy Dried "Scallop" 198

BBQ Mushroom "Steak" with
  Cauliflower Mash 199

Pulled Mushroom "Pork" Tacos with
  Teriyaki Sauce 202

Mushroom Jerky 204

Eggplant Unagi Don.............................. 206
Sushi Rice 207
King Oyster "Calamari" 208
Lemon Dipping Sauce 209
Orange Teriyaki "Scallops" with Japanese
    Dashi Rice 210
Japanese Dashi Rice.............................. 211
Poi 212

LIFE'S LITTLE LUXURIES ❧ 215

Haupia and Meyer Lemon Curd 216
Dalgona Whipped Coffee 218
Custard with Spicy Pineapple 219
Berry Chia Pudding 220
Avocado Chocolate Mousse 222
Chocolate Covered Strawberries........... 223
Mermaid Açai Bowl 225
Crunchy Granola.................................... 226
Lemon Berry Oatmeal Bars 227
Stuffed Dates.. 228
Chocolate Sauce 228
Chocolate Bark 230
PB&J Cookie Sandwich 232
Berry Chia Jelly..................................... 233
Impossible Snicky Bites 235
Rocky Beach Road 236
Pumpkin Pie Slice 237
Baked Vegan Cheesecake with
    Macadamia Nut Crust........................... 238

GLOSSARY AND SUBSTITUTIONS........ 240
INDEX 246
ABOUT THE AUTHOR 258

FOREWORD

When I went vegan years ago, I had a major concern. I was worried I would miss out on the culture of food, alienate myself from the celebration of new dishes and gatherings with people from around the world to try their favorite local cuisine. As a global traveler and human deeply passionate about food and exploring new cultures, I feared that a plant-based lifestyle would close doors and limit my experiences. Today I am thrilled to tell you, I was wrong.

In fact, the opposite started happening. I discovered hundreds of new unique fruits, vegetables, spices, local treats, and small businesses. I met countless people exploring the vegan lifestyle with the same level of passion for food. I tasted truly creative dishes that delighted my senses in inexplicable ways. I became part of something special—a community of compassionate eaters, chefs, restaurants, cafes, small business owners, and entrepreneurs who were redefining culture through their food creations and choices. Doors were not closing, worlds were opening.

Lillian is a perfect example of a beautiful human being and pioneer who has dedicated herself to showing us what's possible. Through her work, she educates and empowers us to continue enjoying all of the cultural staples and favorites of a glorious place like Hawai'i, vegan-style. If you've ever tasted her teriyaki pineapple burger, oyster mushroom "scallops," or jackfruit sliders, you don't need much more convincing of her talent. Lillian brings a level of love, high-frequency energy, and out-of-the-box brilliance to ensuring that every plate is a party and every dish a delight.

Whether you live on a Hawaiian island, on the mainland, or in some other magical far-off land, everything this author and her book represent can be appreciated and incorporated into your life—good food, good vibes, and good people.

If you have picked up this book, you are in for a beautiful journey full of health, kindness, creativity, sensory pleasure, and the countless doors that will open for you. What a gift to enjoy the bread we break and those we have to break it with. So, whether you eat at a party of one, or gather around a crowded table, may you always be nourished, may you always be delighted. May you always be "full."

Brian Rashid
Founder and CEO
Brian Rashid Global

FOREWORD

*L*et me start by saying I am a meat and seafood lover. Before I met Chef Lillian Cumic, I don't recall ever having eaten vegan cooking. Once I tasted her vegan cooking, I had a whole new appreciation for the plant-based diet, from the preparation to the end result. I have sampled countless vegan dishes prepared by Lillian and have never been disappointed. I honestly didn't know vegan cooking could taste so good and her presentation rivals any five-star restaurant.

Furthermore, during my travels, I couldn't help but notice that plant-based options are catching on in restaurants all over the country. Lillian's latest cookbook, *Tasting Hawai'i Vegan Style*, is leading the way as it binds the unique taste of Island cooking with a wide variety of trending dishes and vegan options. The recipes are laid out in such a way that anyone can prepare a scrumptious plant-based and gluten-free Hawaiian-inspired dish at home.

From the moment Lillian arrived, she has taken Hawai'i by storm in a very short time, enlightening so many of us to the wonders and health benefits of the plant-based diet. I have no doubt her second book will encourage more people to eat more plant-based and more consciously in harmony with the aloha spirit.

Peter Pawling
Major General (Ret)

ACKNOWLEDGMENTS

I'm eternally grateful to all the people who make the world a better place and inspire me to keep promoting the vegan lifestyle.

I have to start by thanking my extraordinary husband and best friend, Dave Molinaro. None of this would have been possible without "Mr. Wonderful." From reading early drafts to giving me advice on recipes to taking the cover shot and making sure my glass of bubbles is always chilled come sunset time on the lānai. Your undeniable support is breathtaking, and this book would never have reached its full potential without you. You inspire me to live greatly. Lulu says stop chasing her around. It's not funny. *Ai shiteruyo.*

Much love to my family in Sydney who did not buy a copy of my first book but are waiting for me to bring them free copies next time I visit. My nephews, Hudson, Marlon, Chad, and Liam, who make me so proud to be their favorite Auntie. You don't have to say it, I just know. Mummy, thanks for being there throughout these months. I get you just wanted to talk to Lulu during our tea breaks, but I enjoyed them anyway. The Chuna Sandie recipe is for you. Love you to bits! Tell my brother, Frank, he owes me dinner.

A huge mahalo to my 'ohana in Hawai'i. My neighbors and friends who always make sure I have something to eat at our get-togethers and spoil me with vegan goodies. How you pulled off the surprise book launch party for *Hawai'i A Vegan Paradise* was nothing short of sneaky and absolutely brilliant! Your support and encouragement are beyond words. George is the favorite, though. I mean, his wine!

Thank you to Peter Pawling and his wife, Marcia Anderson, for co-writing the Foreword. You live life greatly and are an inspiration to us all. Also, many thanks to Brian Rashid for sharing your vegan journey in the Foreword. The Big Island is lucky to have you!

To my Facebook and Instagram friends, some of whom I've never met but have built warm friendships with that are definitely "real." You guys rock!

Special thanks to:

Mutual Publishing, for going another round with me—publisher, Bennett Hymer, whose support for local writers is encouraging and motivating; production director Jane Gillespie, the greatest editor and layout designer I could ever imagine. Glad I get to do this with you again! And thanks again to Lili and Ella of Hamburg, Germany, for getting their grandfather interested in vegan eating and cooking.

Joleen Oshiro, CRAVE Magazine Food Editor—the foreword you wrote for my first book was amazing! Thank you for the wonderful article and review in CRAVE.

Ron Nagasawa, *MidWeek* Director of Content—Thank you so much for setting up the cover feature story in *MidWeek*. What an honor. Your weekly stories are a hoot and my weekly entertainment by the pool!

Paige Takeya, *MidWeek* writer—Many thanks for the amazing cover story you wrote about my first book. I've never been prouder in my life, and it was released just in time for the holidays which helped immensely in getting it into a lot of Christmas stockings around the nation.

Jay Fidell, ThinkTech Hawaii Founder, President and CEO—It's an honor being a host and part of the ThinkTech team. Having a platform to share my passion for the vegan lifestyle to the world is something I do not take for granted.

Finally, sincere thanks to the people of Hawai'i and everyone who enjoyed my first book. Your wonderful comments, messages, and online reviews bring tears to my eyes. There are no words for how grateful and blessed I am by your love and support. Thank you for encouraging me to write another one. This is for you!

Fresh Exc
Island Fru

Apple Banana
🍍 Sweet Pinea
Mango 🍎 Lyche
🌰 Rambutan
Soursop Papa

INTRODUCTION

Welcome to Hawai'i—a vegan paradise. With year-round access to some of the most luscious produce and top-notch restaurants, Hawai'i is an inspiration to vegans and a blessing for the health conscious. Honolulu's culinary scene is pioneering in exceptional meat-free dishes with a farm-to-table approach and plenty of farmers markets to lend support along the way. *Tasting Hawai'i Vegan Style* is a collection of innovative and exciting dishes trending Island-wide; all plant-based and gluten-free. You'll find weeknight favorites for the home cook who enjoys traditional classics and comfort food; exotic restaurant remakes; elegant dishes for entertaining; and an assortment of pūpū entrées and sweets for any occasion.

Enjoying plant-based options doesn't mean the end of delicious food! There are plant-based cheeses to bedazzle the biggest skeptics and mock meat recipes guaranteed to convert even the staunchest carnivores. Awaken your senses to the myriad of plant-based cooking possibilities! Let's discover what this book can do for you and what I can do to make the art of cooking an enjoyable experience creating food from plants you never thought possible. Making the switch to a plant-based diet doesn't have to be complicated. There's no need to get a degree in nutrition—just eat more of the good stuff in all the colors of the rainbow. Approach it gradually and positively. The mantras to follow are "progress over perfection" and "moderation not deprivation." Food takes center stage in every home and is what unites us around the table for the most rewarding time of the day—nourishing the body. Explore the fascinating world of vegan cooking through *Tasting Hawai'i Vegan Style* and let it be your stepping-stone to a new mindset and healthier you. Eating consciously is within reach!

The Vegan Life

The term "vegan" was coined by the Vegan Society co-founders Dorothy Morgan and Donald Watson in 1944 by combining the first and last letters of the word "vegetarian." Vegetarians differ in their approach to diet and may eat certain animal products such as fish, eggs, or dairy. Whereas a vegan avoids consuming all animal products including meat, fish, poultry, eggs, dairy, and animal by-products such as honey, gelatin, whey, and casein. Ethically, vegans don't want to hurt animals and are opposed to the use of animals for clothing, science, or entertainment. Veganism is a lifestyle, it's not just a diet. It's an active stance toward environmental awareness, a powerful means of preventative medicine, and a boycott against animal suffering. By eating vegan, you are reshaping the world and contributing to a healthier planet, a healthier body, and a healthier mind. There is no evidence suggesting humans need to eat meat in order to survive. It sounds easier said than done, but you can train yourself to live happily without meat, just like the millions around the world who have already given up knives for forks. When you substitute meat and dairy for plants, you open yourself up to a world full of color, spice, and variety like never before. You are one small bite away from changing your world and the world around you!

Hawaiian Food

Not every dish in Hawai'i is Hawaiian food. Polynesian voyagers transported plants and animals to the Islands in the pre-contact period (300AD-1778). They planted taro, coconuts, sugarcane, and sweet potatoes, and cooked fish and meat wrapped in taro leaves in an imu—pit oven. This type of cuisine is what we now refer to as traditional Hawaiian food. In 1778, missionaries and whalers arrived in the Hawaiian Islands to build sugarcane plantations, bringing with them European and American cuisine. In 1852, the first laborers arrived from China to work on the plantations, introducing a culture of festive banquets and a vast array of exotic dishes with no agenda except to eat. When Japanese, Korean, Filipino, Puerto Rican, and Portuguese immigrants made their way to the Islands, the cuisine changed further. The Japanese influence on Hawaiian food was highly prevalent and likely saw more cross-pollination in the villages than other cultures. When you look at a typical Hawaiian plate, it is simply a deconstructed bento box. Today, Hawai'i's signature fusion-esque cuisine has evolved into a mélange of local food and ethnic fare. This multicultural society is quickly becoming a hip scene on the culinary front and a vegan lover's paradise. My first book *Hawai'i A Vegan Paradise* is testament to the diversity of the food on the Islands and a great read for anyone who loves Hawaiian food.

Vegan Food

The list is shorter if you ask a vegan what they "don't" eat rather than what they "do" eat. Eliminate animal prod-

ucts from the equation and that's what vegans eat—everything else! Here's the scoop—whatever you crave, there's a plant-based version. Many vegans fill up on whole foods including fruits, vegetables, nuts, seeds, legumes, beans, and grains, rather than packaged and processed foods. Some splurge on plant-based versions of comfort food favorites like pizza, tacos, cakes, donuts, and the perennial favorite—burgers and fries. Others stay focused on mainly healthy meals with a little side of naughty.

Remember my mantra, "moderation over deprivation." It's time to dispel the myth that vegan food is boring. Innovations with plant-based cheeses and plant-based dairy is creating giant ripples in the dairy industry resulting in a worldwide boom of impressive plant-based alternatives. Plant-based seafood is gaining in popularity as well. Flip through the pages and you'll find Lobsta Roll, Vegan Scallop Roll, Phishcakes with Sweet Chili Sauce, and King Oyster "Calamari" so realistic in mouth feel and flavor profile you'll swear it was from the briny deep! Bottom line—anything is possible with plants!

The key to a nutritiously sound vegan diet is variety. When you break up the word "healthy," it becomes "heal" "thy." We are creatures of habit and most people reach for the same comfort food, but that all stops now! Start looking at food as a way of healing thy self and your meals will start to look different too. A fountain of nutrients come in a rainbow of color. Purple and blue foods like beets, blackberries, and blueberries are packed with antioxidants. Green foods such as spinach and kale are rich in vitamin K essential for blood and bone health. Bright orange and yellow carrots, pumpkin, and sweet potato are filled with vitamin C and carotenoids for healthy vision and cell growth. Red fruit and veggies contain phytochemicals with cancer-fighting benefits that may help to reduce the risk of diabetes and heart disease. White and brown foods such as garlic, ginger, cauliflower, white beans, soybeans, and dates also contain a multitude of nutrients your body needs and craves. Get painting, Picasso, your plate is a clean slate.

Baby Steps

Developing new eating habits takes time as you adjust your mindset and train your palate to a new way of feeding your body. It can be hard switching to a plant-based diet if you try to change overnight. Unfortunately, there is no magic wand, but the good news is you can train your brain to like certain tastes by eating them more frequently. Your taste buds regen-

GLUTEN-FREE

This book is intended to be vegan-friendly and gluten-free friendly. Gluten is a family of proteins found in certain grains which can cause harmful effects in people with celiac disease, an auto-immune disorder. People with non-celiac gluten sensitivity, gluten ataxia, or wheat allergies also experience sever discomfort when they consume gluten. A gluten-free diet excludes foods containing gluten, including

wheat, barley, rye, and tricitale, a cross between wheat and rye. Oats are naturally gluten-free but may be contaminated during production with other grains. It's crucial you check ingredients and look for the certified "gluten-free" label when buying oats or any other food product. People with other food allergies will also have to scrutinize labels and adjust recipes according to their dietary needs. When you see ingredients listed as "soy sauce or gluten-free liquid aminos," always use the gluten-free option if you are following a gluten-free diet and see the glossary section for products I like to use. People who are not following a gluten-free diet don't necessarily have to use the gluten-free options. It's your choice. Here are some gluten-free alternatives for ingredients listed in this book. When a recipe calls for:

- "Soy sauce or gluten-free liquid aminos" use Braggs liquid aminos or coconut aminos

- "All-purpose flour or gluten-free flour" use Red Mill's 1-1 baking flour, gluten-free all-purpose flour, or any certified gluten-free flour (see Glossary, p. 240)

- "Panko or gluten-free breadcrumbs" use certified gluten-free breadcrumbs, crushed nuts, or Mac Parm (p. 23)

erate every two weeks which opens the door of opportunity for trying new foods as time goes on. As you acclimate your tastes to the new, you can also learn to dislike something as well. Recognize that eating patterns are merely habits we can make or break at any time. You control the way you eat! Replace regular dairy milk with plant-based versions—almond, cashew, soy, or creamy oat milk. Last slice of cheese gone? Go shopping for vegan cheeses and buy a few varieties to taste test. Swap your butter and yogurt with plant-based alternatives and your honey with maple syrup. You're not giving up any of the foods you love, only replacing them with healthier options that taste almost the same. Once your mindset changes its perceptions of food

and is open to developing new eating habits you'll be transitioning from "yuck" to "yum" in no time.

Meatless Monday is a global movement to encourage the reduction of meat consumption one day a week. Challenge yourself to a plant-based fare at least one day a week and make it an adventure. Pour over vegan cookbooks and recipes online for inspiration, then go hunting for ingredients. Health food stores and farmers markets offer the best seasonal produce and can be a useful place to get tips from vendors on how to use their fresh offerings. Quaint little Asian and Indian grocery stores carry some of the most mysterious ingredients and exotic spices sure to send you into sensory overload as soon as you step into their aromatic emporiums. Take advantage of weekends to explore the plethora of vegan-friendly staples you can add to your new pantry collection—you never know what secret treasures you'll come across. I discovered kala namak (black salt) in a tiny Indian marketplace in Honolulu on one of my treasure hunts and my eggless dishes have rocked ever since! When it comes to getting started on a plant-based diet, my answer is to get into the kitchen and

start experimenting. After a bit of trial and error, you'll be able to create all the food you thought you'd have to give up by going plant-based.

Farmers Markets

Shop local! Connect with your community and know where your food originates. Farmers markets are business opportunities for small farmers, food manufacturers, and local artisans keeping the money you spend on food in your community. Stroll among the outdoor stalls on a sunny day to really motivate you to "eat greatly." Every farmers market is unique, offering access to the freshest locally-grown organic foods at the peak of the growing season; produce that you may not find in your average grocery. Who knows, maybe you'll learn a farmer's secret on the wondrous ways to eat poi or how to prepare a unique vegetable. The farmers market is a supportive and nurturing environment with trendy food items; health and wellness products; pet food for our furry friends; herbs and plants to help spruce up and bring healing energy to your abode; aromatic bath and body treats; and quirky gems from local artisans.

You can often find me on a sunny Saturday morning at the Kaka'ako farmers market in Honolulu doing book signings alongside some of my favorite vendors sharing their tantalizing vegan delights.

KITCHEN TOOLS

People assume I'm an appliance junkie and expect to see my kitchen packed with gadgets. However, that's not the case. As a chef, I've certainly collected some useful equipment over the years, but prefer to keep things simple and tidy. (Dave jokes his shock collar goes off when he enters my domain.) Apart from the obvious knife collection and pots and pans, here are some useful tools I recommend you add to your kitchen arsenal.

- Tofu press—You simply cannot embark on a plant-based cooking journey without a tofu press. Inexpensive, easy to clean, and compact. It gets the job done within 15 to 30 minutes resulting in evenly pressed tofu every time. If you're an avid tofu eater, I highly recommend springing for one.

- Air fryer—Invention of the century! Food is lightly sprayed with oil and placed into a perforated basket in the air fryer which circulates hot air around the food producing a crispy layer on the outside without all the oil. Get one!

- Blender—Frozen treats in seconds, soup purée silky and smooth, cashew cheese mixture blended to perfection, and cocktail creation made easy. Invest in a high-speed blender and make healthy cooking easier.

- Food processor—Why do all the chopping when a machine will do it

Stocking Your Vegan Pantry

The less toxic chemicals in your system the better! When it comes to stocking your pantry, spending a few extra dollars in the organic section can be a bit expensive, but is really a great investment in your health. Start a mason jar collection of dried foods to store your goodies and keep your pantry neat and tidy. A nice-looking spice rack encourages you to get familiar with the seasonings and flavors that often make a dish satisfying and inspire you to get out the apron and start cooking. Stock your kitchen with these basic staples to help you get started.

- Dried foods—dried fruit, chia seeds, grains, ground flaxseed, legumes, nori, nuts (almonds, cashews, pecans, walnuts), oats, pumpkin seeds, gluten-free pasta and noodles, dried seaweed, sesame seeds, dried shiitake, soy curls, rice, vegan chocolate chips

- Bottled/Canned foods—black beans, fire-roasted tomatoes, garbanzo beans, jalapeño, hearts of palm, lentils, tomato paste and sauce

- Refrigerator items—plant-based milk, peanut butter, lemons, limes, miso paste, tofu (soft, firm, extra-firm), vegan butter, vegan cheese, vegan mayonnaise, vegan yogurt

- Liquids—agave nectar, apple cider vinegar, balsamic glaze, balsamic vinegar, coconut aminos, maple syrup, mirin, molasses or blackstrap molasses, liquid aminos, sake, soy sauce, white wine vinegar, white vinegar

- Oils—extra-virgin olive oil, cold-pressed flaxseed oil, sesame seed oil, vegetable oil

- Spices, seasoning, and powders—Ground cinnamon, cumin, ginger, curry powder, garlic powder, Italian seasoning, kala namak (black salt), kombu dashi powder (kelp granules), mushroom seasoning, onion powder, nutritional yeast, smoked paprika, vegetable stock powder

for you? A godsend in the kitchen.

- Immersion blender—Also known as a hand blender or stick blender, it's a lightweight tool that can accomplish essential blending tasks directly in a pot, measuring cup, or jar making cleanup effortless. I recommend a cordless type for easy maneuvering.

- Kitchen scale—Measuring by weight ensures accuracy and good old measuring cups just don't measure up! Baking is a precise science that requires accurate measurements; nothing should be "eye-balled" unless you're very familiar with the recipe. Digital scales display the weight in both grams and ounces simultaneously, making weight conversions instantly, while saving time by eliminating the need to clean multiple cups.

- Microplane—The surgical sharp blade shreds, grates, and zests with ease; it's one of the best gadgets a home cook can have. Slice garlic cloves or chunks of ginger directly over a salad to amp up the nutrients. Grate chocolate for a fine dusting over desserts or smoothies for extra specialness, and zest your lemons or limes before cutting them open to squeeze (just avoid the white pith which can very bitter). Citrus zest adds a ton of flavor and fragrance to spruce up any pasta dish, sauce, dressing, dessert, or homemade mayo.

- Electric wine opener—No brainer!

Reg Flag Ingredients

Reading labels is serious business for vegans! You should always be aware of what you're putting into your body and will need to learn how to read labels fast! Steer clear of bizarre ingredients contained in many packaged foods. Unrecognizable ingredients can be hidden amongst the lengthy list of ingredients making the label reading process trickier. Read the small type. It's easy to spot the obvious meat ingredients, while fish, eggs, and dairy are often stated under the allergy information list and a clear indicator the product is not vegan. Keep an eye out for these red flag ingredients that contain animal by-products: Cochineal/carmine, chitin, gelatin, glycerin, isinglass, "natural" flavorings or colorings with numbers, whey, casein, and lactose. Look for the "certified vegan" or "100% vegan" labels on food items. "Natural" or "dairy-free" doesn't always mean the product is vegan.

Is Your Medication Vegan?

Medicine is one of the more difficult products for vegans to avoid. The pharmaceutical industry doesn't have qualms about using animals for testing or in products, which begs the question if something is life-threatening, how far are you prepared to go for your own convictions? Go looking for animal products, and you will find them everywhere. Gelatin shows up in many capsules, pills and tablets, including daily vitamins and supplements. The pinkish or reddish tint in pills could be from cochineal, or carmine, a red dye made from crushed insects, often used in candies too. Lactose is the most common animal-derived ingredient used as a carrier and a stabilizer in order to transport the medication's active ingredient into the body. Anticoagulants like heparin are made from the intestinal mucous membranes of pigs, and although fondaparinux is a synthetic substitute that is technically vegan, it may increase the risk of hemorrhage. Vegans also have to worry about amino acid infusions and hormone preparations and finding alternatives to such products can often be impossible. Medicine is undoubtedly a complicated topic which brings into question a variety of different moral dilemmas for many a conscientious patient. I can only recommend you open up a discussion with your doctor or healthcare professional about options.

Alcohol

Which brings me to alcohol. Sorry to be the bearer of bad news, but not all alcohol is vegan. Surprised? Isinglass is a fining agent made from fish bladders used to remove impurities in some wine and beer. Casein (egg whites) and gelatin (made from animal collagen) are also widely used during processing or included in the drink itself. Unfortunately, liquor manufacturers are exempt from the labeling requirements so the only way you'll know if your booze is vegan-friendly is to look it up. Mustard is generally vegan friendly, but the verjuice (acidic juice made from unripe grapes) used in Dijon mustard undergoes the same filtering process which typically contains animal by-products. Other mustards that contain wine may also not be suitable for someone avoiding animal products. For new vegans, apps are great sources that can scan a food or drink product's barcode and voilà, it will tell you if it's vegan or not. You'll figure it out. Just remember—baby steps!

Do the Research

Documentaries offer a treasure-trove of information and have been known to turn people instantly vegan. Guests on my show, "Lillian's Vegan World," have said they gave up meat after seeing clips of slaughterhouse footage. Although heart-wrenching to watch, there is some validity in saying, "the truth shall set you free." The Australian documentary, *Dominion,* exposes everything that happens in the meat, dairy, egg, clothing, and entertainment industries through drones, handheld cameras, and hidden footage. Like Paul McCartney once said, "If slaughterhouses were made of glass, everyone would be vegetarian." Environmental issues have increasingly become a hot topic as well. From climate change, land and ocean conservation, and waste production, these binge-worthy films are as educational as they are inspiring and brings awareness to the impact our food choices have on our Islands (and planet). *Cowspiracy*, produced by Leonardo DiCaprio, explores the impact of animal agriculture on the environment, covering issues such as global warming, water use, deforestation, and ocean dead zones. Others gain insight from documentaries about professional athletes who thrive on a plant-based diet and learn about the protein problem that isn't. In fact, Americans have formed an obsession around protein getting around twice as much as they need, believing they can only attain it by eating meat. Spoiler alert: All protein is made initially by plants, not animals. Dr. Milton Mills sets the record straight in the documentary, *What The Health?* He explains, "It is not necessary to eat animal tissue in order to get protein. Only plants have the ability to actually take nitrogen from the air, break those molecules apart, and incorporate that nitrogen into amino acids, and then make protein. Any protein you get from an animal is simply recycled protein." *The Game Changers* is another revolutionary documentary which many people claim motivated them to embark on a plant-based diet. Produced by athletes and famous celebrities such as James Wilks, Novak Djokovic, Arnold Schwarzenegger, Jackie Chan, and James Cameron, it delves into everything you need to know about meat, protein, and strength. This award-winning film showcases elite athletes, special ops soldiers, visionary scientists, and everyday heroes on a quest to find the optimal diet for human performance. You may not become an avid plant-based eater after watching these shows, but I guarantee and you'll never look at meat the same way again.

Know Your Nutrients

The recommended dietary reference intake (DRI) for protein is 0.36g per pound of body weight, yet most of us are getting almost twice the amount we need. Plant-based foods provide plenty of protein with soy products, legumes, whole grains, and nuts at the top of the list. Again, do the research! I have yet to meet a person (vegan or not) who suffers from protein deficiency, although many of us are clearly lacking other crucial nutrients.

Fiber has been associated with promoting weight loss, lowering blood sugar levels, and maintaining bowel health. There is no fiber in meat, dairy, or sugar. The average American is getting only about half the daily recommendation of 30g of fiber per day. Most studies suggest the average daily fiber intake to be around 25g for women and 38g for men. Beans, vegetables, whole grains, and chia seeds are all high in fiber.

Another important nutrient is calcium, which is vital for bone health and plentiful in almonds, broccoli, collard greens, fortified plant-based milk and orange juice, kale, tahini, and tofu.

Iron is an essential mineral that helps transport oxygen throughout your body. Up the iron intake with beans, lentils, green leafy vegetables, seaweed, and even blackstrap molasses, an ingredient you'll see in a number of the recipes in this book.

Omega-3 fatty acids keep your heart healthy and protects against stroke. There are three types of omega-3 fatty acids. ALA is the only one found in plant sources, while the other two, EPA and DHA, come from fish. Chia, flax and hemp seeds, walnuts, tofu, edamame, and seaweed contain ALA, but you'll need to consume a lot to achieve the same quota as a fish eater. Vegan DHA supplements are available, just make sure you chat with your doctor about how much you need as expert opinions vary between 250-500mg per day for healthy adults.

HOW TO USE THIS BOOK

• A pinch of—A pinch of an ingredient is about 1/8 of a teaspoon or less, the tiny bit of salt or pepper you pick up between your index finger and thumb.

• Season with salt and pepper to taste—This means add the amount of salt and pepper to taste that you think will be enough in a dish. When a recipe calls to "season with salt and pepper to taste," I usually add a pinch or two of salt (depending on the volume of the dish) and twist a pepper grinder a few times followed by a quick shake to remove any excess pepper from the grinder.

• Salt—Few ingredients are as powerful as salt; choose wisely. Whether you use kosher salt, Himalayan salt, or Hawaiian sea salt, it is the foundation of any dish and contributes immensely to the taste. Some salts are pricier for a reason and should be used as a finishing salt or in a recipe where their complexity is not lost during cooking. In short, save the expensive salts for sprinkling just before eating. When a recipe calls for "1 teaspoon of salt," I am referring to any type of salt you are comfortable with using. If you're watching your intake of sodium, then adjust the amount accordingly. You may only want to use half that amount or none at all. Adjusting ingredients is perfectly fine, but will inevitably affect the outcome of the dish. As long as you're happy with how a dish tastes in the end, do not take my word for granted.

• Mushroom seasoning and kombu dashi powder— The secret to creating delicious food is hidden in plant-based umami. There are five basic taste qualities: sweet, sour, salty, bitter, and what is commonly known as the fifth taste receptor being "umami." Umami is the meaty, or savory, flavor that spreads across the tongue and lingers in the mouth longer than other flavors pro-

moting salivation, helping you taste and enjoy food more. Umami is found in foods with high levels of glutamate, a naturally occurring amino acid that triggers the umami taste receptors. Plant-based sources include miso, mushrooms, seaweed (in particular kombu), and seasonings such as mushroom seasoning, kombu dashi powder, soy sauce or liquid aminos, and nutritional yeast flakes. Salt is not the only flavor enhancer and a good recipe knows in order to have that deep, rich, savory factor, some type of umami needs to be present. Make your own mushroom seasoning by blending dried shiitake, onion powder, and salt to taste until a fine powder is achieved.

- Pepper—Always use a pepper grinder (or mill) filled with black peppercorns to create freshly ground pepper. When the centers of the peppercorn crack open for the first time, intense flavors release and oils excrete from them adding even more flavor to your dishes.

- Sugar—Unfortunately, not all sugar is vegan. White sugar gets its color from a refining process using bone char from animals. Look for labels with the words "certified vegan," "organic," "unrefined," "natural," and "raw" when buying sugar to ensure its vegan. I personally use raw organic cane sugar anytime a recipe calls for sugar. Coconut sugar, beet sugar, and date sugar are also all vegan-friendly. Liquid sweeteners offer a nice alternative to sugar but can change the consistency and texture of a dish, especially when it comes to baking. Maple syrup and agave syrup are often used in plant-based recipes and are available in most supermarkets. Molasses is the umami king of liquid sweeteners containing more antioxidants than honey, maple syrup, and agave. It's made by extracting liquids from sugarcane and beets that are boiled down to form crystals. Molasses is the thick, brown syrup left over after the crystals have been removed. The syrup is then boiled three times producing a light molasses from the first boiling, dark molasses from the second, and blackstrap molasses from the third boiling. I'm a huge fan of blackstrap molasses which has the thickest consistency and the richest flavor. It's much more intense in flavor than other liquid sweeteners so use it sparingly.

- Oil—This is without a doubt the trickiest part of recipe developing. There is a lot of conflicting noise over which oil is right for you and how much. Some studies link extra-virgin olive oil to better heart health, while others claim all kinds of oils, including olive oil, contribute to arterial damage and also the progression of heart disease. Many vegans following a strict whole foods plant-based diet are giving up oil all together. The beauty of cooking your own food means you get to make all these judgment calls on your terms. If you want to omit oil from a recipe, just use water. Seriously, it's that simple, although the end result of the dish may differ. When a recipe tells you to sauté the vegetable in 1 tablespoon of extra-virgin olive oil, just use a 1:1 replacement of water. Add more water if the food starts to stick to your skillet or pan. Another option is to use an air fryer that requires little or no oil at all. Air fryers are a brilliant invention creating a crispy crust similar to foods that have been deep-fried in oil. If you are going to deep-fry food, neutral oils have higher smoking points, the point when oil starts to burn and smoke. Heating oil past its smoking point harms the flavor and many nutrients in the oil degrade releasing harmful compounds called free radicals. Canola, coconut, corn, grapeseed, peanut, safflower, and vegetable oil are all considered neutral oils making them suitable for frying.

- **Store in the refrigerator for up to 1 week**—My recommendations for how long you can store food are only guidelines. You should always use your best judgment when storing leftovers. If in doubt, when anything looks or smells strange, be safe and throw it away. Sterilizing your mason jars and using clean, dry, airtight containers are crucial factors when it comes to storing food successfully.

Vitamin B12 is only found in animal and fortified foods and is responsible for cell division and blood. A B12 deficiency can cause anemia and nervous system damage. Fortunately, there are plant-based foods like nutritional yeast fortified with this important nutrient. This deactivated yeast powder makes everything taste cheesy, nutty, and savory and contains high levels of the essential vitamin B12. Vegans should take a daily B12 supplement containing 2.4 micrograms (mcg), the recommended dietary allowance (RDA), or eat foods fortified with B12.

This information should not be treated as professional medical advice. Always consult with your doctor or nutritionist before drastically changing your diet in any way.

Dining Out

Want to know why food tastes "better" when you eat out or order take out? Apart from the fact that professionally trained chefs make it their sole mission to prepare tasty meals, often restaurant food tastes good because it's laden with fat, salt, and sugar in order to get you hooked and wanting more. So many of us are petrified of cholesterol and early death by salt and sugar overdose, yet we are willing to forego those fears when it comes to other people cooking for us. I love eating out and discovering new dishes, but I'm aware many establishments aim to please and spoil the diner with a tasty experience rather than a healthy one—with exceptions, of course. Continue supporting your local restaurants, but choose your food wisely. Remember "moderation over depravation!"

While many restaurants are adopting vegan options on their menus, they can also be breeding grounds for cross-contamination, the transfer of bacteria from one food item to another. It's standard practice to use the same deep-fryer or grill for meat and vegetables, meaning those fries or veggie spring rolls are likely to end up in the same batch of oil as the fried chicken. Another cross-contamination hazard is a plant-based ingredient being cut on a chopping board also used for meat or fish. Ever been to a sushi bar and ordered a vegan roll only to see it being sliced on the very same board someone else's tuna roll was segmented on? The pizza base and sauce may be vegan, but once they scoop out the toppings, your mushrooms and bell peppers have been cross-contaminated with meat or seafood by the "double-dipping" server handling one ingredient to another without changing their gloves. Unless you dine in a dedicated vegan restaurant, it can be tough eating out.

Another factor often overlooked when dining out is ambience, which is critical to our perception of food. It can be a challenge at home with the noise, kiddie distractions, and grumpy husband. Even truly great dishes can seem lackluster in that environment. Now, imagine your creation on a beautifully set table with candles, a flower in a pretty vase, and music in the background. A mediocre meal can be transformed into a special moment if the presentation and environment is appealing. Recreating that restaurant atmosphere is one way to turn your home dining into something to look forward to—and you don't have to spend big bucks or time! Ask your keiki to pick some flowers from the garden, tell "Mr. Wonderful" to turn on some music, and pull out Nona's flatware to make it a special occasion. If you're really motivated, take your meal outside and enjoy a beautiful sunset while catching up with your 'ohana.

Progress Over Perfection

Learning to live without meat and dairy is merely a matter of breaking habits and starting new ones. It isn't easy to adjust to the plant-based life and you may be overwhelmed by change. Be patient with the transition. Introduce new things into your diet slowly and start eliminating the foods that aren't serving you well, one by one. Stock your pantry and refrigerator with food that will encourage healthy eating habits at home. Stay positive when you "cheat" by remembering my mantra "progress over perfection." With all the exciting dishes and diverse cultural cuisines to explore in this book, your plant-based journey is just beginning. Set goals and write them down. I'm a big believer in vision boards. Displaying images and words that embody your aspirations and dreams spark your motivation to take action and manifest them. Happiness comes when we live with integrity and align our values and morals with what really matters to us.

THE SPIRIT OF ALOHA

Literally meaning "the breath of life," Aloha is the spirit of the Hawaiian culture, its people, and the lifestyle. Aloha is deeper than just a greeting or farewell, it's a way of life and an essence of being. Aloha includes treating others with love, affection, respect, kindness, patience, mercy, empathy, compassion, and oneness; living in harmony with everything around you and creating positive energy, thoughts, and feelings around us and flowing between us. It's a state of mind that connects us through conscious choices. *Tasting Hawai'i Vegan Style* is a taste of living vegan in the spirit of Aloha, from my kitchen to yours.

FAVORITE CONDIMENTS GONE VEGAN

Condiments enhance the taste of a dish and bring attitude to the table, but can pose a real problem for vegans as animal products are found in most. It's best you master a few, if for nothing more than bragging rights. One of those perennial favorites to master is Vegan Honey (p. 38)—Oh yes, my friends, vegan honey is happening; right here, right now. But don't be blown away just yet. There's Pineapple Ginger Honey (p. 38) and Hot Honey (p. 38) to lift your spirits, too! Drizzle over anything and tell me you're not falling in love with this joyous goo.

Hawaiian Chili Pepper Water (p. 33) is another condiment you should become familiar with. This stuff has a unique depth of sour and tang capable of making any dish pop with Island flavor. Japanese Furikake will also become your buddy throughout this book, so make sure you have some handy at all times. The XO Sauce (p. 36) is incredible! Just trust me. Dip, dunk, sprinkle, and enjoy these delightful condiments with any of the dishes in the book. Get testing and make food people will talk about for a long time to come.

FUN IDEA: Start collecting glass jars with lids in interesting shapes and sizes for your condiments. They make attractive gifts to entice your friends to try some of your new vegan creations. Explore craft stores or magazines for decorating ideas and at-home hacks to give your vessels a ative makeover without

1. ALMOND MAC PARM
2. PECAN MAC PARM
3. BLACK SALT CASHEW MAC PARM
4. PISTACHIO MAC PARM
5. DRY-ROASTED MAC PARM
6. CHILI WALNUT MAC PARM

CHOOSE YOUR MAC PARM

Yield: about 1 cup

This Mac Parm is the king of all condiments with that familiar saltiness and crumbled texture we all know and love. You'll notice it's used throughout the book as a garnish, topping, or crispy coating in many dishes. You won't miss processed packaged chips after you try the Mac Parm Kale Chips on p. 68. The cool part is you can create your own flavors by swapping nuts and adding different seasonings. Your household will be eating this on the regular, so make sure you have a jar handy at all times. Happy sprinkling!

BASIC MAC PARM

¾ cup (90g) toasted macadamia nuts (see **CHEF'S TIP**)

¼ cup (30g) toasted or raw cashews (or choose a
    different nut from list below)

2 teaspoons nutritional yeast

1 teaspoon salt

Pulse all ingredients in a food processor until a fine meal is achieved. Store in an airtight container in the refrigerator for up to 1 month.

Create your own Mac Parm by swapping the cashew nuts for other nuts below:

- Almond Mac Parm—Toast almonds for added flavor (see **CHEF'S TIP**).

- Black Salt Cashew Mac Parm—Use black Hawaiian sea salt instead of regular salt.

- Dry-Roasted Nut Mac Parm—Unsalted or salted dry roasted nuts.

- Glazed Pecan Mac Parm—Glazed Pecans (Candied Hurricane Popcorn with Pecans p. 62) add a terrific sweetness to the Parm.

- Pine Nut Mac Parm—Toast pine nuts for better results.

- Pistachio Mac Parm—Remove as much skin as possible from the pistachios before adding.

- Chili Walnut Mac Parm—Add ½ to 1 teaspoon crushed red pepper and use walnuts.

- Furikake Mac Parm—Add 2 to 3 tablespoons Furikake Seasoning (p. 24) to any of your Mac Parms for a Japanese twist.

JAPANESE FURIKAKE

Yield: about 1 cup

You'll see furikake-crusted items on menus everywhere in Hawai'i. Could this be the magical sprinkle that helps food taste better? Upgrade your sprinkle to this exotic seasoning loaded with umami and notes of the sea. You'll come across it in the Phishcakes (p. 48) that are divine! Candied Hurricane Popcorn (p. 62) is another winner with all ages. Fortunately, seaweed and sesame seeds happen to be high in vitamins and minerals, so feel free to shake your new flavor maker on everything!

3 sheets nori, torn into small pieces
½ cup (70g) toasted black sesame seeds
½ cup (70g) toasted white sesame seeds
1 teaspoon mushroom seasoning or
    kombu dashi powder
1 teaspoon salt

Pulse all ingredients in a food processor until nori has broken up and sesame seeds are partially ground. Store in an airtight container in the refrigerator for up to 2 weeks.

VARIATION: Make your own flavored furikake by adding 'alaea salt (Hawaiian red salt), black cracked pepper, chili powder, crushed red pepper, garlic powder, ginger powder, Li Hing powder, mustard powder, shiso powder, or wasabi powder.

SPICY CHILI CRISP

Yield: about 2 cups

Consider this your new fiery hot sauce condiment! Spicy Chili Crisp is an infused chili oil condiment available in most Asian supermarkets. Spicy and salty with an addictive umami flavor packed with spice and crunch and filled with garlic, ginger, chili, and toasted sesame seeds to brighten any dish. Adjust the seasoning, heat, and add your own personal touches like some crushed nuts or black peppercorns for extra punch. People have been known to put this on their ice cream! But don't take my word for it.

1 cup (240ml) grapeseed, peanut oil, or
   vegetable oil
20 garlic cloves, finely chopped
¼ cup (25g) finely chopped fresh ginger
1 cinnamon stick
½ cup (40g) crushed red pepper
¼ cup (30g) chili powder
¼ cup (60ml) soy sauce or gluten-free
   liquid aminos
3 tablespoons Sichuan peppercorns,
   roughly chopped
2 tablespoons white toasted sesame seeds

2 teaspoons mushroom seasoning
½ teaspoon Chinese five spice powder

Heat oil in a saucepan over medium-low heat. Add garlic, ginger, and cinnamon stick. Simmer for 4 to 5 minutes without burning it, or until ginger and garlic brown. Discard cinnamon stick and stir in remaining ingredients. Simmer for another 2 minutes then remove from heat and cool to room temperature. Once cooled, store in an airtight container in the refrigerator for up to 6 months.

NUTTY BUTTER

Yield: about 1 cup

Did you know that peanut butter is just blended peanuts? You can easily create your own funky and delicious version of this globally adored spread in a mixer in just minutes. Once you master blending the techniques for your own nut and seed butters, finding a combination tailor-made for you is fun and the choices are endless. Roasted chipotle flavored macadamia blends into the most divine nut butter anywhere. Get really fancy and make the Peanut Butter Cookies on p. 232 using your own nut butters. You'll be a star!

PLAIN PEANUT BUTTER
2 cups (280g) dry roasted peanuts (salted or unsalted)

ALMOND BUTTER
2 cups (280g) roasted almonds (salted or unsalted)

MACADAMIA BUTTER
2 cups (280g) roasted macadamia nuts (salted or unsalted)

CHOCOLATE BUTTER
2 cups (280g) roasted hazelnuts or dry roasted peanuts (salted or unsalted)
¼ cup Chocolate Sauce (p. 228)

2 tablespoons maple syrup
1 teaspoon vanilla essence

SPICY PEANUT BUTTER
2 cups (280g) dry roasted peanuts (salted or unsalted)
¼ cup hot sauce
2 tablespoons maple syrup or agave syrup

SUNFLOWER OR HEMP SEED BUTTER
3 cups (400g) raw sunflower seeds or hulled hemp seeds (also known as hemp hearts)
¼ cup maple syrup or agave syrup
2 tablespoons melted refined coconut oil
Pinch of salt

Blend nuts or seeds in a food processor for 5 to 6 minutes, or until smooth and creamy. The nuts go in stages from crumbs to a dry ball to a smooth and creamy peanut butter. Transfer to a bowl and stir in additional flavorings. Do not blend once you've added the flavorings—the butter can harden and crumble. Store nut or seed butter in an airtight container in the refrigerator for up to 3 months.

OIL-FREE TOFU MAYO

Yield: about 1 cup

As most people in Hawai'i are mayo-lovers, I decided it was time to put together an oil-free version that doesn't just taste like blended tofu. This is my take and it worked! No saturated fat or cholesterol in this creamy homemade mayo. Great as a sandwich topping, dipping sauce, or salad dressing, this yummy guilt-free spread won't have you counting calories.

½ block (7oz/200g) silken tofu, drained
1 tablespoon red or white wine vinegar
2 teaspoons agave syrup
2 teaspoons lemon juice
1 teaspoon nutritional yeast

½ teaspoon apple cider vinegar
½ teaspoon onion powder
½ teaspoon salt
½ teaspoon yellow mustard
¼ teaspoon garlic powder

Blend all ingredients until smooth and creamy. Store in an airtight container in the refrigerator for up to 3 to 5 days.

Stir in additional ingredients to make different flavored mayo combos:

- FURIKAKE MAYO—Add 1 tablespoon Japanese Furikake (p. 24)

- PICKLE MAYO—Add 1 tablespoon sweet relish or chopped pickles, 2 teaspoons finely chopped parsley, 1 teaspoon minced garlic, freshly cracked black pepper to taste

- PARMESAN MAYO—Add 2 tablespoons grated vegan Parmesan or Mac Parm (p. 23), freshly cracked black pepper to taste

- SPICY MAYO—Add 1 tablespoon sriracha, 1 teaspoon minced garlic, ¼ teaspoon smoked paprika, pinch of crushed red pepper for garnish

- WASABI MAYO—Add ½ to 1 teaspoon wasabi paste, 1 teaspoon soy sauce or gluten-free liquid aminos, 1 teaspoon toasted white sesame seeds

THAI BASIL PESTO

Yield: about 1 cup

Take a stroll around Chinatown or Asian supermarkets and you will find the freshest herbs like Thai basil. A member of the mint family, Thai basil has a stronger, slightly peppery flavor, with hints of anise and licorice. The leaves have purple stems that make pretty garnishes for your dish, too. Serve this pesto alongside a beautiful piece of roasted kabocha, mashing together directly on the serving plate. Thai basil pesto is fantastic as a dip for fresh veggie sticks, mixed into mashed potatoes, fried rice, pasta, or gnocchi. Check out the Lemon Zucchini Pasta with Thai Basil Pesto (p. 153) for more inspiration on how to Thai things up!

PESTO

2 to 3 cups (100g) Thai basil leaves
¼ cup (60ml) extra-virgin olive oil
½ cup (80g) raw cashews
2 tablespoons nutritional yeast
2 tablespoons lemon juice
1 tablespoon roasted garlic or 3 to
   4 cloves Garlic Confit (p. 32)

Salt and freshly cracked black pepper

ROASTED KABOCHA

⅛ kabocha slice (per person), deseeded
Extra-virgin olive oil cooking spray
Salt and freshly cracked black pepper

Blend all pesto ingredients until smooth, or pulse and leave chunky style. Season with salt and pepper to taste. Chill in the refrigerator until ready to use.

For kabocha, preheat oven to 400°F (200°C). Place kabocha on a baking sheet lined with parchment paper. Spray with oil on all sides and season with salt and pepper to taste. Bake for 25 to 30 minutes, or until tender.

CHEF'S TIP: In lieu of Thai basil, swap with different greens/herbs: basil, baby arugula, cilantro, parsley, spinach, or a combination of a few. Pine nuts, walnuts, or pepitas can substitute the cashews and a few slices of jalapeño can give the pesto an extra kick.

GARLIC CONFIT

Yield: 1 cup

This is the ultimate solution when you want your garlic and the flavors it brings forth without the garlicky breath. The French word "confit" simply means to preserve by slowly cooking it in a liquid. In this case, the raw cloves are cooked at a low temperature in a bath of oil that strips the acidity and sharp heat, while concentrating their sweetness. The cloves literally melt in your mouth with a flavor so mellow and sweet. Spruce up any of your dishes with these sublime cloves or spread on some bread and top with homemade Sun-Dried Tomato (p. 56) for a quick nibble.

1 cup (170g) peeled garlic cloves   1½ cups (360ml) extra-virgin olive oil

Preheat oven to 200°F (100°C). Place garlic in a small oven-proof dish. Cover with olive oil and bake for 2 to 3 hours, or until garlic cloves are soft when poked with a toothpick. Cool to room temperature and store in the refrigerator for up to 3 weeks.

HAWAIIAN CHILI PEPPER WATER

Yield: about 2½ cups

This is Hawai'i's version of the all-time favorite hot sauce sometimes referred to as "pepper water." The first time I tried it, I was hooked at first splash. As I started creating my own recipe, I quickly realized how versatile this liquid gold can be. Keep it traditional or add a splash of pineapple juice, soy sauce, or gluten-free liquid aminos. Sriracha really amplifies the flavor as well. Customize as you like for a Hawai'i hot sauce treat.

2 cups (480ml) distilled water or boiled
  water
½ cup (120ml) white vinegar or rice
  vinegar
5 red chili peppers

2 tablespoons sriracha
1 teaspoon Hawaiian sea salt
1 teaspoon sugar
1-inch sliced ginger, smashed (optional)
1 clove garlic (optional)

Combine ingredients in a large mason jar and place in the refrigerator for 1 to 2 days to allow flavors to meld. Remove ginger and garlic, if using, and store in the refrigerator for up to 6 months.

WORCESTERSHIRE SAUCE

Yield: about 2 cups

Worcestershire sauce is probably not one of things you think about making yourself until you become vegan. Traditional versions are made with anchovies or fish sauce, meaning you will have to either give it up or practice self-reliance and make your own. Swapping molasses for tamarind (which can be tricky to find) will also provide the key "umami" from the absent anchovies. The acidity level in orange juice gives just the right balance in flavor. Something not right about a soup? Just add a dollop of Worcestershire. Stew a bit bland? A few drops save the day!

½ cup (120ml) apple cider vinegar
¼ cup (60ml) malt vinegar
¼ cup (60ml) molasses
¼ cup (60ml) orange juice
¼ cup (60ml) soy sauce or gluten-free
   liquid aminos
2 tablespoons pickle brine or caper brine
2 teaspoons sugar

1 teaspoon garlic powder
1 teaspoon onion powder
½ teaspoon ground ginger
½ teaspoon mustard powder or
   1 teaspoon yellow mustard
½ teaspoon pumpkin spice
¼ teaspoon ground black pepper
2 dates, deseeded, roughly chopped

Whisk together all ingredients in a saucepan and bring to a boil over medium-high heat. Reduce heat to medium and cook until liquid thickens slightly, about 10 to 12 minutes. Remove from heat and blend until smooth. Cool to room temperature and store in an airtight container in the refrigerator for up to 3 months.

BAKED POTATO WEDGES

Cut 4 russet potatoes into wedges. Toss with 2 tablespoons extra-virgin olive oil, 1 tablespoon smoked paprika, 1 teaspoon onion powder, and 1 teaspoon garlic powder. Season with salt and pepper to taste. Bake in a preheated oven at 400°F (200°C) for 40 to 50 minutes, or until golden brown, flipping halfway through. For air fryer, bake at 350°F (180°C) for 30 to 35 minutes. Serve drizzled with Worcestershire Sauce.

XO SAUCE

Yield: about 2 cups

"XO" is used to denote anything of high-quality, prestige, and luxury. Hong Kong's most beloved chili sauce gets its name from fine XO (extra-old) cognac, even though it contains none of France's most notable export. Traditionally made with dried scallops, this shiitake version will not disappoint. However, if you're after a more authentic version, try adding some chopped Conpoy Dried Scallop (p. 198) to your batch. A dollop of XO will elevate any dish to the next level.

10 dried shiitake mushrooms
1½ cups (360ml) hot water
¼ cup (60ml) sesame oil (or vegetable, grapeseed, peanut oil)
1 cup (50g) green onion, minced
5 garlic cloves, finely chopped
¼ cup (30g) finely chopped fresh ginger

¼ cup (60ml) soy sauce or gluten-free liquid aminos
1 tablespoon blackstrap molasses or sugar
1 tablespoon chili powder (I use Korean gochugaru—see **NOTE**)
1 tablespoon crushed red pepper (add up to 3 tablespoons for a spicy version)
1 teaspoon mushroom seasoning
½ teaspoon Chinese five spice powder

Soak shiitake in hot water for 30 minutes, or until softened. Drain and squeeze out excess water from the shiitake reserving ¾ cup (180ml) of the soaking liquid. Remove stems and discard. Finely chop the shiitake caps or pulse in a food processor to save time.

Heat oil in a saucepan over medium heat. Add shiitake, green onion, garlic, and ginger; sauté for 5 minutes. Add remaining ingredients and reserved soaking liquid. Simmer for 5 minutes, or until the liquid is almost gone. Cool to room temperature and store in an airtight container in the refrigerator for up to 2 weeks.

NOTE: Gochugaru is a Korean red chili powder made from sun-dried peppers without the seeds. It has a nice balance of heat with sweet undertones.

XO EDAMAME

Yield: 4 to 6 servings

Cook 1 pack frozen edamame according to package instructions. Drain and toss with XO Sauce to taste. Serve warm or chilled.

ROASTED XO ASPARAGUS

Yield: 4 servings

Toss asparagus spears with extra-virgin olive oil and season with salt. Bake in oven at 425°F (220°C) for 12 to 15 minutes, or until tender. Sprinkle with XO Sauce to taste and serve hot or chilled.

SPICY COLD XO TOFU

Yield: 4 to 6 servings

Cut silken tofu into 6 pieces and top with XO Sauce to taste.

VEGAN HONEY

Yield: about 1 cup

Honey is one of those things most frequently mistaken as vegan-friendly, but it is not. Luckily, you can have your honey, too. "Celebrate good times, come on!" (Playing in the background.) Vegans don't consume animal byproducts, and many believe honey is made by bees for bees; without it they would starve. Their health can be sacrificed when it's harvested, so leave the honey for the bees and let's talk about this star recipe. Surprise someone you know with a jar of homemade Vegan Honey and watch their reaction. It's magical! Even the calories in this honey are completely worth it. Drizzle over the cashew cheeses in Chapter 8 and send me a thank you card later. You're welcome.

1 cup (240ml) 100% apple juice from
   concentrate
1 cup (200g) sugar

1 tablespoon lemon juice
2 chamomile tea bags (see **NOTE**)

Combine all ingredients in a saucepan over medium-high heat and bring to a soft boil. Squeeze and remove chamomile tea bags as soon as liquid comes to a boil. (The tea bags can leave a bitter aftertaste if left in the "honey" for too long.) Reduce heat to medium and simmer until liquid is reduced to about half, 15 to 20 minutes.

"Honey" is ready when it darkens and starts to thicken. Watch it constantly so it doesn't boil over, caramelize, or burn. Test "honey" on a cold plate for consistency or see how the syrup drips from the back of the spoon. It will continue to thicken as it cools down. Cool to room temperature and store in an airtight container. "Honey" will keep for a long time as long as your jar has been thoroughly sterilized. (See Sterilizing p. 39)

HOT HONEY

Add ¼ cup (60g) hot sauce after you remove the tea bags from the syrup and follow remaining recipe instructions.

PINEAPPLE GINGER HONEY

Use 100% pineapple juice instead of apple juice and add 2 teaspoons fresh ginger juice or 1 teaspoon ground ginger. To make ginger juice, grate peeled fresh ginger and squeeze to remove juice.

{ FAVORITE CONDIMENTS GONE VEGAN }

NOTE: Use different teas to flavor your honey: Earl Grey, Hibiscus, Mint, Orange Blossom, Tropical Fruit, Thyme, Dandelion, Lavender—the possibilities are endless!

CHEF'S TIP: Vegan Honey can crystallize if you cook off too much of the liquid or if it has been stored for a long time. You can try saving it by reheating in a pot with more apple juice or pineapple juice and getting it to the right consistency again. This is one recipe where trial and error is the only way you'll learn!

STERILIZING: To sterilize jars and lids, wash in hot soapy water and rinse, then submerge in boiling water for 10 minutes. Carefully remove from boiling water; drain and allow to air-dry. Alternatively, you can place clean, wet jars and lids in a preheated oven at 350°F (180°C) for 15 minutes.

CHAPTER 2

COCKTAIL HOUR PŪPŪ

There is a time-honored tradition called "pau hana" in Hawai'i. Roughly translated to "finish work," pau hana is the equivalent of "cocktail hour" and is used as an excuse for leaving early to catch one of Hawai'i's stunning sunsets over a drink. Hawai'i cocktail hour is any time of the day (I kid you not!). But don't think pau hana involves only alcohol. On the contrary, bartenders here are masters at concocting the perfect mocktails in every color of the rainbow to satisfy your cravings. Sunset get-togethers are a huge component of social life here on the Islands, right down to the teeny-tiniest of pūpū—an assortment of hot or cold, usually small serving appetizers, enjoyed with pau hana drinks. Pūpū dishes are the life of the party and no Island-style potluck would be complete without these Hawai'i-inspired *hors d' oeuvres*. There is something for everyone in this collection of appetizers to get the pā'ina (party) started.

FUN IDEA: Get a bunch of pals together and dress in Hawaiian outfits—Aloha shirts and flip flops for the boys; fresh lei and colorful skirts for the ladies. Make it a potluck and ask guests to bring a Hawaiian-inspired pūpū or a pre-mixed Hawaiian cocktail to share.

BANG BANG BROCCOLI

Yield: 4 servings

My husband and I both agree this is a winner. Dave claims it tastes like chicken, and I have to agree it loses all of its broccoli-ness and transforms into a meaty bite that is so stupefying. This tastes amazing cold, so cook it ahead of time and let it sit for the crust to thicken and firm. Bang bang cauliflower, Brussels sprouts, kabocha, or tofu and you'll get it. I'm impressed!

BANG BANG SAUCE
½ cup (120g) vegan mayonnaise
2 tablespoons Spicy Chili Crisp (p. 25)
   or ¼ cup (60ml) sweet chili sauce
1 tablespoon apple cider vinegar
1 tablespoon hot sauce
1 tablespoon lemon juice
1 tablespoon maple syrup or agave syrup
1 tablespoon toasted white sesame seeds

BATTER
1 tablespoon apple cider vinegar
1 cup (240ml) plant-based milk
¾ cup (100g) all-purpose flour or
   gluten-free flour
½ cup (60g) cornstarch

2 tablespoons hot sauce (add more for
   extra spicy)
1 teaspoon garlic powder
1 teaspoon onion powder
½ teaspoon ground black pepper
½ teaspoon salt

1 cup (50g) panko or gluten-free bread-
   crumbs
1 teaspoon onion powder
1 teaspoon lemon pepper seasoning

1 medium broccoli (about 300g), trimmed
   into bite-sized florets

GARNISH
2 tablespoons thinly sliced green onion

Mix all the sauce ingredients in a bowl and set aside. Preheat oven to 400°F (200°C) and line a baking sheet with parchment paper.

Pour the apple cider vinegar into the milk into a large bowl and allow to sit for 10 minutes to thicken. Add remaining batter ingredients and mix to combine. Combine panko, onion powder, and lemon pepper seasoning in a separate bowl. Toss the broccoli florets in the batter (all at once), then dredge in panko mixture, one at a time. Arrange on baking sheet and bake for 25 to 30 minutes, or until golden brown. Remove from oven and toss the baked broccoli in the bang bang sauce. Return to oven and bake another 5 minutes. Remove from oven and garnish with green onion.

NOTE: For air fryer, bake at 350°F (180) for 20 to 25 minutes.

BEET THESE ARANCINI

Yield: 8 rice balls

Beets are becoming a popular restaurant item in Honolulu with more people looking for healthier menu options, and these crispy rice balls are a perfect way to embellish them. They are among the most nutritious foods on the planet and have been shown to support the detoxification process in the body by helping to capture toxins and flush them out of your system. Beet powder is also making a buzz. That rich red pigment from belatains is often added to plant-based meats in the liquid or powder form to create a realistic meaty color. The Moxtail Stew recipe p. 192 or the Mushroom Jerky p. 204 are delicious examples of how you can use beet powder.

RICE

2 cups (400g) cooked white or brown rice
2 small, cooked beets (about 150g), peeled, finely chopped (see **NOTE**)
1½ cups (300ml) plant-based milk
2 tablespoons nutritional yeast
1 teaspoon mushroom seasoning
½ teaspoon onion powder
¼ teaspoon garlic powder

Salt and freshly cracked black pepper

BATTER

½ cup (120ml) plant-based milk
¼ cup (30g) all-purpose flour or gluten-free flour
½ cup (60g) panko or gluten-free bread-crumbs

Vegetable oil or other neutral oil for frying

GARNISH

Oil-Free Tofu Mayo (p. 28) to taste

Combine all rice ingredients in a small pot and heat over medium-high for 4 to 5 minutes, or until rice is just hot. Season with salt and pepper to taste. Transfer to a bowl and cool to room temperature. Wet fingers to avoid sticking and roll mixture into 8 balls; set aside.

To make batter, mix together milk and flour in a large bowl. In a separate bowl, add panko. Coat the rice balls in the batter, then dredge in panko. Heat two inches of oil to 365°F in a large pot. Fry rice balls in batches on both sides for about 2 to 3 minutes, or until golden brown. Drain on paper towels and serve with Oil-Free Tofu Mayo.

NOTE: Cover whole beets in foil and bake at 400°F (200°C) for 50 to 60 minutes, or until tender when poked with a fork. Once slightly cooled, use a paper towel to rub the beets and the skin should just slide off. For air fryer, bake at 380°F (190°C) for 25 to 30 minutes. To save time, buy pre-cooked beets in vacuum-sealed packs.

STUFFED MINI PEPPERS

Yield: 16 stuffed mini peppers

I'm not sure if it's the sweet roasted peppers that are the star of this dish or the rice filling that brings it all together. All I know is every time I make these pretty and colorful poppers the entire plate gets completely demolished. What gets me through the day is knowing I'm eating all the colors of the rainbow and sneaking in essential nutrients for the lucky ones around the table as well. A delicious and healthy bite-size appetizer perfect for parties, game days, holidays, or late night snacks.

8 sweet mini peppers, cut in half lengthwise, seeds and membrane removed
1 tablespoon extra-virgin olive oil
Salt and freshly cracked black pepper

RICE FILLING
2 cups (450g) cooked rice
½ cup (120ml) plant-based milk
¼ cup (10g) chopped fresh coriander
2 tablespoons finely sliced green onion
2 garlic cloves, minced
1 chipotle pepper in adobo sauce, finely
   chopped
1 tablespoon nutritional yeast

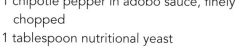

1 teaspoon Cajun seasoning
1 teaspoon mushroom seasoning
1 teaspoon onion powder
Freshly cracked black pepper

CRUST
¼ cup (30g) Mac Parm (p. 23) or panko
   or gluten-free breadcrumbs

GARNISH
8 lemon wedges
1 to 2 tablespoons Balsamic Glaze
   (p. 125)

Preheat oven to 400°F (200°C). Place peppers in an oven dish and drizzle with olive oil. Season with salt and pepper to taste. Combine rice filling ingredients in a bowl and season with pepper to taste. Stuff rice filling into peppers and sprinkle with Mac Parm to give tops a nice crust. Bake for 25 to 30 minutes, or until peppers are tender. Serve with lemon wedges and drizzle with Balsamic Glaze.

PHISHCAKES WITH SWEET CHILI SAUCE

Yield: 8 phishcakes

You'll put a smile on a everyone's face with this vegan twist on a classic appetizer. If you're new to plant-based cooking, then let me reassure you there are plenty of fishy plant-based dishes out there you can enjoy. Hearts of palm crumble into flaky pieces just like fish and are excellent in getting that seafood texture you love at a price you'll love too—it is cheaper to make than a batch of real fish cakes. Dip into the sweet chili sauce and rest assured, you've got this.

PHISHCAKES

1 can (15 oz) hearts of palm or artichoke hearts, drained

1 can (15 oz) garbanzo beans, drained and rinsed

1 cup (50g) gluten-free panko or bread-crumbs

¼ (60g) cup vegan mayonnaise

¼ cup (30g) green onion, finely chopped

2 tablespoons finely chopped fresh cilantro or parsley

2 garlic cloves, finely chopped

2 sheets nori, crumbled

1 tablespoon miso paste

1 teaspoon Old Bay seasoning

1 teaspoon soy sauce or gluten-free liquid aminos

1 teaspoon yellow mustard

½ teaspoon salt

⅛ teaspoon ground black pepper

½ cup (60g) panko or gluten-free bread-crumbs

Vegetable oil or other neutral oil for frying

GARNISH

Sweet Chili Sauce

8 lemon wedges

Pulse the garbanzo beans and hearts of palm in a food processor. Leave mixture partially chunky for more texture. Transfer to a large bowl and mix in remaining ingredients. Shape mixture into 8 phishcakes and place in the refrigerator for 30 minutes to set.

Dredge the phishcakes in panko. Heat two inches of oil to 365°F (185°C) in a large pot. Fry phishcakes for about 2 to 3 minutes on each side, or until golden brown; drain on paper towels. Serve with lemon wedges and Sweet Chili Sauce (p. 49).

VARIATION: For air fryer, bake at 350°F (180°C) for 15 to 20 minutes. For oven, bake at 400°F (200°C) for 25 to 30 minutes, or until golden brown, flipping halfway through.

SWEET CHILI SAUCE

¼ cup (60ml) rice vinegar
¼ cup (50g) sugar
¼ cup (60ml) water
2 cloves garlic, minced
1 teaspoon crushed red pepper
1 teaspoon sriracha

¼ teaspoon soy sauce or gluten-free liquid
  aminos

SLURRY
2 teaspoons cornstarch mixed with
  1 tablespoon water

Whisk together all ingredients in a saucepan and bring to a boil over medium-high heat. Once sugar has dissolved, add slurry to thicken and remove from heat. Serve sauce warm or chilled.

TATER STACKS
Yield: 12 stacks

A delightful dish of crispy, thinly sliced potatoes that start letting off hints of rosemary and thyme as each stack bakes away turning your kitchen into a fragrant haven. When fries just won't cut it, this is another way to enjoy the beloved spud, stunning in all its potato glory.

2 pounds (1kg) potatoes, peeled, sliced
⅛-inch thick (I use Yukon gold)
¼ cup (60ml) extra-virgin olive oil
4 garlic cloves, minced
2 tablespoons cornstarch (optional, but will help potato slices stick together)
2 tablespoons chopped fresh parsley or
1 teaspoon dried parsley
2 tablespoons fresh rosemary leaves or
1 teaspoon dried rosemary
2 teaspoons fresh thyme leaves or ½ teaspoon dried thyme
1 teaspoon onion powder
1 teaspoon salt
Freshly cracked black pepper

Extra-virgin olive oil cooking spray

Preheat oven to 375°F (190°C). Toss potato slices with remaining ingredients in a large bowl to coat; season with pepper to taste. Spray a 12-cup muffin pan with cooking spray. Stack the potatoes into the muffin cups one handful at a time. Bake for 40 to 45 minutes, or until potato is tender and golden brown on the edges and tops. Use a small spatula to remove stacks from muffin pan and serve hot.

MISO YAKI GRILLED TOFU

Yield: 4 servings

Miso is a traditional Japanese seasoning and protein-rich paste made primarily from fermented soybeans. The word "yaki," meaning grilled in Japanese, suggests some kind of grilling or searing will be involved. Slather this sweet, savory miso sauce on anything from veggies to rice balls to grilled tofu. The perfect pūpū for any occasion and a yummy way to introduce tofu into your diet.

MISO SAUCE
¼ cup (60ml) sake
¼ cup (50g) sugar
¼ cup (70g) white miso
3 tablespoons mirin (read label to make sure it's gluten-free)

1 (12oz/340g) vacuum-packed, deep-fried tofu, drained, cut into 2-inch triangles (I use Aloha brand)

GARNISH
½ cup (60g) thinly sliced green onion
1 tablespoon toasted white sesame seeds
1 to 2 thinly sliced fresh or bottled jalapeños (optional)

Whisk together miso sauce ingredients in a saucepan and bring to a boil over medium-high heat. Once sauce starts to bubble, cook for 1 more minute then remove from heat. Chill in the refrigerator until ready to use.

Heat grill or grill pan to high. Place tofu on the grill and sear for 3 to 4 minutes on each side to create sear marks. Arrange tofu on a dish and drizzle miso sauce to taste. Top with green onion, sesame, and jalapeño, if using.

CRISPY BAKED TOFU

Yield: 2 to 3 servings

It's time to talk about the other white (non) meat. Tofu is a powerhouse plant-based protein high in potassium and iron, and low in fat. The best way to spruce up tofu is to make sure you press it and season it properly. Cornstarch is the key element that crispens tofu when baking, so be generous! This soy marvel can be added to stir-fries, salads, or served in a pūpū platter with a sauce on the side for dipping. Don't miss the Crispy Tofu Watercress Poke on p. 85 or the Candied Hurricane Crispy Tofu on p. 65.

1 (14-ounce/400g) block firm or extra-firm tofu, drained, patted dry with a towel, cut into ½-inch cubes

½ tablespoon extra-virgin olive oil or oil of choice

1 tablespoon soy sauce or gluten-free liquid aminos

2 tablespoons cornstarch

½ teaspoon cracked black pepper or other seasoning (see **CHEF'S TIP**)

SUGGESTED GARNISHES
Oil-Free Tofu Mayo (p. 28)
Dengaku Sauce (p. 54)
Thai Basil Pesto (p. 31)
Sriracha
6 lemon wedges

Preheat oven to 400°F (200°C) and line a baking sheet with parchment paper. Place tofu in a large bowl and drizzle with olive oil: toss gently to coat. Add soy sauce and toss again. Sprinkle with cornstarch and toss one more time making sure the cornstarch has soaked into the tofu. Sprinkle with pepper or other seasoning. Bake for 25 to 30 minutes, or until golden brown and crispy. Serve with choice of suggested garnishes.

CHEF'S TIP: Use flavorful spices and herbs to perk up your tofu. Try 'alaea salt (Hawaiian red salt), BBQ rub, crushed red pepper, curry powder, dried herbs, garam masala, kala namak, Italian seasoning, lemon pepper seasoning, sesame seeds, smoked paprika, taco seasoning, or turmeric. You can also coat tofu with sriracha, BBQ sauce, teriyaki sauce, mayonnaise, or sauce of choice before baking to add flavor. However, adding sauces to the tofu may affect its crispiness.

NOTE: For air fryer bake at 350°F (180°C) for 15 to 20 minutes.

CHOY SUM WITH DENGAKU SAUCE

Yield: 4 servings

If your miso is neglected and pushed to the back of the refrigerator, it's time to reach for it and try this sweet and savory glaze. Miso lends an incredible depth of flavor to dishes, giving food an umami flavor that keeps you coming back for more. This is a light Japanese dish you can serve as an appetizer or over rice.

1 pound (500g) choy sum, cut into 2-inch pieces, steamed or boiled until tender, chilled

DENGAKU SAUCE
¼ cup (60ml) mirin

¼ cup (70g) miso paste (check ingredients for barley, wheat, or rye to make sure it's gluten-free)
¼ cup (50g) sugar
1 teaspoon toasted white sesame seeds

Whisk together mirin, miso, and sugar in a saucepan. Bring to a boil over medium-high heat. Once it starts to boil, reduce heat to medium and simmer until sugar is dissolved and sauce has thickened, about 1 minute. Remove from heat and add sesame seeds. Toss choy sum with dengaku sauce and serve.

VARIATION: Try the dengaku sauce with Miso Yaki Grilled Tofu (p. 51) or baked eggplant in the Eggplant Unagi Don recipe (p. 206).

MUSHROOM WALNUT PÂTÉ

Yield: 1 cup

This amazing spread is a delicious take on liver pâté, only meatless and way better for you. When you start thinking outside of the box, you'll come to realize anything can be veganized. Your pūpū platter will sparkle with this unique pâté as the centerpiece. If wine and happy hours are your thing, serve this to your guests at your next get-together and watch the bowl empty very quickly.

1 tablespoon extra-virgin olive oil
1 cup (150g) chopped onion
2 cloves garlic, minced
Pinch of salt
1 pound (500g) cremini mushrooms, sliced
½ cup (50g) chopped fresh parsley
2 teaspoons chopped fresh rosemary or
   ½ teaspoon dried rosemary

1 teaspoon mushroom seasoning
¼ teaspoon ground black pepper

½ cup (50g) walnuts

GARNISH
Gluten-free bread, crackers, or fresh
   vegetable sticks

Heat oil in a skillet over medium-high heat. Add onion, garlic, and a pinch of salt. Cook for 5 to 6 minutes, or until onion turns translucent. Add remaining ingredients and cook until the mushrooms are tender and reduced in size by half, about 5 to 6 minutes. Transfer to a blender and add the walnuts. Pulse until you reach a smooth pâté texture. Chill in the refrigerator for at least 4 hours, or overnight to allow flavors to meld. Serve with crackers, bread, or vegetable sticks.

SUN-DRIED TOMATO
AND SUN-DRIED TOMATO CASHEW BUTTER

Yield: 4 to 6 servings

One of the joys that have come out of our post-pandemic lifestyle is that many of us are cooking more and creating things from scratch. You will gain great satisfaction from making your own sun-dried tomatoes, then bottling to infuse in the luscious oil. Make sure you have some clean mason jars ready, and if it you can find the strength to part with these beautiful gems, they make great omiyage!

SUN-DRIED TOMATO

1 pound (500g) cherry tomatoes, sliced in
   half lengthwise
1 tablespoon extra-virgin olive oil

1 tablespoon chopped fresh oregano,
   basil, or thyme
Salt and freshly cracked black pepper

Preheat oven to 225°F (110°C) and line a baking sheet with parchment paper. Toss tomatoes with olive oil and fresh herbs in a large bowl; season with salt and pepper to taste. Arrange tomatoes on baking sheet and bake for 4 to 5 hours, or until tomatoes are dried out. (If you prefer your tomatoes semi-dried, bake for only 2 to 3 hours.) Serve on bread or crackers with pesto and Tofeta.

CHEF'S TIP: Place sun-dried tomatoes in a mason jar and fill with extra-virgin olive oil. Add garlic cloves or fresh herbs. Seal and store for up to 2 weeks in the refrigerator. Use the infused oil in salad dressings or for stir-frying.

SUN-DRIED TOMATO CASHEW BUTTER

Blend or pulse ½ cup (80g) raw cashews, 15 sun-dried tomatoes, ¼ cup (60ml) extra-virgin olive oil, 1 tablespoon nutritional yeast and 1 tablespoon lemon juice; season with salt and pepper to taste.

DARRY & LEE'S SANGRIA

Yield: about 1½ bottles

A visit to this sassy couple's beautiful home in Kailua is not complete without a glass of their famous sangria. It's summer entertaining at its best, and when you live in a warm climate like Hawai'i, unexpected guests in flip flops can turn up on your doorstep unannounced and thirsty. This Scottish beauty and her partner in crime know how to make a boozy sangria that's light with citrus notes and just the right amount of sliced fruit to give it that punch flair. For an authentic version, show up for a surprise visit and sample a glass of Darry and Lee's sangria and some of that warm Aloha spirit. Don't say I sent you!

1 bottle Wild Vines Blackberry Merlot or Red Blend
1 cup (240ml) orange juice (Tropicana no pulp preferred)
12 ounces (350ml) Captain Morgan's Spiced Rum
¼ cup (50g) sugar

GARNISH
1 slice each lemon, lime, and orange per glass

Mix ingredients together and chill for 1 hour before serving. Fill glasses with ice and top with sangria. Garnish with fruit slices.

VARIATION: Use non-alcoholic wine for a mocktail version.

DAVE'S HYDRO GIN

Yield: 1 serving

Dave writes, "A most appropriate libation for a vegan cookbook, this refreshing and energizing concoction symbolizes the most common and useful element in the universe—hydrogen. While enjoying your first green sip, make a toast in honor of those dedicated to capturing and converting hydrogen via renewable energy in the quest to save mankind (and animals) from the folly of fossil fuels." Here here!

GINGER SYRUP (MAKES ABOUT ¾ CUP)

4 ounces (200g) ginger, peeled and thinly sliced
2 cups (400g) sugar
2 cups (480ml) water
Pinch of salt

FRESH GINGER ALE

1 cup (240ml) seltzer tonic water or seltzer
2 tablespoons ginger syrup
1 tablespoon lemon or lime juice

 ## GARNISH

Colored ice balls (see **CHEF'S TIP**)
1 slice lemon or lime

Combine ginger, sugar, and water and a pinch of salt in a saucepan. Bring to a boil over medium-high heat. Once mixture starts to bubble, reduce heat to low and simmer, uncovered for 30 minutes. Strain through a sieve into a mason jar. Set aside ginger slices to make Candied Ginger (p. 59). Store ginger syrup in an airtight container in the refrigerator for up to 2 weeks.

Fill glass with ice. Add tonic or seltzer, ginger syrup to taste, and lemon or lime juice. Stir, then adjust to taste. Garnish with lemon or lime slice.

COCKTAIL VERSION

Add 2 ounces gin, or to taste.

CHEF'S TIP: Freeze candied ginger in ice balls or cubes to use in this drink as a surprise treat. Adding food coloring, pieces of fruit, whole strawberries, and jalapeño slices or fresh herbs to the water in your ice molds before freezing lends an elegant touch to your mocktails and cocktails.

CANDIED GINGER

Yield: about ½ cup

Arrange leftover ginger slices on a baking sheet lined with parchment paper and sprinkle with a little sugar to coat. Dry in the warm setting of your oven at 170°F (80°C) for 5 to 6 hours, or until you're happy with the texture. Store in an airtight container for up to 3 months.

CHAPTER 3

BY THE BEACH

Hawai'i is loved for its laid-back surf culture and sandy stretches where honeymoon couples fly thousands of miles for the ultimate photo-op. Although there are too many stunning beaches on this Pacific Island to visit in one lifetime, you can certainly picnic your way around as many as possible with some fun food. There's a bunch to consider when packing meals for the beach like the heat, cooler space, level of messiness, and the sand with its magnetic ability to get into everything. When I think of a picnic by the shore, handheld options like sweet and savory snacks or hearty sandwiches are your best bet should you encounter an unexpected gust of wind. In case you do get messy from the whims of Mother Nature, the water is just in front of you. Skip the utensils and napkins for this collection of beach staple faves. Now go hit the waves to work up an appetite!

FUN IDEA: Have your group of day-trippers each take a bunch of photos you can upload to a share file and turn into a short memory video of your day in the sand you can post on your social media. You could also turn the photos into a collage on a postcard and give to your friends on July 30 to celebrate International Friendship Day.

CANDIED HURRICANE GLAZE DONE 3 WAYS

I'm happy to offer you my twist on the popular Island-style hurricane seasoning with a spicy furikake glaze. Tiny drool? I approach my food very seriously and if I'm going to indulge, I'm going all out! It's sweet and salty, savory and spicy, in a mixture that brings all of the spices together in the most heavenly glaze you could imagine. Here are my four favorite candied hurricane dishes that are worth every single calorie. But who's counting? Take any of these creations to the beach or outdoor gathering and prepare yourself for compliments galore!

CANDIED HURRICANE POPCORN WITH PECANS

Yield: 4 cups

Hurricane popcorn is a local snack with a very well-deserved following. I've searched high and low for vegan-friendly versions to no avail. So here it is! Furikake adds a Japanese twist to this sweet and salty crunchy snack you are going to fall madly in love with. Enough said. The world needs this.

HURRICANE GLAZE
¾ cup (150g) sugar
3 tablespoons Japanese Furikake (p.30)
2 tablespoons hot sauce
1 tablespoon water
2 teaspoons crushed red pepper

½ teaspoon salt

3½ ounces (100g) ready-made plain
   popcorn
½ cup (50g) toasted pecans

Heat sugar in a large skillet until it starts to melt and bubble, about 2 to 4 minutes. Add remaining glaze ingredients and mix well to combine. Add popcorn and pecans; toss well to combine. Popcorn will still be sticky but will harden as it cools down. Pour onto a lined baking sheet to cool. Popcorn and nuts may clump up. Break apart into small pieces and store in an airtight container in the refrigerator until ready to use.

VARIATION: Skip the popcorn and try this Hurricane Glaze recipe using 1½ cups (150g) of mixed nuts.

CANDIED HURRICANE SWEET POTATO

Yield: 3 to 4 servings

This is my version of a traditional Japanese treat called **Daigaku Imo**, *"university potatoes," in Japanese. This candied sweet potato snack was popular in universities during the earlier part of the century, hence the name. The addition of Japanese Furikake adds just the right toasted umph packed with enough calories to get anyone through an all-nighter.*

1 medium Japanese sweet potato, peeled, cut into 1-inch pieces

½ tablespoon sesame oil

Salt

1 batch Hurricane Glaze (p. 62)

Heat oven to 400°F (200°C) and line a baking sheet with parchment paper.

Toss sweet potato with sesame oil in a bowl and season with salt to taste. Arrange sweet potato on baking sheet and bake for 25 minutes. Remove from heat and allow to cool slightly.

Prepare Hurricane Glaze and add sweet potato; toss well to coat. Remove from heat and pour onto a lined baking tray to cool. Chill in the refrigerator for at least 1 hour before serving.

NOTE: For air fryer, bake at 350°F (180°C) for 15 to 20 minutes.

CANDIED HURRICANE CRISPY TOFU

Yield: 2 to 4 servings

You will never look at tofu the same way again after you give this a try. Beyond delicious!

1 batch Hurricane Glaze (p. 62)
1 batch of Crispy Baked Tofu (p. 53)

Prepare Hurricane Glaze and add Crispy Baked Tofu; toss to coat. Remove from heat and pour onto a lined baking tray to cool. Chill in the refrigerator for at least 1 hour before serving.

PEANUT BUTTER OAT BITES

Yield: about 12 balls

Instead of scarfing down sugar laden granola bars, try making your own. Dried fruit, dates, sesame seeds, a lot of things end up in my mix and the choices are endless. Start your day off right with a morning stroll on the beach or a walk around your neighborhood, then treat yourself to this delicious snack. Breakfast done!

DRY INGREDIENTS
1 cup old fashioned rolled oats
¼ cup (50g) vegan chocolate chips
½ cup (50g) toasted coconut flakes
2 tablespoons ground chia or flaxseed (or a mixture of both)

WET INGREDIENTS
½ cup (120g) peanut butter
⅓ cup (110g) maple syrup or agave syrup
1 teaspoon vanilla extract

SUGGESTED ADD-INS (OPTIONAL)
Vegan chocolate chips
Dried fruit (berries, cranberries, dates, raisins)
Nuts (almonds, cashews, hazelnuts, macadamia nuts, peanuts, walnuts)
Seeds (hemp, pumpkin, sunflower)

¼ cup (30g) toasted white sesame seeds

Combine dry ingredients in a bowl. In a separate bowl, mix together wet ingredients and fold into the dry ingredients. Mix in 2 to 3 tablespoons of suggested add-ins, if using. Chill in the refrigerator for 20 minutes to firm. Form mixture into about 12 balls then roll in sesame seeds. Store in an airtight container in the refrigerator for up to 1 month.

VARIATION: Add chopped dates and cocoa powder to your mixture for extra flavor, or skip the sesame seeds and dip the balls in melted vegan chocolate for a heavenly choc-coated version.

CORN RIBS

Yield: 8 corn ribs

Corn ribs are a hot topic on social media and for good reason. Cooked and seasoned to savory perfection, they leave your hands and mouth covered in sticky goodness. I suggest you watch a video online to see how you can hack through the corn cobs successfully. Overall, the process is pretty simple. Some of them even curl up like a curvature of a rib when baked (especially in the air fryer), adding to the whole "rib" experience. A beach picnic essential!

2 corn ears

SEASONING
2 tablespoons extra-virgin olive oil
1 tablespoon Old Bay seasoning
1 teaspoon smoked paprika
½ teaspoon liquid smoke

Salt and freshly cracked black pepper

GARNISH
1 batch Tangy Chipotle Mayo (p. 76) (optional)

Preheat oven to 400°F (200°C) and line a baking sheet with parchment paper.

Remove husk from corn and cut off ends. Stand corn up vertically on the larger flat end. Cut in half down the center of the core, then cut the halves into quarters. Go slowly as the core is quite tough and will require concentration.

Whisk together seasoning in a large bowl. Add corn "ribs' and toss well to coat; season with salt and pepper to taste. Lay the ribs in a single layer on the baking sheet and bake for 25 to 30 minutes, flipping halfway through, or until corn kernels are tender and slightly charred.

VARIATION: For air fryer, bake at 350°F (180°C) for 12 to 15 minutes.

MAC PARM KALE CHIPS

Yield: 4 servings

When my part-time vegan husband said, "These are great!" I knew I was onto something good. The truth is this low-calorie nutritious snack has unwittingly caused people to eat more kale. Fill some large mason jars with this superfood crunch to avoid sand ruining your munch and pass them around the beach site. Save the kale stems for your smoothies!

1 bunch kale leaves (5oz/150g), stems removed, torn into 1 to 2-inch pieces (kale must be washed, rinsed, and dried thoroughly)

2 tablespoons extra-virgin olive oil

½ cup (30g) Mac Parm (p. 23)

Preheat oven to 300°F (150°C) and line 2 baking trays with parchment paper. Place kale in a large bowl and drizzle with olive oil; toss to coat. Sprinkle with Mac Parm and toss again. Bake for 10 minutes then flip kale and bake another 10 to 12 minutes, or until crisp. Allow to cool on tray before serving.

VARIATION: For air-fryer, bake at 250°F (120°C) for 7 to 10 minutes.

VEGAN "SCALLOP" ROLL

Yield: 4 rolls

The beguiling scallop roll made with king oyster mushrooms is a sandwich that will keep you up at night as the leftovers will be a siren call from your refrigerator at 3:00 am. Seared "scallops" tossed with a light dressing makes this picture-perfect roll a delectable delicacy. Not into the bun? Dress some fresh crispy greens and turn it into a vegan seafood salad.

"SCALLOPS"
1 tablespoon vegan butter
4 king oyster mushrooms, cut into ½-inch
  pieces.
2 garlic cloves, minced
½ teaspoon Old Bay seasoning
¼ teaspoon mushroom seasoning

DRESSING
2 to 3 tablespoons lemon juice
2 tablespoons vegan mayonnaise
1 tablespoon chopped fresh dill, parsley,
  or tarragon
1 tablespoon minced onion
1 tablespoon sweet relish or chopped

pickles
Freshly cracked black pepper

4 bread rolls or gluten-free rolls toasted
  with Garlic Herb Butter (p. 141)
1 cup (30g) baby leaf greens or baby
  spinach leaves

GARNISH
8 lemon wedges
1 tablespoon chopped fresh parsley

Heat butter in a skillet over medium-high heat. Add mushrooms and cook for 3 minutes. Stir in garlic, mushroom seasoning, and Old Bay. Cover with a lid and allow to steam for 2 to 3 minutes or until "scallops" are tender. Flip "scallops" a few times to brown. Remove from heat and cool to room temperature.

Whisk together dressing ingredients in a bowl and season with pepper to taste. Fold into "scallop" mixture and chill in the refrigerator for at least 1 hour before serving to allow flavors to meld. Fill bread with baby leaf and "scallop" mixture. Garnish with lemon wedge and parsley.

CARROT SMOKED "SALMON" AND CASHEW CREAM CHEESE

Yield: 4 to 6 servings

For those of you who enjoyed smoked lox prior to giving up animal products, carrots are one way you can still enjoy "salmon" on a plant-based diet. This convincingly fish-friendly seafood alternative is the perfect complement to Cashew Cream Cheese served over crackers or a bagel for a special breakfast, party snack, or cocktail hour pūpū. All made possible by plants. Yes, really!

"SALMON"
3 medium carrots (do not peel)
½ teaspoon salt

MARINADE
1 cup (240ml) hot water
3 tablespoons caper brine or pickle brine
3 tablespoons soy sauce or gluten-free liquid aminos
2 tablespoons extra-virgin olive oil
1 teaspoon rice vinegar
1 tablespoon capers
½ tablespoon kombu dashi powder (kelp granules) or
    mushroom seasoning
1 tablespoon miso paste
1 teaspoon onion powder
½ teaspoon garlic powder
½ teaspoon liquid smoke

GARNISH
Cashew Cream Cheese (recipe following)
Gluten-free crackers or bread
Thinly sliced red onion
1 tablespoon fresh dill or ½ teaspoon dried dill
Freshly cracked black pepper

Preheat oven to 350°F (180°C) and line a baking sheet with parchment paper. Wash carrots and place on baking sheet while still wet. Sprinkle with salt and rub onto the outside of the carrots. Bake for 55 minutes. Remove from oven and cool to room temperature. Slice into strips using a peeler to resemble "salmon."

Combine all marinade ingredients in a large mason jar. Seal with lid and shake to mix. Add "salmon" and gently swish around to coat. Cover and allow to marinate in the refrigerator for 1 to 2 days, or at least overnight to allow flavors to meld.

Spread Cashew Cream Cheese onto crackers or bread and top with "salmon" and red onion slices. Garnish with fresh or dried dill and season with pepper to taste.

NOTE: I don't recommend using an air fryer to bake the carrots as they can get a little crispy on the edges. The carrot should be soft enough to peel, but still firm enough so that it doesn't crumble when peeling or slicing into strips.

CASHEW CREAM CHEESE

Yield: about 1 cup

½ cup (80g) raw cashews, rinsed, boiled in water for 25 minutes, drained (see **NOTE**)
½ cup (100g) coconut cream (see **NOTE** on p. 239)
2 tablespoons non-dairy milk
1 tablespoon apple cider vinegar

2 teaspoons lemon juice
2 teaspoons maple syrup or agave syrup
1 teaspoon onion powder
1 teaspoon salt

½ teaspoon dried dill (optional)

Blend all ingredients, except dill, until smooth and creamy. Add more milk if cream cheese is still thick. Stir in dill, if using, and chill for at least 1 hour before serving. Store in an airtight container in the refrigerator for up to 5 days.

NOTE: Cashews must always be raw (not cooked or toasted), and boiled until soft to ensure a creamy consistency. Boil cashews longer if you feel they're still too hard or use raw cashews that have soaked in water overnight for guaranteed softness.

CHUNA SANDIE

Yield: 6 servings

This "chuna" filling of mashed garbanzo beans creates a flaked consistency remarkably similar to tuna that even my tuna sandie-addict mom would approve. For many of us, a sandwich was the first meal we attempted to make for ourselves as kids. When you think about the fundamental principles of sandwich construction, it all comes down to whether it's filling and fulfilling. Start with good bread. Gluten-free or not, toasted or untoasted. A fatty spread will help insulate and waterproof the bread from becoming soggy. The Sun-Dried Tomato Cashew Butter on p. 56 makes an excellent spread and will complement the flavors in this "chuna" salad. Vegan butter or mayo also provide a nice barrier to keep your bread intact. Find your spot on the sand and take it all in, one delicious bite after another. Best beach food ever!

CHUNA

2 cans garbanzo beans, drained
½ cup (120g) vegan mayonnaise
¼ cup (25g) finely chopped celery
¼ cup (60ml) lemon juice
¼ cup (25g) finely chopped onion
2 tablespoons chopped parsley or cilantro
1 tablespoon whole grain mustard

¼ teaspoon mushroom seasoning or
    kombu dashi powder (optional)
Salt and freshly cracked black pepper

12 slices bread or gluten-free bread,
    toasted or untoasted

SUGGESTED FILLINGS

Vegan mayonnaise to taste
Leafy greens or baby spinach leaves
Sprouts (I use broccoli sprouts)
Sliced tomato
Sliced cucumber
Pickles
Pickled jalapeño slices
Grated beets
Vegan cheese

Roughly mash garbanzo beans in a large bowl using a potato masher or fork. Mix in remaining chuna ingredients and season with salt and pepper to taste. Chill in the refrigerator for 1 hour to allow flavors to meld. Build your sandwich with any of the suggested fillings.

LOBSTA ROLL

Yield: 4 servings

There's no denying the lobster roll is the summertime sandwich of choice, which of course can be veganized. Pink Lobster mushrooms are about as hard to come by as a winning lottery ticket, but if you can find them, the more power to you. Pink oyster mushrooms are the next best choice with a meaty texture so similar to lobster it's uncanny. Treat your beach buddies to this East Coast classic and make sure someone brings the wine. A sparkling wine, dry rosé, or a rich, barrel-fermented Chardonnay will really compliment the rolls.

LOBSTA
1 tablespoon vegan butter
10 ounces (300g) pink oyster mushrooms, bottom stem removed, pulled apart into 1-inch pieces
1 to 2 cloves garlic, minced (optional)
Salt and freshly cracked black pepper
1 teaspoon Old Bay seasoning
½ teaspoon kombu dashi powder (kelp granules) or mushroom seasoning

DRESSING
2 tablespoons vegan mayonnaise
1 tablespoon minced celery
1 tablespoon chopped fresh parsley, tarragon, or dill (or a combination of all)

1 tablespoon minced onion
1 tablespoon sweet relish or chopped pickles
3 to 4 tablespoons lemon juice, or to taste
Salt and freshly cracked black pepper

ROLL SUGGESTIONS
Gluten-free bread roll toasted with Garlic Herb Butter (p. 141)
Gluten-free tortilla you can roll up
Leafy greens
Tomato
Cucumber
Pickled vegetables (p. 134)
Fresh herbs

Heat butter in a skillet over medium-high heat. Add mushrooms and cook for 3 minutes, stirring constantly. Add garlic and season with salt and pepper to taste. Cook for another 4 to 5 minutes, or until mushrooms are tender. Mix in Old Bay seasoning and kombu dashi powder. Remove from heat and transfer to a bowl; cool to room temperature.

Whisk together dressing ingredients in a small bowl. Mix into the lobsta mixture and season with salt and pepper to taste. Add more lemon juice, if desired. Chill in the refrigerator for at least 1 hour to allow flavors to meld. Build your bread roll or tortilla roll with suggested garnishes. Top with lobsta and garnish with fresh herbs.

CORN OKRA FRITTERS

Yield: 10 fritters

I was greeted by my neighbor, George, and his daughter, Lauren, with a plate of corn okra fritters. They were so good I knew I had to create my own recipe. Whether you're on "team okra" or not, these crispy fritters are a treat and may just change the way you see these sticky "lady's fingers." Visit your local farmers market during the summer months for fresh okra or use the frozen stuff and enjoy anytime of the year. This Southern staple is a nice nibble on a sunny day hang at the shore. Don't even get me started about the chipotle mayo. It's good. Really, really, good.

TANGY CHIPOTLE MAYO
½ cup (120g) vegan mayonnaise
2 tablespoons chipotle in adobo sauce
   (sauce only)
1 tablespoon apple cider vinegar
1 tablespoon lemon juice
1 teaspoon minced garlic
Salt and freshly cracked black pepper

FRITTERS
½ cup (120ml) plant-based milk
½ cup (100g) silken tofu, mashed with a
   fork
2 cups (250g) fresh or canned corn kernels
1 cup (about 10 okra/150g) thinly sliced
   okra
½ cup (15g) chopped fresh cilantro
¼ cup (15g) thinly sliced green onion

1 to 2 fresh or bottled jalapeño, chopped
   (optional)

DRY INGREDIENTS
½ cup (100g) all-purpose flour or
   gluten-free flour
½ cup (70g) cornmeal
2 teaspoons Cajun seasoning
1½ teaspoons salt
1 teaspoon baking powder
1 teaspoon onion powder
¼ teaspoon ground black pepper

Vegetable oil or other neutral oil for frying

GARNISH
10 lemon wedges

Whisk together Tangy Chipotle Mayo ingredients in a small bowl; cover and chill in the refrigerator until ready to use.

To make fritters, whisk together the milk and tofu in a large bowl. Mix in the corn, okra, coriander, and green onion. Whisk the dry ingredients in a separate bowl and add to the corn mixture; mix well to combine.

Heat two inches of oil to 365°F in a large pot. Fry fritters on each side for about 2 to 3 minutes, or until golden brown; drain on paper towels. Serve with Tangy Chipotle Mayo and lemon wedges.

VARIATIONS: For air fryer, bake at 350°F (180°C) for 15 to 20 minutes. You may need a light coating of flour and cooking spray before baking. For oven, arrange on a lined baking sheet and bake at 400°F (200°C) for 25 to 30 minutes, flipping half-way through, until golden brown.

OYSTER BACON CHICKPEA FRITTATA

Yield: 12 muffins

Who said you have to give up egg dishes when you go vegan? I'm not kidding when I say expect amazing! First thing on your shopping list is kala namak, Himalayan black salt. Light pink or pinkish gray in color (contrary to what its name suggests), kala namak is an Indian volcanic rock salt with a sulfurous, pungent smell that turns any dish "eggy." Fold in some Oyster Bacon and make this a frittata worth talking about.

FRITTATA BATTER

2 cups (240g) chickpea flour (also called garbanzo flour or gram flour)
2 cups water

OYSTER BACON

¼ cup (60g) vegan butter
10 ounces (270g) oyster mushrooms, bottom stem removed, chopped into ¼-inch pieces
1 teaspoon BBQ seasoning or taco seasoning
Salt and freshly cracked black pepper

FRITTATA SEASONING

¼ cup (15g) nutritional yeast
1 tablespoon melted vegan butter or extra-virgin olive oil
1 tablespoon tapioca starch
1 teaspoon baking powder
1 teaspoon garlic powder
1 teaspoon kala namak
1 teaspoon onion powder
1 teaspoon smoked paprika
⅛ teaspoon ground nutmeg

FILLING

½ cup (100g) shredded vegan cheese
½ cup (50g) sliced green onion
½ cup (10g) parsley, chopped
2 tablespoons chopped fresh chives
Salt and freshly cracked black pepper
Extra-virgin olive oil cooking spray

Whisk together chickpea flour and water in a bowl and set aside for 30 minutes. (The batter tastes better when it has had time to rest.)

In the meantime, prepare Oyster Bacon. Heat butter in a skillet over medium-high heat. Add mushrooms and cook for 3 minutes. Once mushrooms start to brown, turn heat down to medium and cook for 15 to 20 minutes, or until "bacon" is golden brown and crispy. Add barbecue seasoning and season with salt and pepper to taste; set aside.

Heat oven to 375°F (190°C) and spray a 12-cup muffin pan with cooking spray.

Add frittata seasoning ingredients to the chickpea mixture and whisk to combine. Mixture should be thin and smooth like a pancake batter. Stir in filling ingredients and Oyster Bacon. Pour frittata mixture evenly into the muffin cups and bake for 25 minutes. Cool slightly before gently lifting the frittata out of the muffin pan using a small spatula. Drizzle with vegan honey and hot sauce to taste.

CHAPTER 4

BEYOND POKE VEGAN STYLE

I could probably write a whole book on this casual Hawaiian cuisine locals and tourists knock back any time of day. Poke (pronounced poh-kay), the Hawaiian word for "to slice," is a raw sushi-in-a-bowl concept made with sashimi grade 'ahi tuna, sweet onions, limu (seaweed), 'ina-mona (roasted kukui, or candlenut), and green onion. While modest poke bowls are still part of the culinary landscape in the Islands, modern creations are being served at restaurants with new flavor com-binations including house-made chili paste, wasabi, kim-chi, mayonnaise, fresh lemon, roasted garlic, ume (pickled plum), ja-lapeño, and even tahini. In my obsession with con-cocting the perfect vegan version of this Hawaiian favor-ite, I quickly realized I would need to give this poke phenomenon a whole chapter of its own—and Beyond Poke Vegan Style was born.

Pause briefly for a moment and take a quick look at the Watermelon Chuna Poke Bowl on p. 87. Once you're able to wrap your head around the fact that baked watermelon is just 'ahi in disguise, you'll quickly learn, once again, that anything can be veganized. The poke bowl is merely a canvas in which you can perform. Top freshly steamed rice with at least three types of poke and throw in some pickled avocado (p. 134) for crunch. You could well go bonkers dreaming about the myriad of ways you can enjoy this true taste of Hawai'i—vegan style. It's an exotic trip for the taste buds that will take you back to the smell of the ocean and your toes hitting the sandy beaches of this beautiful paradise. Now go forth and make poke magic!

POKE DRESSING

Yield: about 2 cups

Who knew it was so easy to bring your favorite Hawaiian dish home? Even if you don't want to eat fish, you can still be part of the poke trend. The dressing functions as ambassador in poke bowls and comes in many different guises. Getting it right is key to a banging poke dish! The beauty of this dressing is it's so easy to make and is the ideal combination of sweet, salty, spicy, crunchy, and sticky. Your poke obsession starts now!

¼ cup limu seaweed, chopped (substitute with kizami arame, hijiki, or wakame, see **NOTE**)

½ cup (120ml) soy sauce or gluten-free liquid aminos

½ cup (30g) finely chopped Maui onion or sweet onion

½ cup (60g) finely sliced green onion

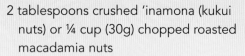

2 tablespoons crushed 'inamona (kukui nuts) or ¼ cup (30g) chopped roasted macadamia nuts

¼ cup (60ml) toasted sesame oil

2 tablespoons sugar

2 teaspoons toasted white sesame seeds

2 thinly sliced Hawaiian chili peppers or ½ teaspoon crushed red pepper

1 teaspoon minced fresh ginger

½ teaspoon 'alaea salt (Hawaiian red salt) or salt of choice

Mix together all ingredients in a bowl and chill until ready to use. Store dressing in the refrigerator for up to 2 to 3 days

NOTE: Limu, seaweed in Hawaiian, sometimes referred to as ogo, is reddish-brown with lacy, branching tendrils that taste like the sea. This is the seaweed that is likely to show up in your poke bowl in Hawai'i. Dried seaweed such as kizami arame, hijiki, or wakame can be easily rehydrated by soaking in hot or cold water (follow package instructions) for just a few minutes, then draining. Two tablespoons dried seaweed yields about ¼ cup (30g) rehydrated seaweed.

ROASTED KABOCHA POKE

Yield: 3 to 4 servings

Kabocha, or Japanese pumpkin, has got to be my favorite winter squash taking on the taste and texture of roasted chestnuts or sweet potatoes when cooked. Drizzled with the umami-rich poke dressing, the combination of flavors highlights the sweetness in the kabocha in the best possible way.

1 whole kabocha, deseeded (not peeled), diced into ½-inch pieces
Extra-virgin olive oil cooking spray
½ teaspoon salt
Poke Dressing (p. 82)

GARNISH
1 tablespoon chopped roasted macadamia nuts

Preheat oven to 400°F (200°C) degrees and line a baking sheet with parchment paper. Place kabocha in a large bowl and drizzle with oil. Add salt and toss well to coat. Arrange on prepared baking sheet and bake for 20 to 25 minutes, or until kabocha is tender. Transfer kabocha to a large bowl and mix in Poke Dressing to taste. Sprinkle with macadamia nuts.

NOTE: The kabocha pumpkin skin is edible and does not require peeling. When cooked, it becomes tender and also has a higher concentration of nutrition in the skin.

VARIATION: For air fryer, bake kabocha at 350°F (180°C) for 15 to 20 minutes.

BEETIFUL POKE

Yield: 3 to 4 servings

Serve this vibrant beet poke over rice, noodles, quinoa, or in a salad with nuts, avocado, radishes, or crunchy veggies. Beets become more and more flavorful as they marinate in the dressing, so try and allow time for the beets to soak in the dressing before creating your delicious vegan poke bowl.

5 beets, leaves cut off, scrubbed thoroughly
Poke Dressing (p. 82) to taste

GARNISH
2 tablespoons roughly chopped macadamia
   nuts

Preheat oven to 400°F (200°C). Line a baking sheet with parchment paper. Wrap beets individually in foil and bake for 50 to 60 minutes (Small beets will cook more quickly than larger ones.) They're done when a fork or skewer slides easily into the center of the beet. Remove from oven and allow to cool to room temperature. Once cooled, peel away skin and dice into ½-inch cubes. Place in a bowl, drizzle with Poke Dressing to taste, and sprinkle with nuts.

NOTE: You can also steam, boil, or use precooked beets for this recipe.

CRISPY TOFU WATERCRESS POKE

Yield: 2 to 3 servings

Trust me, swapping raw fish for crispy tofu in this vegan twist on Hawaiian poke is the perfect complement to the bold and powerful flavors in the poke dressing. As for the rest of the bowl? Fill it with as many colors and textures as possible: vibrant purple cabbage, shaved rainbow carrots, crunchy radishes, and other scraps from your refrigerator. The only rule is to have fun with it!

CRISPY TOFU

1 (14-ounce/400g) block firm or extra-firm tofu, drained, patted dry with a towel, cut into ½-inch cubes
1 tablespoon sesame oil or oil of choice
1 tablespoon soy sauce or gluten-free liquid aminos
2 tablespoons cornstarch

1 cup (220g) watercress, cut into small pieces
Poke Dressing (p. 82)

GARNISH
6 lemon wedges

Preheat oven to 400°F (200°C) and line a baking sheet with parchment paper. Place tofu in a large bowl and drizzle with sesame oil; toss gently to coat. Add soy sauce and toss again. Sprinkle with cornstarch and toss one more time making sure the cornstarch has soaked into the tofu. Bake for 25 to 30 minutes, or until golden brown and crispy.

Transfer tofu to a large bowl. Mix in watercress and Poke Dressing to taste. Serve with lemon wedges.

VARIATION: For air fryer, bake tofu at 350°F (180°C) for 15 to 20 minutes.

EDAMAME "'AHI" POKE

Bake 2 whole red bell peppers at 425°F (220°C) for 40 minutes. Peel, remove seeds and membrane, and cut into ½-inch pieces. Mix with 1 cup (150g) shelled edamame and add Poke Dressing (p. 82) to taste. Serve chilled.

MUSHROOM POKE

Cook 1 pound (450g) button mushrooms in 1 tablespoon extra-virgin olive oil for 4 to 5 minutes, or until tender. Add Poke Dressing (p. 82) to taste. Sprinkle with 2 tablespoons sliced green onion and serve chilled.

OKRA NATTO POKE

Boil 10 okra in salted water for 2 to 3 minutes, or until just tender. Place in a bath of cool water to stop the cooking process; drain and cut into ½-inch slices. Mix 2 packs (80g) natto vigorously with chopsticks until frothy. Combine with okra and add Poke Dressing (p. 82) to taste. Serve chilled.

WATERMELON CHUNA POKE BOWL

Yield: 4 servings

1 batch Sushi Rice (p. 207)
Watermelon Chuna Poke (p. 87)
Cucumber Sukemono
Wasabi Mayo Dressing

GARNISH
1 avocado, diced or sliced, drizzled with 1 tablespoon lemon
  juice
1 sheet nori, crumbled
2 tablespoons sliced green onion

Divide rice into 4 bowls. Top with Watermelon Chuna Poke, Cucumber Sukemono, avocado, nori, and green onion; drizzle with dressing.

WATERMELON CHUNA POKE

Yield: 4 servings

WATERMELON CHUNA
1 pound (500g) watermelon, cut into ½-inch cubes
¼ cup (60ml) Poke Dressing (p. 82)
2 teaspoons tahini
½ teaspoon sriracha (optional)

Preheat oven to 375°F (190°C) and line a baking sheet with parchment paper.

Arrange watermelon on lined sheet and bake for 45 minutes,

stirring halfway through baking. Remove from oven and pour into a colander; allow to drain for 10 minutes. You should see liquid still coming out from the watermelon. Place watermelon in a large bowl. Whisk together the poke dressing, tahini, and sriracha (if using) in a small bowl; add to watermelon and toss to combine. Cover and chill in the refrigerator for at least 2 hours or overnight to allow flavors to meld. Store watermelon poke in the refrigerator for up to 1 week.

CUCUMBER SUKEMONO
(JAPANESE PICKLED CUCUMBER)

3 tablespoons sugar
2 teaspoons salt
1 teaspoon Japanese karashi (hot mustard)
½ teaspoon mushroom seasoning

3 Japanese or Persian cucumbers, sliced
¼-inch thick on the diagonal

GARNISH
2 teaspoons toasted white sesame seeds
¼ nori sheet, crumbled

Mix together sugar, salt, mustard, and mushroom seasoning in a zip-lock bag. Add cucumber and rub mixture over the cucumbers to coat. Squeeze out the air from the bag and seal. Marinate for at least 2 hours or overnight to allow flavors to meld. Discard liquid. Garnish with sesame seeds and nori.

WASABI MAYO DRESSING

½ cup (115g) vegan mayonnaise
2 tablespoons plant-based milk
2 tablespoons rice vinegar

2 tablespoons wasabi powder or
    2 teaspoons wasabi paste
1 tablespoon soy sauce or gluten-free
    liquid aminos

Mix together ingredients in a bowl and chill in the refrigerator before serving.

CHAPTER 5
THE SOUPA BOWL

Think of soup as an opportunity to cash in on nature's bounty and get your daily quota of veggies. You should know by now my love affair with the local farmers market, and when my refrigerator is overloaded with produce, it's time to create a big pot of comforting goodness. Here's what I can share with you that will instantly turn your soups into worthy meals. Tip number one; roast your veggies first! They'll gain intense flavors by squeezing out the moisture that boiling just can't offer. That slight char with its smoky tang and caramelization deepens the flavors of the spices as well, propelling your batch into soup stardom. A touch of extra-virgin olive oil and some seasoning is all you need. Once you've roasted your veggie combos simply add them to a pot with vegetable broth or plant-based milk and heat. SO easy! These roasted soups are even better on the second or third day once you've allowed them to hang for a while, allowing the flavors to harmonize. They also freeze well, so double or triple the batch then store in airtight containers in the freezer. For the busy bees, I've included a Soup To Go (p. 116) I think you're going to find useful. My signature Kombu Dashi Broth (p. 104) is fit for any soup or noodle dish and will take your soups to a whole new level of umami. Make your own vegetable broth with leftover veggie scraps using a ratio of 1:1 veggies to water. Place in a big pot and simmer for about one hour with your choice of herbs and spices. Strain and enjoy! Now without further ado, get cracking in the kitchen and into a hearty bowl of vegan heaven. It's soupa good!

FUN IDEA: Throw a Soupa Bowl party! Make four or five of the soups ahead of time (remember you can freeze them). Set up your soup station with big warm pots of soup and condiments. Show off your collection of homemade condiments from Chapter 1. Stack mugs and bowls around your soup station in every shape you can find and tuck in!

NOTE: Peeled garlic can turn bitter when baked. Bake garlic cloves in their skin and discard peel after baking.

ALMOST BORSCHT ROASTED BEET SOUP

Yield: 4 to 6 servings

If you're spending any time at a farmers market, chances are you'll discover the most beautiful beets on the planet. Keep an eye out for these gorgeous beetroots that come in various colors from red to yellow and candy-striped. I like to use the red ones and build that deep crimson shade for this "almost borscht" soup—my Ukrainian friends, Ilona and Anna, would never forgive me if I claimed this to be an authentic version of their country's most loved staple. Feel free to clean out your refrigerator and throw in any veggies you find. Soup is very forgiving in the sense it can handle stray ingredients and still come together in harmony. It's personal (table etiquette gets thrown out the door when soup is involved), but I like to dip my bread straight into the bowl and scoop it all up with no shame at all.

SOUP BASE

1 can (16oz/454g) butter beans, rinsed and drained

1 pack (10oz/300g) pre-cooked beets, diced (steamed, baked, or boiled)

1 large onion, diced

1 large carrot, diced (no need to peel the carrot when using organic)

2 tablespoons chopped fresh dill or 1 teaspoon dried dill

2 tablespoons extra-virgin olive oil

2 tablespoons fresh rosemary leaves or 1 teaspoon dried rosemary

2 whole garlic cloves, unpeeled

Salt and freshly cracked black pepper

1 cup (240ml) vegetable broth

3 tablespoons sweet relish or chopped pickles

SUGGESTED GARNISH

Chopped nuts or seeds

Chopped parsley or leafy herb

Reserved roasted vegetables and beans

Vegan sour cream or yogurt

Preheat oven to 400°F (200°C). Combine soup base ingredients in an oven dish and season with salt and pepper to taste. Bake for 35 to 40 minutes, or until vegetables are tender and slightly charred. Remove from oven and set aside ¼ cup of the roasted butter beans, beets, and carrots for garnishing. Squeeze out garlic cloves into veggies and discard skin. Transfer roasted vegetables to a large pot; mix in vegetable broth. Use an immersion stick to blend the soup, or ladle into a mixer and blend the soup in batches. Pulse for chunky style or purée until creamy. Stir in sweet relish. Add a little more vegetable broth or water if soup is too thick; adjust seasoning, if necessary. Warm soup over medium heat. Ladle into bowls and top with suggested garnishes. A nice dollop of vegan sour cream or yogurt is excellent with this soup.

CASHEW CHEESE
OF MUSHROOM SOUP

Yield: 4 to 6 servings

Imagine for a moment, the creamiest mushroom soup served in a toasted bread bowl straight from the oven. It is what vegan dreams are made of—but some credit has to go to the luscious Cashew Cheese Sauce that brings this thick chowder together. Gluten-free bread is easily found on supermarket shelves so you should have no trouble getting your hands on a good-sized bun that works for your dietary needs. To make an edible bread bowl, hollow out the inside of a round bun, saving the insides as a garnish for the soup. Brush the inside with olive oil creating a seal and bake at 350°F (180°C) for 10 to 15 minutes, or until crispy. Fill with warm soup and serve, or top with vegan cheese and return to oven to lightly brown. Talk about a soup to remember!

SOUP BASE

1 pack (8oz/227g) mushrooms, sliced

2 large potatoes, diced

1 large onion, diced

3 whole garlic cloves (see **NOTE**)

2 tablespoons chopped fresh parsley or
1 teaspoon dried parsley

1 tablespoon fresh thyme leaves or
¼ teaspoon dried thyme

2 teaspoons mushroom seasoning

Freshly cracked black pepper

1 batch Cashew Cheese Sauce (p. 160)

2 cups (480ml) vegetable broth

GARNISH

Freshly cracked black pepper

Sliced fresh or bottled jalapeño

Chopped fresh parsley or leafy herb

Gluten-free toasted bread or croutons

Preheat oven to 400°F (200°C). Mix together soup base ingredients in an oven dish and season with pepper. Bake for 35 to 40 minutes, or until vegetables are tender and slightly charred. Remove from oven and set aside ¼ cup of the roasted mushrooms for garnishing. Squeeze out garlic cloves into veggies and discard skin. Transfer roasted vegetables to a large pot. Add Cashew Cheese Sauce and vegetable broth. Use an immersion stick to blend the soup, or ladle into a mixer and blend the soup in batches. Pulse for chunky style or purée until creamy. Add a little more vegetable broth or water if soup is too thick; adjust seasoning, if necessary. Warm soup over medium heat. Ladle into bowls (or bread bowls) and top with suggested garnishes.

NOTE: Peeled garlic can turn bitter when baked. Bake garlic cloves in their skin and discard peel after baking.

CREAMY CHARRED BRUSSELS SPROUTS SOUP

Yield: 4 to 6 servings

The secret to the best Brussels sprout soup is a good char. It may just be the solution to make non-believers a fan of these cute mini cabbages. This winter veggie grows in a spiral pattern along a huge stalk. Some supermarkets sell them unplucked when in season and you can pull them off straight from the stalk. When roasted, crispy sweet and caramelized layers develop that are full of flavor and complexity. Keep this nice and chunky so you get a good taste of the sprout. It's a comforting meal for seriously hungry folks on a chilly night. Drizzle with Balsamic Glaze and top with Oyster Bacon (p. 78) to up the game!

2 cups (480ml) vegetable broth
1 tablespoon nutritional yeast
2 tablespoons chopped sun-dried tomato
   in oil, drained

SOUP BASE

1 pound (500g) Brussels sprouts
2 tablespoons extra-virgin olive oil
1 teaspoon Italian seasoning
Salt and freshly cracked black pepper

1 can (16oz/454g) large butter beans,
   rinsed and drained

SUGGESTED GARNISH

Reserved charred Brussels sprouts
Chopped fresh parsley or leafy herb
Pumpkin seeds
Balsamic Glaze (p. 125)

Preheat oven to 400°F (200°C). Combine soup base ingredients in an oven dish and season with salt and pepper to taste. Bake for 20 to 25 minutes, or until Brussels sprouts are tender and slightly charred. Remove from oven and set aside ¼ cup of the charred Brussels sprouts for garnishing. Transfer roasted sprouts to a large pot; mix in butter beans, vegetable broth, and nutritional yeast. Use an immersion stick to blend the soup, or ladle into a mixer and blend the soup in batches. Pulse for chunky style or purée until creamy. Stir in sun-dried tomato and add a little more vegetable broth or water if soup is too thick; adjust seasoning, if necessary. Warm soup over medium-high heat. Ladle into bowls and top with suggested garnishes.

NOTE: Peeled garlic can turn bitter when baked. Bake garlic cloves in their skin and discard peel after baking.

CURRY KABOCHA SOUP

Yield: 4 to 6 servings

Two words I love to hear, and preferably in the same sentence, are curry and kabocha—and boy do we love kabocha in Hawai'i. In other parts of the country, it's known as butternut squash or Japanese pumpkin. Baking brings out its sweet, nutty flavor becoming tender and almost creamy. The skin is soft and edible and has lots of nutrients, so don't peel. Kabocha marries really well with curry flavors and coconut making this a creamy meal-in-one to lift any mood.

SOUP BASE

2 cups (300g) kabocha pumpkin, deseeded, cut into ¼-inch pieces

2 large potatoes, diced

1 large onion, diced

1 can (8oz/227g) tomato sauce

2 tablespoons extra-virgin olive oil

2 tablespoons chopped fresh cilantro

3 whole garlic cloves (see **NOTE**)

1 tablespoon curry powder

1 teaspoon garam masala

1 teaspoon minced fresh ginger

½ teaspoon coriander seeds

Salt and freshly cracked black pepper

2 cups (480ml) vegetable broth

¾ cup (180ml) canned coconut milk

SUGGESTED GARNISH

Reserved roasted kabocha

Chopped fresh cilantro or leafy herb

Pumpkin seeds

Drizzle of chili oil

Preheat oven to 400°F (200°C). Combine soup base ingredients in an oven dish and season with salt and pepper to taste. Bake for 20 to 25 minutes, or until vegetables are tender and slightly charred. Remove from oven and set aside ¼ cup of the roasted kabocha for garnishing. Squeeze garlic cloves into veggies and discard skin. Transfer vegetables to a large pot; add vegetable broth and coconut milk. Use an immersion stick to blend the soup, or ladle into a mixer and blend the soup in batches. Pulse for chunky style or purée until creamy. Add a little more vegetable broth or water if soup is too thick; adjust seasoning, if necessary. Warm soup over medium-high heat. Ladle into bowls and top with suggested garnishes.

NOTE: Peeled garlic can turn bitter when baked. Bake garlic cloves in their skin and discard peel after baking.

DA HAWAIIAN TARO SPINACH SOUP

Yield: 4 to 6 servings

This moss green soup is so pretty it may just win a beauty pageant, but that's not what I'm aiming for. Mock lū'au is my intention here. I understand traditional Hawaiian lū'au is made by cooking fresh lū'au leaves (taro leaves), which can be pretty complicated and unfortunately not easy to find outside of Hawai'i. Spinach is an excellent alternative resulting in a gravy-like mishmash you know is so good for you. It's green, right? Finish with a splash of Hawaiian Chili Pepper Water (p. 33) or make the King Oyster Calamari on p. 208 and stir it into this soup for a modern version of squid lū'au.

SOUP BASE

1 pound (500g) taro, peeled, cut into
 ¼-inch pieces

1 pack (12oz/340g) chopped frozen
 spinach

1 large onion, diced

½ cup vegetable broth (to help the taro
 cook)

¼ cup roughly chopped Thai basil leaves
 or fresh cilantro

3 whole garlic cloves (see **NOTE**)

2 tablespoons extra-virgin olive oil

1 tablespoon mushroom seasoning

1 teaspoon minced fresh ginger

1 teaspoon onion powder

¼ teaspoon crushed red pepper

Salt and freshly cracked black pepper

1½ cups (360ml) vegetable broth

¾ cup (180ml) canned coconut milk

SUGGESTED GARNISH

Reserved roasted spinach

Thai basil or leafy herb

Preheat oven to 400°F (200°C). Combine soup base ingredients in an oven dish and season with salt and pepper to taste. Bake for 35 to 40 minutes, or until vegetables are tender and slightly charred. Remove from oven and set aside ¼ cup of the roasted spinach for garnishing. Squeeze garlic cloves into veggies and discard skin. Transfer vegetables to a large pot; mix in vegetable broth and coconut milk. Use an immersion stick to blend the soup, or ladle into a mixer and blend the soup in batches. Pulse for chunky style or purée until creamy. Add a little more vegetable broth or water if soup is too thick; adjust seasoning, if necessary. Warm soup over medium-high heat. Ladle into bowls and top with suggested garnishes.

JAPANESE CURRY BROTH FOR SOUPS, STEWS, AND NOODLES

Yield: about 2 cups

Japanese curry differs from other curries you'll find in Asia. It's slightly sweet and less spicy than its Indian counterpart, although most renditions come straight from a package. Curry roux has become quite the lifesaver for a lot of home cooks, and I get it. Unfortunately, not many of them are vegan. This tried and tested curry "broth" is great in soups or risotto, as a base for stews, or can be enjoyed with any type of noodles. Enjoy this aromatic broth in soup recipes for just the right curry boost, any time of day.

4 cups (1 liter) vegetable broth (or less if you prefer a thicker broth)

½ cup (120ml) tomato sauce

¼ cup (40g) raw cashews, cooked in boiling water for 15 minutes, drained (see **CHEF'S TIP**)

2 tablespoons mushroom seasoning

1 tablespoon blackstrap molasses

1 tablespoon curry powder

1 tablespoon nutritional yeast

1 tablespoon tapioca starch

2 teaspoons garam masala

1½ teaspoons salt

1 teaspoon li hing powder or 1 tablespoon lemon juice

1 teaspoon onion powder

1 teaspoon soy sauce or gluten-free liquid aminos

½ teaspoon garlic powder

½ teaspoon smoked paprika

¼ teaspoon chili powder

¼ teaspoon ground ginger

Blend all ingredients until smooth and creamy. Transfer to a pot and bring to a boil over medium-high heat. Use immediately as a substitute for vegetable broth, as a base for stews, or to enjoy with any type of noodles you like. Prepare 2 to 3 cups baked, steamed, boiled or stir-fried mixed veggies, tofu, beans or whatever you have on hand. Make the Japanese Curry Broth, add cooked veggies, water or more vegetable broth as needed, heat, and serve.

CHEF'S TIP: Always buy organic cashews when you can and save money by getting the broken bits. Whole ones are more expensive and will end up in your blender anyway.

JAPANESE NABE WITH KOMBU DASHI BROTH

Yield: 4 servings

Nabe, *or* nabemono, *is Japanese hot pot. The most important piece of equipment for making* nabe *is the pot itself. If this is going to be your thing, I recommend investing in a* donabe, *traditional earthenware pot made with clay which retains and distributes heat evenly. A cast iron pot also works well. Place a portable gas burner or electric burner in the middle of the table and place the* nabe *on top. I like to fill a tea pot with the kombu dashi broth and set it next to the pot adding as the broth starts to disappear. Heat and enjoy, refilling with veggies as you go. Only thing left to do is* kampai *with sake for an authentic Japanese dining experience.*

KOMBU DASHI BROTH

Yield: 8 cups/2 liters

KOMBU DASHI

2 (4-inch) pieces dried kombu

5 dried shiitake mushrooms

8 cups (2L) water

1 (2-inch) piece fresh ginger, peeled, and smashed with a knife (this allows for easy infusion into the soup)

Reserved shiitake, sliced

½ cup (120ml) mirin

½ cup (120ml) soy sauce or gluten-free liquid aminos

2 tablespoons mushroom seasoning or kombu dashi powder

1 tablespoon sugar

½ teaspoon salt

To make kombu dashi, soak kombu and shiitake in water overnight (at least 8 hours), then remove dried kombu and discard. Transfer to a saucepan and bring to a boil over medium-high heat. Reduce heat to medium and simmer for another 5 minutes. Strain through a mesh sieve or cheesecloth, reserving shiitake. Transfer kombu dashi to a large pot, or Japanese *nabe*. (Some people actually stop here and use only the kombu dashi for the *nabe,* but it's quite bland in my opinion.) Add reserved shiitake and remaining ingredients to the kombu dashi and heat for 1 minute. Use immediately or chill in the refrigerator overnight to allow flavors to meld. Store in an airtight container in the refrigerator for up to 1 week.

JAPANESE NABE

Yield: 4 to 6 servings

1 batch kombu dashi broth
   (recipe above)

SUGGESTED ADD-INS
Baby spinach leaves
Bok choy, sliced in quarters
Sliced burdock root
Shredded napa cabbage
Carrots, julienned
Sliced daikon
Dried seaweed—kizami
   arame, hijiki, or wakame
   (rehydrate seaweed in
   water for 10 minutes,
   then drain before using)
Sliced green onion
Mochi
Mushrooms—sliced button,
   cremini, enoki, king
   oyster, shiitake, shimeji
Cooked rice (zosui is usually served last)
Rehydrated rice noodles or cooked
   noodles (usually served last)
Tofu—soft, firm, extra-firm, fried, aburaage
   (deep-fried tofu)

GARNISH
XO Sauce (p. 36)
ichimi togarashi (Japanese chili powder)

Arrange your vegetables in the *nabe* or pot. Add kombu dashi broth to cover. Bring it to a boil over medium-high heat, covered. Remove lid, turn heat down to medium and cook until vegetables are tender. Once you start eating, turn heat down to low and continue adding vegetables, tofu, or noodles and broth as you go. You may need to increase the heat as the pot cools down. Serve with XO Sauce and ichimi togarashi. For *shime*, to finish up the dish, cooked noodles or zosui (cooked rice) are often added at the end to soak up the leftover dashi and flavors from the vegetables that have developed.

LEMONY CREAM OF BROCCOLI

Yield: 4 to 6 servings

It's no secret that people will consume more vegetables if they're camouflaged, and creamy soups hide veggies well. Broccoli is a great source of protein, fiber, and an array of vitamins and minerals. Broc on!

SOUP BASE

1 pack (12oz/340g) frozen broccoli florets
  (use fresh broccoli if you prefer)
2 large potatoes, diced
1 large onion, diced
3 whole garlic cloves (see **NOTE**)
1 to 2 tablespoons extra-virgin olive oil
2 tablespoons chopped fresh parsley or
  1 teaspoon dried parsley
2 teaspoons lemon pepper seasoning
1 teaspoon Italian seasoning
Salt and freshly cracked black pepper

½ lemon

2 cups (480ml) plant-based milk
1 tablespoon nutritional yeast

GARNISH

Drizzle of chili oil
Sliced black olives
Chopped fresh parsley or leafy herb
Cracked black pepper
Reserved roasted broccoli

Preheat oven to 400°F (200°C). Combine soup base ingredients in an oven dish and season with salt and pepper to taste. Place half a lemon, cut side up, in the center of the dish. Bake for 35 to 40 minutes, or until vegetables are tender and slightly charred. Remove from oven and set aside ¼

cup of the roasted broccoli for garnishing. Squeeze garlic cloves into veggies and discard skin. Transfer roasted vegetables to a large pot. Squeeze juice from roasted lemon into the vegetables and discard. Add plant-based milk and nutritional yeast. Use an immersion stick to blend the soup, or ladle into a mixer and blend the soup in batches. Pulse for chunky style or purée until creamy. Add a little more plant-based milk or water if soup is too thick; adjust seasoning, if necessary. Warm soup over medium heat. Ladle into bowls and top with suggested garnishes

NOTE: Peeled garlic can turn bitter when baked. Bake garlic cloves in their skin and discard peel after baking.

{ THE SOUPA BOWL }

PEA, BASIL, AND MINT SOUP

Yield: 4 to 6 servings

This vibrant pea, mint, and basil soup is like spring in a bowl. There are so many green herbs out there I have to force myself not to add too many in my soups, but the wealth of polyphenols found in herbs makes it well worth the overdose. I reckon the more herbs the merrier! For more of an Asian flavor, you can use Thai basil instead of plain basil and add baby spinach to amp up the nutrients. Spring-tastic!

SOUP BASE

2 cups (260g) frozen peas

1 can (16oz/454g) large butter beans, drained

1 large onion, diced

¼ cup roughly chopped basil leaves

¼ cup roughly chopped mint leaves

2 tablespoons extra-virgin olive oil

Salt and freshly cracked black pepper

2 cups (480ml) vegetable broth

SUGGESTED GARNISH

Basil or mint leaves

Drizzle of chili oil

Reserved roasted peas and butter beans

Preheat oven to 400°F (200°C). Combine soup base ingredients in an oven dish and season with salt and pepper to taste. Bake for 35 to 40 minutes, or until onion is translucent and slightly charred. Remove from oven and set aside ¼ cup of the roasted peas and butter beans for garnishing. Transfer roasted vegetables to a large pot and add vegetable broth. Use an immersion stick to blend the soup, or ladle into a mixer and blend the soup in batches. Pulse for chunky style or purée until creamy. Add a little more vegetable broth or water if soup is too thick; adjust seasoning, if necessary. Warm soup over medium-high heat. Ladle into bowls and top with suggested garnishes.

CHEF'S TIP: A little trick to help bring back some of the color from the peas to the soup which cooking takes away is to add some thawed frozen peas at the final blending stage. This will also add that fresh pea taste.

RICH CAULIFLOWER POTAGE

Yield: 4 to 6 servings

Caramelized notes develop when you roast cauliflower, creating a depth of flavor so irresistible it is hard to stop at one bowl. This soup calls for basic ingredients but delivers amazing flavor with a savory goodness and lightly charred bits that will delight your senses. Keep blending if you want to achieve a creamy potage. Cauliflower is low in carbs with fewer calories than potatoes and just as creamy when mashed. Absolutely worth dirtying the blender for this one.

Salt and freshly cracked black pepper
½ lemon

3 cups (720ml) vegetable broth
2 tablespoons nutritional yeast

SOUP BASE

1 pound (500g) cauliflower florets
2 large potatoes, diced
1 large onion, diced
1 tablespoon fresh thyme leaves or
  ½ teaspoon dried thyme
⅛ teaspoon ground nutmeg

SUGGESTED GARNISH

Drizzle of extra-virgin olive oil or chili oil
Reserved roasted cauliflower
Chopped nuts or seeds (I recommend
  toasted pine nuts)
Chopped fresh parsley or leafy herb
Pinch of ground turmeric

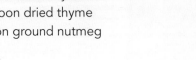

Preheat oven to 400°F (200°C). Combine soup base ingredients in an oven dish and season with salt and pepper to taste. Place the lemon half in the center of the dish, cut side up, and bake for 35 to 40 minutes, or until vegetables are tender and slightly charred. Remove from oven and set aside ¼ cup of the roasted cauliflower for garnishing. Squeeze juice from roasted lemon into the vegetables and discard or use as a garnish. Place roasted vegetables in a large pot. Add vegetable broth and nutritional yeast. Use an immersion stick to blend the soup, or ladle into a mixer and blend the soup in batches. Pulse for chunky style or purée until creamy. Add a little more vegetable broth or water if soup is too thick; adjust seasoning, if necessary. Warm soup over medium heat. Ladle into bowls and top with suggested garnishes.

ROASTED CORN CHOWDER

Yield: 4 to 6 servings

If you're new to plant-based corn chowder, prepare yourself for a wonderful experience. It's mega creamy and loaded with that irresistible sweet corn flavor we all love. Corn can be planted all year round in Hawai'i, giving local growers three to four harvests a year. However, frozen or canned corn is an acceptable substitute if summer is the only time you can get your hands on the fresh ears. Maize well dig in!

SOUP BASE

3 cups (390g) corn (use fresh when possible, but frozen or canned will work too)

1 can (15oz/425g) garbanzo beans, rinsed and drained

1 onion, diced

2 tablespoons extra-virgin olive oil

2 teaspoons lemon pepper seasoning

2 teaspoons onion powder

1 teaspoon Italian Seasoning

Salt and freshly cracked black pepper

2 cups (480ml) plant-based milk

2 tablespoons nutritional yeast

GARNISH

Cracked black pepper

Drizzle of chili oil

Reserved roasted corn and garbanzo beans

Sliced fresh or bottled jalapeño

Chopped fresh parsley or leafy herb

Preheat oven to 400°F (200°C). Combine soup base ingredients in an oven dish and season with salt and pepper to taste. Bake for 35 to 40 minutes, or until onion is translucent and slightly charred. Remove from oven and set aside ¼ cup of the roasted corn and garbanzo beans for garnishing. Transfer roasted vegetables to a large pot. Add plant-based milk, reserved bean liquid and nutritional yeast. Use an immersion stick to blend the soup, or ladle into a mixer and blend the soup in batches. Pulse for chunky style or purée until creamy. Add a little more non-dairy milk or water if soup is too thick; adjust seasoning, if necessary. Warm soup over medium heat. Ladle into bowls and top with suggested garnishes.

ROASTED EGGPLANT AND CHICKPEA SOUP

Yield: 4 to 6 servings

The time has come to cozy up to a hearty bowl of eggplant soup with a Mediterranean twist. It's the perfect meatless entrée for entertaining. Throw some fresh bread on the table with a salad and voilà! Dinner done. Serve with a nice Pinot Noir and pour yourself a glass while you wait for your guests to arrive. The right temperature for serving Pinot is between 55-60°F (12-15°C). Since Burgundy is the spiritual home of Pinot Noir, a Burgundy glass is most suited for this wine. Cheers and bon appétit!

SOUP BASE

1 large eggplant, cut into ¼-inch pieces
1 large onion, diced
1 can (15oz/425g) garbanzo beans,
   drained
1 can (8oz/227g) tomato sauce
2 tablespoons extra-virgin olive oil
1 tablespoon smoked paprika
2 teaspoons mushroom seasoning
½ teaspoon ground cumin
½ teaspoon crushed red pepper
¼ teaspoon ground nutmeg

Salt and freshly cracked black pepper

½ lemon

2 cups (480ml) vegetable broth
3 tablespoons roughly chopped fresh
   cilantro

SUGGESTED GARNISH

Sliced black olives
Drizzle of chili oil
Chopped fresh parsley or leafy herb
Reserved roasted garbanzo beans
Roasted pumpkin seeds
Pickled vegetables (I made pickled carrots
   from p. 134)

Preheat oven to 400°F (200°C). Combine soup base ingredients in an oven dish and season with salt and pepper to taste. Place the lemon half in the center of the dish, cut side up, and bake for 35 to 40 minutes, or until vegetables are tender and slightly charred. Remove from oven and set aside ¼ cup of the roasted garbanzo beans for garnishing. Squeeze juice from roasted lemon into the vegetables and discard. Transfer roasted vegetables to a large pot. Add vegetable broth and reserved bean liquid. Use an immersion stick to blend the soup, or ladle into a mixer and blend the soup in batches. Pulse for chunky style or purée until creamy. Stir in cilantro and add a little more vegetable broth if soup is too thick; adjust seasoning, if necessary. Warm soup over medium heat. Ladle into bowls and top with suggested garnishes.

CHEF'S TIP: Roasted corn is a nice addition to this soup.

SWEET POTATO AND BLACK BEAN SOUP

Yield: 4 to 6 servings

This is like eating a Mexican taco without the actual taco. Let it sit for a day or two in the refrigerator to thicken into a nice mash you can use in a taco, tortilla, or quesadilla turning it into something completely different. The sweet and smoky roasted flavors and aromas will surely get your appetite going. Garnish as you would a taco—fresh avocado cubes, a dollop of vegan sour cream, cilantro, and a splash of lime juice adds brightness to the dish. Serve it in a big pumpkin at Halloween or Thanksgiving to binge on and avoid a candy overdose!

SOUP BASE

1 pound (500g) sweet potatoes, diced

1 can (15oz/425g) black beans, rinsed and drained

1 can (14.5/411g) fire-roasted diced tomatoes

1 large onion, diced

3 whole garlic cloves (see **NOTE**)

2 tablespoons chopped fresh parsley or 1 teaspoon dried parsley

2 tablespoons extra-virgin olive oil

1 tablespoon smoked paprika

2 teaspoons Cajun seasoning

½ teaspoon ground cumin

¼ teaspoon crushed red pepper

Salt and freshly cracked black pepper

2 cups (480ml) vegetable broth

GARNISH

Drizzle of chili oil

Chopped fresh cilantro or leafy herb

Sliced fresh or bottled jalapeño

Reserved sweet potato and black beans

Pumpkin seeds

Preheat oven to 400°F (200°C). Combine soup base ingredients in an oven dish and season with salt and pepper to taste. Bake for 35 to 40 minutes, or until vegetables are tender and slightly charred. Remove from oven and set aside ¼ cup of the roasted sweet potato and black beans for garnishing. Squeeze garlic cloves into veggies and discard skin. Transfer roasted vegetables to a large pot and add vegetable broth. Use an immersion stick to blend the soup, or ladle into a mixer and blend the soup in batches. Pulse for chunky style or purée until creamy. Add a little more vegetable broth or water if soup is too thick; adjust seasoning, if necessary. Warm soup over medium heat. Ladle into bowls and garnish as you like.

NOTE: Peeled garlic can turn bitter when baked. Bake garlic cloves in their skin and discard peel after baking.

SOUP TO GO

Yield: 1 jar per person

The soup jar is a no-brainer for soup lovers who want to eat something warm on their lunch break, not to mention healthier and tastier than the instant ones in stores. Nothing is off the table when it comes to packing for this jar of goodness. Open up your refrigerator and go for it! Thin cellophane noodles soften quickly in hot water and are filling without leaving you feeling bloated. Invest in some colorful chopsticks and a nice holder. Some studies say about 20 billion pairs of chopsticks are produced each year around the world, meaning roughly 20 million trees are felled to produce the disposable utensils. Watch your carbon footprint at all times!

SUGGESTED ADD-INS

Cellophane noodles

Fresh herbs

Baby spinach leaves

Sliced bell peppers

Steamed broccoli

Shredded cabbage

Carrots, julienned

Fresh, frozen, or canned corn

Steamed cauliflower florets

Sliced celery

Kale leaves

Dried seaweed—kizami arame, hijiki, or
    wakame

Sliced green onion

Mushrooms—sliced button, cremini, enoki,
    king oyster, shiitake

Tofu

SUGGESTED HERBS

Chopped basil, cilantro, parsley, oregano,
    thyme

SUGGESTED SEASONING

'Alaea salt (Hawaiian red salt)

Cavender's Seasoning (p. 196)

Crushed red pepper

Curry powder

Garam masala

Kombu dashi powder

Mushroom seasoning

Salt

Sesame seeds

Smoked paprika

Pepper

FOR EXTRA FLAVOR

Fresh chili slices

Lemon or lime slices

Pickles

Ponzu

Red or white wine vinegar

Rice vinegar

Soy sauce or gluten-free liquid aminos

XO Sauce (p. 36)

Stack your mason jars with veggies and noodles, adding seasoning and condiments for extra flavor and store in the refrigerator until ready to use. Take the jar out of the refrigerator 15 minutes before you're ready to eat as pouring hot water into a cold jar can sometimes cause it to crack. Pour in hot water and set aside for 5 to 10 minutes to heat. Stir and enjoy!

{ THE SOUPA BOWL }

CHAPTER 6

EXOTIC SALADS OF THE ISLANDS

For a humble but decadent weeknight dinner, go the salad route and make it da bomb! When you think about healthy eating, salads are most likely to come to mind. What used to be considered a lackluster "side" we all had to get through to make us feel better we ate something green for the day, has now become an integral part of our meals. A satisfying salad should consist of a combination of crispy veggies, greens, protein, and healthy carbs—who said anything about lettuce? When a pile of leaves just won't satisfy, turn to your oven, grill, or pickle barrel. Introduce powerful dressings, veggies in all the colors of the rainbow, or fermented tea leaves—yes, you read correctly! Ever heard of a Burmese tea leaf salad? It may turn out to be one of the best salads of your life, and I have a recipe for it on p. 128. Don't even get me started on avocado. When that craving for a nice soft, buttery avocado comes along only to find the supply of ripe ones is pau, heck! Don't wait for that avocado to ripen—pickle it! Throw them into your leafy salads for a crispy nudge to balance out the textures. Think of your salad as a seesaw adding additional ingredients that bring contrast in texture and flavor; add sweet to salty or bitter, acid (vinegar) to rich (oily), crunchy to soft, creamy (avocado) to thin (vinaigrette).

The best chefs don't start with handfuls of baby spinach, and neither should you. Take a trek to the farmers market and explore the offerings your local vendors have in season and make salad with an attitude!

PARADISE SALAD

Yield: 4 to 6 servings

Kiss boring salads goodbye because this green papaya version knocks it out of the park! The word paradise brings forth feelings of happiness and delight, while the word salad conjures up images of color, texture, and crispy cool crunch which is exactly what you'll find in this dish—Gochujang tofu, smashed Chinese long beans, and shredded papaya enveloped in a sweet and sour mango dressing reminiscent of Island-style flavors. This paradise salad is so flavorsome you'll never want to make a mediocre salad again

GOCHUJANG TOFU

1 (14-ounce/400g) block firm or extra-firm tofu, drained, patted dry with a towel, cut into ½-inch cubes

1 tablespoon sesame oil

2 tablespoons soy sauce or gluten-free liquid aminos

1 tablespoon gochujang (mild or hot)

2 tablespoons cornstarch

3 Chinese longs beans, cut into 2-inch pieces

MANGO DRESSING

½ cup (120g) fresh or canned mango, roughly chopped (see **NOTE**)

2 tablespoons agave syrup

2 tablespoons rice vinegar

1 tablespoon stone ground mustard

1 tablespoon toasted white sesame seeds

2 teaspoons minced fresh ginger

1 clove garlic, minced

1 to 2 fresh red chilies, sliced, or ¼ teaspoon crushed red pepper

1 teaspoon soy sauce or gluten-free liquid aminos

1 teaspoon sriracha

¼ teaspoon salt

1 small green papaya (200g), peeled, seeds removed, shredded

8 to 10 Thai basil leaves, basil, or mint, roughly torn

GARNISH

2 tablespoons dry roasted peanuts, roughly chopped

6 lemon wedges

Preheat oven to 400°F (200°C) and line a baking sheet with parchment paper. Place tofu in a large bowl and drizzle with olive oil; toss gently to coat. Add soy sauce and gochujang; toss to coat. Dust with cornstarch and toss one more time making sure the cornstarch has soaked into the tofu. Bake for 25 to 30 minutes, or until golden brown and crispy. Remove from oven and set aside.

{ EXOTIC SALADS OF THE ISLANDS }

Cook beans in boiling salted water for 3 to 4 minutes, or until crisp-tender. Rinse under cold water and pat dry with a towel. Gently pound beans using a mortar and pestle or smash on a chopping board using a rolling pin, just enough so that they split and allow the dressing to soak in. (Many traditional papaya salad recipes call for the beans to be slightly pounded or crushed after cooking.)

Whisk together mango dressing ingredients in a large bowl. Add beans, papaya, Thai basil, and gochujang tofu; toss well to combine. Garnish with nuts and lemon wedge.

NOTE: Depending on the variety or the ripening process, some mangoes can be very fibrous and stringy with an unpleasant mouth feel. Just strain the mango and discard the stringy parts using only the soft flesh.

SPINACH AND ORANGE QUINOA SALAD

Yield: 4 to 6 servings

I'm blown away by how nutty quinoa becomes when you toast it before cooking! Quinoa salads are easy to customize and suitable for almost every dietary preference. Add pomegranate seeds when they're in season, or swap the orange for crispy apple or pear. This dish is seriously bursting with flavor the health-conscious among us will really appreciate. Quinoa is a versatile ingredient ideal as a replacement for rice, potatoes, and pasta. This stuff is darn good, and darn good for you!

½ cup (90g) quinoa, unwashed (see **NOTE**)
1 teaspoon extra-virgin olive oil (see
  CHEF'S TIP)
1 cup (240ml) vegetable broth

BALSAMIC VINAIGRETTE
¼ cup (60ml) extra-virgin olive oil
2 tablespoons balsamic vinegar
1 tablespoon stone ground mustard
1 tablespoon maple syrup
1 clove garlic, minced

1 tablespoon chopped fresh thyme or
  ¼ teaspoon dried thyme
½ teaspoon salt
Freshly cracked black pepper

1 pack (5oz/150g) baby spinach leaves
2 oranges, peeled and segmented
  (discard white pith)
¼ cup (30g) dried cherries or dried
  cranberries
¼ cup (25g) toasted walnuts
¼ cup (30g) pumpkin seeds or pepitas

Place quinoa in a saucepan and toast for 2 to 3 minutes, stirring constantly, until it starts popping. Pour quinoa into a strainer and rinse under cold water; drain and return to the saucepan. Add vegetable broth to the quinoa and bring to a boil over medium-high heat. Reduce heat to low, cover and simmer for 15 minutes. Remove from heat and let stand for 10 minutes, covered. Fluff quinoa with a fork and place in a large bowl to cool.

Whisk together vinaigrette ingredients until thick and emulsified; season with pepper to taste. Pour half of the vinaigrette over the quinoa and toss to coat. Add baby spinach, orange segments, dried cherries or cranberries, and remaining vinaigrette; toss well to combine. Garnish with walnuts and pumpkin seeds.

NOTE: I recommend rinsing your quinoa after you've toasted it. You'll get a more even toast on a dry seed.

CHEF'S TIP: That tiny bit of oil makes all the difference giving the quinoa a nice toasty coating. Do not skip this step!

LOMI
BELL PEPPER
"'AHI"
AVOCADO

Yield: 4 servings

The name lomilomi is taken from the method of preparation used for fish. Literally meaning "to massage" in Hawaiian. Lomi lomi 'ahi and salmon are a must-have for any Hawaiian lū'au and are an integral part of most Hawaiian meals. I've seen posh restaurants on the Islands serve up lomi lomi 'ahi (tuna) mixed with avocado which I've always thought to be very pretty and very veganizable. The poke dressing really pulls this dish together, but don't forget to splash some Hawaiian Chili Pepper Water on top for a taste of Island heat!

2 avocados, halved, seed removed
1 roasted bell pepper for "'ahi" (Caprese
   recipe p. 164)
5 cherry tomatoes, quartered
Poke Dressing (p. 82)

GARNISH
4 lemon wedges

Scoop out the flesh of the avocado using a spoon. Roughly chop the avocado and roasted bell pepper. Place in a bowl with cherry tomato and add poke dressing to taste; mix to combine. Spoon mixture into avocado shells and garnish with lemon.

GRILLED WATERMELON
AND TOFETA SALAD WITH BALSAMIC GLAZE
Yield: 4 to 6 servings

Is it possible the summer salad of your dreams is tangy Tofeta and grilled watermelon drizzled with a thick,-syrupy Balsamic Glaze? Pop a bit of all that in your mouth and tell me your world didn't just flip upside down. Enough said.

12 watermelon slices, cut into ½-inch thick
    triangles or wedges
¼ cup (60ml) extra-virgin olive oil
Pinch of crushed red pepper (optional)

GARNISH
½ cup (100g) Tofeta (p. 166)
1 to 2 tablespoons Balsamic Glaze (see
    NOTE)
3 tablespoons chopped fresh mint leaves

Brush both sides of watermelon with oil. Heat grill pan over medium heat (or use an outdoor grill). Add the watermelon and grill for 2 to 3 minutes on each side, or until grill marks appear. Transfer to a plate and season with crushed red pepper, if using. Crumble Tofeta over the watermelon, drizzle with Balsamic Glaze to taste, and sprinkle with mint leaves.

CHEF'S TIP: Add arugula, fresh basil leaves, and thinly sliced red onion to make a refreshing tossed salad perfect for a picnic or outdoor gathering.

NOTE: To make Balsamic Glaze, heat 1 cup (270g) balsamic vinegar and 1/4 cup (50g) sugar or ¼ cup (60ml) maple syrup in a saucepan over medium heat for 10 to 15 minutes, or until vinegar reduces and is thick enough to coat the back of a spoon.

CRUNCHY WARM CHEESE AND SPINACH ROMAINE SALAD

Yield: 4 to 6 servings

I took my husband out to a romantic dinner for his birthday and he ordered the Caesar salad as an appetizer. This is the same guy who lamented, "I could never eat salads everyday." Now here we are three years later, and this Wisconsinite starts his dinners with a big bowl of leafy greens. Back to the salad. A rustic stack of crispy romaine lettuce piled up on a plate with slivers of Parmesan cheese came to the table, and my mind immediately went into veganize mode. Two days later I created my rendition of the romaine salad using a warm cheese and spinach sauce. You can add croutons if you like, but the salad is so crunchy anyway you won't miss them. Added bonus—the sauce is so light and creamy with a cheesy accent the kiddos won't even notice they're eating spinach!

1 batch Cashew Cheese Sauce (p. 160)
1 pack (8oz/227g) baby spinach leaves
2 small heads romaine lettuce
Freshly cracked black pepper

GARNISH
¼ cup (60g) shaved vegan Parmesan
cheese (I use Violife, see Glossary
p. 260) or Mac Parm (p. 23)
6 lemon wedges

Prepare Cashew Cheese Sauce according to the recipe. Once it starts bubbling, stir in spinach leaves and cook 1 to 2 minutes, or until spinach is wilted. Remove from heat and pour cheese sauce in a large bowl. Add romaine lettuce and toss gently to coat; season with pepper to taste. Stack coated lettuce leaves in a serving dish and drizzle over any leftover sauce. Use a vegetable peeler to shave vegan Parmesan over lettuce or sprinkle with Mac Parm.

CHEF'S TIP: Before you heat the Cashew Cheese Sauce to thicken, add 2 to 3 cloves of chopped garlic and the zest of 1 lemon for extra flavor.

TEA LEAF SALAD

Yield: 4 to 6 servings

Laphet is a fermented tea leaf dressing and the savory star of this dish. It can take up to a month for the tea leaves to ferment, but I've found a shortcut that produces the same signature flavors using miso. A Burmese restaurant in Honolulu serves the best tea leaf salad many of us locals have fallen in love with, and it's surprisingly easy to make. Now let's talk tea. The volcanic soil in this state makes Hawai'i a tea-growing paradise, the heart of the tea producing industry being on the Big Island. The Hilo climate is ideal for growing tea with distinct flavor profiles. Its green teas taste generally fresh and crisp with undertones of citrus. Touted to be one of the healthiest beverages on the planet, green tea is loaded with antioxidants with many health benefits. Depending on your caffeine tolerance you may experience an after "buzz" effect that may have you bouncing off the walls. Time this salad accordingly!

TEA LEAF BASE

1 tablespoon green tea leaves (I use sencha)

4 cups (1L) hot water (temperature for brewing green tea should be around 175°F/80°C)

2 teaspoons mushroom seasoning

1 teaspoon miso paste (check ingredients for barley, wheat, or rye to make sure it's gluten-free)

DRESSING

3 tablespoons avocado oil, macadamia nut oil, or sesame oil

3 tablespoons soy sauce or gluten-free liquid aminos

1 tablespoon lemon juice

1 tablespoon rice vinegar

2 teaspoons caper juice (see CHEF'S TIP)

2 cloves garlic, minced

1 teaspoon minced fresh ginger

¼ teaspoon crushed red pepper (optional)

SALAD

7 ounces (200g) coleslaw or Asian mix (cabbage, onion, carrot, spinach, green onion, or other veggies)

10 cherry tomatoes, halved

1 cup (40g) roughly chopped sprouts

¼ cup (20g) roughly chopped fresh
  cilantro
¼ cup (30g) sliced green onion
1 to 2 fresh or bottled jalapeño peppers,
  thinly sliced

Salt and freshly cracked black pepper

GARNISH
3 tablespoons fried onion or garlic chips
3 tablespoons dry roasted nuts, chopped
2 tablespoons (25g) yellow split peas fried
  in oil until crispy, drained (optional)
2 tablespoons toasted white sesame seeds
8 lemon wedges

Preheat oven to "warm" setting, about 170°F (80°C), and line baking sheet with parchment paper.

Steep tea leaves in hot water for 10 minutes (see **NOTE**). Strain tea leaves and squeeze out excess liquid. Mix in mushroom seasoning and miso, then scatter the leaves on the baking sheet and bake for 1½ hours. Drying the leaves out removes some of their bitterness leaving them semi-dried and almost like a paste. Remove from oven and place in a food processor with remaining dressing ingredients; pulse until well-combined. Don't over mix! Cover and chill tea leaf dressing in the refrigerator for 1 hour to allow flavors to meld.

Combine coleslaw mix and tea leaf dressing in a large bowl. Use your hands to scrunch coleslaw together with the dressing. (Coleslaw should shrink to about half.) Add the remaining salad ingredients to the coleslaw and toss to combine; season with salt and pepper to taste. Sprinkle with garnishes and a squeeze of fresh lemon juice, if desired.

CHEF'S TIP: Caper juice is an excellent substitute for fish sauce often used in tea leaf salads with the same salty bite and tangy characteristics. Handy tip to remember when a recipe you're making calls for fish sauce or fish oil.

NOTE: When making green tea to drink, you only need to steep for 3 minutes.

KALE SLAW POTATO SALAD

Yield: 4 to 6 servings

Kale meets coleslaw meets potato salad; it will be a hit with the keiki! Per calorie, kale has more iron than beef and more calcium than milk per gram. It also has all the essential amino acids your body needs, plus 9 non-essential ones. Pair this delightful salad with Riesling, or something lightly acidic like Gewurztraminer, to cut through the creaminess in the dish.

4 medium potatoes, peeled, cut into
   1-inch pieces
½ teaspoon salt

CREAMY LEMON DRESSING
½ cup (100g) vegan mayonnaise
½ cup (100g) vegan yogurt
2 tablespoons chopped fresh chives

2 tablespoons lemon juice
1 tablespoon whole grain mustard
Salt and freshly cracked black pepper

KALE SLAW
1 pack (5oz/150g) kale mix (shredded or
   sliced kale, broccoli, carrot, red
   cabbage, radicchio)
3 tablespoons dried cranberries

Salt and freshly cracked black pepper

GARNISH
2 tablespoons Candied Hurricane
   Pecans (p. 62) or nut of choice,
   roughly chopped

Place potatoes in a large pot; fill with water to cover and add salt. Bring to a boil over medium-high heat. Reduce heat to medium and simmer for 12 to 15 minutes, or until tender. Remove from heat; drain and set aside to cool to room temperature.

Whisk together dressing ingredients in a large bowl. Add potatoes, kale slaw, and cranberries and toss gently to coat. Season with salt and pepper to taste. Sprinkle with pecans and serve.

TOFU EGG AND CORN MACARONI SALAD

Yield: 4 to 6 servings

Bento boxes won't be the same after you try this twist on a local side dish favorite. The magical ingredient is kala namak which gives this salad that wonderful egg taste. Don't stop at macaroni salad! Add tofu scramble to any dish when you need that "eggy" fix. Nail the scramble and this mac salad will be a hit at any table. Hush about it being eggless—they won't know!

TOFU SCRAMBLE
1 tablespoon vegan butter
1 block (14oz/400g) extra-firm tofu, drained and patted dry with a towel (no need to press)
2 tablespoons plant-based milk
2 tablespoons nutritional yeast
1 teaspoon kala namak (black salt)
1 teaspoon onion powder
½ teaspoon garlic powder
½ teaspoon salt
¼ teaspoon turmeric (for color)
⅛ teaspoon white pepper

DRESSING
1 cup (240g) vegan mayonnaise
3 tablespoons chopped dill pickles or dill relish
2 tablespoons chopped fresh dill
2 tablespoons lemon juice

1 tablespoon pickle juice or apple cider vinegar

1 cup (125g) dried macaroni or gluten-free macaroni, cooked al dente according to package instructions, rinsed under cold water and drained

SALAD
1 cup (125g) fresh steamed or roasted corn (or canned corn, drained)
½ cup (50g) shredded carrots
½ cup (50g) chopped cucumber
½ cup (70g) frozen peas, thawed

Salt and freshly cracked black pepper

GARNISH
2 tablespoons chopped fresh parsley
1 to 2 teaspoons Japanese Furikake (p. 24)

To make tofu scramble, heat butter in a skillet over medium heat. Crumble in the tofu, add plant-based milk and sauté 3 to 4 minutes, or until liquid has evaporated. Mix in the remaining tofu scramble ingredients and sauté another 2 minutes; remove from heat and set aside to cool. Whisk dressing ingredients in a large bowl. Add cooked macaroni, salad vegetables, and tofu scramble. Toss gently to combine and season with salt and pepper to taste. Chill in the refrigerator for 1 hour to allow flavors to meld. Garnish with parsley and sprinkle with furikake to taste.

ISLAND-STYLE POTATO SALAD

Yield: 4 servings

Say goodbye to ho hum and give a big Aloha to Island-style potato salad meets poke. Tangy and chock full of healthy bits and bobs concealed in tender chunks of potato and "broke da mouth" goodness. Island-style potato salads often include macaroni and mayonnaise which can be a downer if you're watching your calories. This version is full of color, flavor, and texture that will give the traditional version a run for its money. Arrange all the components separately in your salad bowl and toss at the table so everyone can appreciate the diversity of this bountiful dish. Ideal for any friendly bash!

4 medium-sized Yukon potatoes (about 700g), peeled, cut into bite-size pieces
½ teaspoon salt

SEASONING
3 tablespoons soy sauce or gluten-free liquid aminos
2 tablespoons macadamia nut oil or avocado oil
2 cloves garlic, minced
1 tablespoon smoked paprika
1 to 2 red Hawaiian chilies, sliced, or ½ to 1 teaspoon crushed red pepper
1 to 2 teaspoons Hawaiian Chili Pepper Water (p. 33) or hot sauce (optional)
Salt and freshly cracked black pepper

SALAD
5 cherry tomatoes, quartered

¼ cup (5g) chopped fresh cilantro or parsley
½ cup (70g) cooked, shelled edamame or peas
¼ cup (10g) thinly sliced green onion
¼ cup (15g) limu (seaweed), chopped (or rehydrated hijiki, kizami arame, or wakame—see **NOTE**)
¼ cup (30g) chopped roasted macadamia nuts
¼ cup (40g) finely chopped Maui onion

GARNISH
2 tablespoons fried onion chips or garlic chips
1 tablespoon black or white toasted sesame seeds
8 lemon wedges

Place potatoes in a large pot and fill with water to cover. Add salt and bring to a boil over medium-high heat. Reduce heat to medium and simmer for 12 to 15 minutes, or until tender. Drain and place potatoes in a large serving bowl. While potatoes are still hot, add the seasoning ingredients and toss to coat; season with salt and pepper to taste. Place potato mixture in the center of a large bowl or plate. Arrange salad ingredients, individually, around the potato mixture and garnish with onion or garlic chips and sesame seeds. Toss the potato salad at the dining table and serve with lemon wedges.

A WONDERFUL WORLD OF PICKLES

Pickles may become your new kitchen addiction when you see how easy they are to make. You can pickle almost any food, but for many, pickles are synonymous with cucumbers. Ever tried pickling avocado? The firmer the avocado the better when it comes to pickling them. The hardest part of this recipe is peeling and cutting the fruit. You'll need to remove the skin using a knife, rather than a peeler. The traditional method of cutting open the avocado won't work either as the seed is super glued to the flesh before it starts to ripen and loosen up. Use your knife to get as close to the seed as you can to cut away long slices. Cubes work nice as a snazzy addition for a salad or a tangy sushi filling, so don't fret if you can't get even slices. Venture out and try pickling beets, red cabbage, apple, chili, garlic, radish—the world is your oyster! Colorful vegetables take on sweet, salty, acidic notes full of crunch to awaken your taste buds and make you feel like you're nourishing your body.

PICKLING BRINE
2 cups (480ml) water
1½ cups (360ml) rice vinegar
⅓ cup (80g) sugar
1 teaspoon mustard seeds

1 tablespoon salt
½ teaspoon black peppercorns
½ teaspoon coriander seeds
½ teaspoon dill seeds

Combine pickling brine ingredients in a small saucepan and bring to a boil over medium-high heat. Once sugar and salt have dissolved, remove from heat and cool to room temperature.

Pack vegetables into clean mason jars. Pour the brine over the vegetables to cover. Cover and refrigerate for at least 2 days. The pickles will improve with flavor as they age.

GREEN AVOCADO PICKLES

Yield: 1 (18-ounce) canning jar

2 to 3 firm avocados, peeled and thinly
    sliced (avocado must be under-ripe)

1 (16-ounce) mason jar, washed, rinsed
    and set aside to dry completely

Place avocado slices in mason jar. Cover with pickling brine and seal. Refrigerate for at least 2 hours, or overnight, before serving.

CHAPTER 7
ALL ABOUT THE SAUCE

Creating vegan-based sauces may feel daunting and is in fact a cooking art in itself. However, it's not as complicated as you think. A healthy plant-based sauce can add texture, juiciness, sharpness, tanginess, contrast in taste, and a degree of visual excitement. The three most important things to remember when considering your slather—we eat with the eyes, delight with the taste, and savor with the nose. Include color, flavor, and aroma in every dish you prepare. Master some of the fundamental sauces in this book then mix and match as you like. Cashew Cheese Sauce (p. 160), XO Sauce (p. 36), and Poke Dressing (p. 82) provide a nice base for many vegan dishes.

FUN IDEA: Dressings, spreads, and sauces in festive jars are a great way to show your friends you care. Customize your jars with little stickers or printed out messages like, "Keep Pele the Fire Goddess Smiling," "Way Better than Nutella I Tell Ya," and "Your Cooking Won't Suck Anymore XO Sauce." Have fun in the kitchen and you will find the process of making food so much more enjoyable.

BOK CHOY NOODLES
WITH CREAMY XO SAUCE

Yield: 4 servings

Bok choy, a type of Chinese white cabbage, offers a nice crunch with a very mild bitterness. The flavor-booster in this dish is my favorite go-to XO Sauce. A spoonful of this delectable stuff will elevate a mild-manned dish to a neighborhood favorite and leave your friends thinking you've discovered an ancient recipe. Toss with some noodles and you have yourself a darn tasty dish. This pairs nicely with a side of Orange Teriyaki "Scallops" (p. 210).

7 ounces (200g) dried noodles or gluten-free noodles, cooked according to package, drained (I use thick rice noodles)

1 pound (500g) baby bok choy, cut in half through the stem

CREAMY XO SAUCE
2 cups (480ml) non-dairy milk

½ cup (120g) XO Sauce (p. 36)
1 tablespoon mushroom seasoning
1 tablespoon toasted white sesame seeds
Salt and freshly cracked black pepper to taste

GARNISH
¼ cup (30g) sliced green onion
XO Sauce to taste

Steam bok choy for 2 to 3 minutes, or until stems are slightly tender. Mix together creamy XO Sauce ingredients in a skillet and bring to a simmer over medium heat. Add noodles and bok choy. Toss to coat and heat through, about 1 minute; season with salt and pepper to taste. Divide bok choy noodles into 4 bowls. Sprinkle with green onion and serve with a spoon of XO Sauce on the side.

CHARRED BRUSSELS WITH CRANBERRIES AND XO SAUCE

Yield: 4 to 6 servings

Char is everything when it comes to the love/hate relationship people have with Brussels sprouts. Crispy edges, blackened ever-so-slightly with that hint of bitterness from the char is the key to a banging sprout dish. When the first mouthful hits your palate, expect a sweet and sour pop from the cranberries and an umami-packed explosion.

1 pound (500g) Brussels sprouts, cut in quarters through the stem

1 tablespoon extra-virgin olive oil
Salt and freshly cracked black pepper
¼ cup (30g) dried cranberries, soaked in water for 10 minutes, drained
2 to 3 tablespoons XO Sauce (p. 36)

GARNISH
3 tablespoons chopped dry roasted nuts or seeds

Preheat oven to 450°F (230°C) and line a baking sheet with parchment paper.

Toss Brussels sprouts with olive oil in a large bowl; season with salt and pepper to taste. Arrange on baking sheet and bake for 20 to 25 minutes, or until nicely charred on the edges. Transfer to a bowl. Add cranberries and XO Sauce; toss gently to combine. Garnish with nuts.

NOTE: For air fryer, cook Brussels sprouts at 400°F (200°C) for 15 to 20 minutes.

{ ALL ABOUT THE SAUCE }

BAKED OKINAWAN SWEET POTATO WITH GARLIC HERB BUTTER

Yield: 4 servings

Baked potatoes never looked so good! These beautiful tubers (which are part of the morning glory family and not related to the potato), are actually bright purple on the inside. With 150 percent more antioxidants than blueberries, they are fat-free, high in fiber, low in calories, and have a mild sweetness with notes of honey.

GARLIC HERB BUTTER

Yield: about 1 cup

½ cup (120ml) extra-virgin olive oil
¼ cup (60g) vegan butter, softened
4 to 6 garlic cloves, minced
2 tablespoons finely chopped fresh parsley
1 tablespoon finely chopped fresh oregano
1 teaspoon finely chopped fresh thyme
2 tablespoons Mac Parm (p. 23) or vegan Parmesan cheese
1 tablespoon nutritional yeast
½ teaspoon salt
¼ teaspoon smoked paprika
¼ teaspoon pepper

4 Okinawan sweet potatoes, poked with a fork, baked in an oven at 425°F (220°C) for 40 to 45 minutes, or until tender

GARNISH
2 tablespoons chopped fresh parsley

Blend Garlic Herb Butter ingredients until smooth and creamy. Top sweet potato with a dollop of garlic butter toast and garnish with parsley. Store remaining butter in an airtight container in the refrigerator for up to 2 weeks.

CAULIFLOWER STEAK WITH CHEESE PEPPERCORN SAUCE

Yield: 4 servings

A golf course in Kailua serves the best vegan cauliflower steak that is both hearty and satisfying. Terri and Pat got me hooked on this sassy "steak" that's slightly smoky, richly flavored, and addictive in a way you wouldn't think applied to this underwhelming vegetable that is often left behind on veggie trays. Roast in your oven or grill some at your next BBQ.

1 large head cauliflower, rinsed, leaves removed
Extra-virgin olive oil cooking spray

SIMPLE RUB
3 cloves garlic, minced
2 tablespoons smoked paprika
1 tablespoon fresh rosemary leaves
2 teaspoons onion powder
1 teaspoon salt

CHEESE PEPPERCORN SAUCE
1 cup (240ml) water

2 tablespoons raw cashews, cooked in boiling water for 15 minutes, drained
1 tablespoon nutritional yeast
1 tablespoon tapioca starch
½ tablespoon apple cider vinegar
2 teaspoons soy sauce or gluten-free liquid aminos
½ teaspoon mushroom seasoning
½ teaspoon onion powder
¼ teaspoon garlic powder

1 teaspoon cracked black peppercorn
1 clove garlic, minced

Preheat oven to 400°F (200°C) and line a baking tray with parchment paper.

Cut cauliflower into 4 (1-inch thick) "steaks" and arrange on baking tray. Spray generously with cooking spray on both sides. Combine simple rub ingredients in a small bowl; rub onto both sides of each steak using your fingers. Bake for 10 minutes. Flip steaks and bake another 10 to 15 minutes, or until tender.

Blend cheese peppercorn sauce ingredients in a mixer until smooth. Transfer to a saucepan; add peppercorn and garlic. Bring to a boil over medium-high heat, stirring constantly for 2 to 3 minutes, or until mixture starts to bubble. Remove from heat and drizzle over cauliflower steaks to taste.

NOTE: You will probably only need about half of the brown sauce for this recipe. Store the rest in the refrigerator or add some cooked noodles to the stir-fry—there will be enough sauce to coat them nicely.

CHINESE STIR-FRY

Yield: 4 to 6 servings

Consistency and speed are two very important requirements for a good dish, so having an all-purpose brown sauce on hand makes the cooking process a lot easier. Turn the music on, start your rice, chop your veggies and get ready to wok! Try adding bamboo shoots, bean sprouts, baby corn, snap peas, or any of your favorite local market finds. This dinner is a winner!

BROWN SAUCE

1 cup (240ml) water
3 tablespoons soy sauce or gluten-free
    liquid aminos
1 tablespoon blackstrap molasses
1 tablespoon mushroom seasoning
1 tablespoon rice vinegar
1 teaspoon sugar
¼ teaspoon smoked paprika
¼ teaspoon crushed red pepper
¼ teaspoon ground Szechuan pepper or
    ground black pepper

SLURRY

2 tablespoons cornstarch mixed with
    ¼ cup (60ml) water

STIR-FRY

1 tablespoon sesame oil
1 head of broccoli, trimmed into florets,
    stem peeled and sliced on the diagonal
    (discard peel)
1½ cups (120g) mixed red, yellow, and
    orange mini bell peppers, cut into
    ½-inch pieces
2 to 3 cloves garlic, minced
1 tablespoon minced fresh ginger
1 batch Crispy Baked Tofu (p. 53)
¼ cup (40g) cashews
Salt and freshly cracked black pepper

GARNISH

2 tablespoons finely sliced green onion
2 teaspoons toasted white sesame seeds

Combine brown sauce ingredients in a saucepan and bring to a simmer over medium-high heat. Once sauce starts to bubble, stir in slurry to thicken; remove from heat and set aside.

Heat oil in a wok over medium-high heat. Add broccoli and bell peppers and cook for 3 to 4 minutes, or until slightly browned. Stir in garlic and ginger; cook for another 1 minute until fragrant. Stir in tofu and brown sauce to taste (see **NOTE**). Cook for 1 to 2 minutes, or until vegetables are tender. Toss in cashews and season with salt and pepper to taste. Garnish with green onion and sesame seeds.

CRISPY TOFU POCKETS WITH DASHI SAUCE

Yield: 4 servings

It's true, I am obsessed with tofu and thought I'd eaten it all until I devoured a sprout stuffed version known as "Tahu Bakar" at a Burmese restaurant in Honolulu. It's a new approach to spicing up tofu and exotic-looking enough for any Island potluck. Be sure to add your own touches to the stuffing—grated zucchini, crunchy shredded cabbage, or carrots and some fresh herbs can really amplify this already stunning dish. Spice it up with some XO Sauce and enjoy with a nice Shiraz on the side.

2 (12-ounce/340g) vacuum-packed deep-fried tofu, drained, each block cut in half (I use Aloha brand)

2 tablespoons soy sauce or gluten-free liquid aminos (I use a spray bottle)

¼ cup (30g) cornstarch

5-MINUTE DASHI SAUCE

1 cup (240ml) water

1 tablespoon mirin

2 teaspoons soy sauce or gluten-free liquid aminos

1½ teaspoons mushroom seasoning

2 teaspoons sugar

SLURRY

1 tablespoon cornstarch mixed with 2 tablespoons water

1 to 2 teaspoons rice vinegar (optional)

2 cups (40g) broccoli sprouts

GARNISH

1 nori sheet, crumbled

3 tablespoons fried onion chips

2 teaspoons toasted white sesame seeds

Preheat oven to 400°F (200°C) and line a baking sheet with parchment paper.

Brush or spray fried tofu with soy sauce. Sprinkle with cornstarch making sure all sides are coated well. (This will help crispen the tofu.) Bake for 25 minutes. Remove from oven and set aside for 5 minutes to cool. Make a slit in the center of the cut side of the tofu to open up as a pocket.

Combine the dashi sauce ingredients in a saucepan and bring to a simmer over medium heat. Once sauce starts to bubble, stir in slurry to thicken. Remove from heat and mix in vinegar to taste, if using. (I prefer the sauce with vinegar, but it's also great without it.) Drizzle over half the dashi sauce into the tofu pockets to give the tofu some flavor. Stuff with sprouts and drizzle remaining dashi sauce over the top. Garnish with nori, onion chips, and sesame seeds.

{ ALL ABOUT THE SAUCE }

VARIATION: For air fryer, bake tofu at 350°F (180C) for 20 minutes.

TWICE FROZEN TOFU SKEWERS WITH PEANUT DIPPING SAUCE

Yield: 4 to 6 servings

I dedicated an entire section in my first cookbook, Hawai'i A Vegan Paradise on all the ways to prep tofu. The basic principal is the water must first come out (unless you are using soft silken tofu which does not require pressing). Pockets of water run through the tofu and freezing it produces ice crystals. When thawed, the ice melts away making it spongey or porous and ready to soak in flavors. You still need to press the tofu to get rid of the excess water. No amount of boiling, draining, or pressing can minimize sogginess as much as freezing does. It also turns the bean protein slightly yellow, so don't be alarmed by the change in color. Test out the freezing method with any of the tofu dishes in this book and see if it adds a novel twist to your curd.

2 (14oz/400g) blocks extra-firm tofu, pressed, drained, patted dry with a towel
2 tablespoons extra-virgin olive oil
2 tablespoons lemon pepper seasoning
¼ cup (30g) cornstarch

½ cup (60g) panko, gluten-free bread-crumbs or Mac Parm (p. 23)

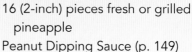

GARNISH
16 (2-inch) pieces fresh or grilled pineapple
Peanut Dipping Sauce (p. 149)

Freeze entire package of tofu for 24 hours. Defrost completely, then freeze a second time for another 24 hours. Defrost again and remove from package. Press for at least 30 minutes; drain and pat dry with a towel.

Preheat oven to 400°F (200°C) and line a baking sheet with parchment paper.

Cut each block of tofu into 8 pieces and place in a large bowl. Drizzle with olive oil and toss gently to coat. Sprinkle over lemon pepper seasoning; toss again. Sprinkle over cornstarch and toss again to coat. Tofu should be sticky enough for panko to stick to it. Dredge in panko and arrange on baking sheet. Bake for 25 to 30 minutes, or until golden brown.

Arrange tofu and pineapple onto skewers and serve with peanut dipping sauce.

VARIATION: For air fryer, bake at 350°F (180°C) for 15 to 20 minutes.

{ ALL ABOUT THE SAUCE }

PEANUT DIPPING SAUCE

Yield: about 1½ cups

½ cup (60g) smooth peanut butter
¼ cup (60ml) water
2 tablespoons lemon juice
2 tablespoons maple syrup or agave syrup
2 tablespoons rice vinegar
2 tablespoons soy sauce or gluten-free
    liquid aminos
2 tablespoons sriracha
2 cloves garlic, minced
1 teaspoon minced fresh ginger
¼ teaspoon red pepper flakes

Whisk all ingredients in a small bowl and
chill in the refrigerator before using.

BAHN MI
WITH SESAME GINGER TOFU

Yield: 4 servings

Bahn mi, or Banh mi, is Vietnamese for bread and refers to a short baguette stuffed with savory ingredients and crunchy homemade pickles. Vietnamese restaurants in Honolulu are serving up their versions of this French roll and with good reason. Squish what you can into your crusty roll and smother in fresh chili to awaken your senses. Give it a good squeeze to deflate (the human jaw can expand only so much), then go in for the bite. Expect mess and flying bits—it's a Bahn mi thing!

1 (12-ounce/340g) vacuum-packed, deep-fried tofu, drained (I use Aloha brand)
1 tablespoon soy sauce or gluten-free liquid aminos
2 tablespoons cornstarch

CARROT DAIKON PICKLES

1 medium carrot, peeled and julienned (cut into matchsticks)
¼ daikon (about 100g), peeled and julienned
½ cup (120ml) Pickling Brine (A Wonderful World of Pickles p. 134)

SESAME GINGER SAUCE

3 tablespoons mirin
2 tablespoons soy sauce or liquid aminos
1 tablespoon minced fresh ginger
1 tablespoon molasses or sugar
1 tablespoon rice vinegar

1 tablespoon sesame seeds
1 tablespoon sriracha
1 fresh red chili, sliced, or ¼ teaspoon crushed red pepper

BEAN SPROUTS

2 teaspoons sesame oil
1 pack (8oz/226g) bean sprouts, rinsed and drained
½ teaspoon mushroom seasoning
1 tablespoon hoisin sauce

4 small baguettes or gluten-free bread rolls

GARNISH

¼ cup (5g) chopped cilantro
¼ cup (30g) sliced green onion
2 tablespoons chopped dry roasted nuts
1 fresh red chili, sliced

Preheat oven to 400°F (200°C) and line a baking sheet with parchment paper. Cut tofu into 1-inch strips and place in a large bowl. Add soy sauce and toss to coat. Sprinkle with cornstarch and toss again. Arrange on lined baking sheet and bake for 25 to 30 minutes, or until golden brown.

While tofu is baking, prepare pickles. Combine the carrot and daikon in a bowl. Pour over pickling brine to cover; set aside to marinate for 30 minutes, or overnight to allow flavors to meld. Drain before using.

Once tofu is done baking, remove from oven and set aside. Whisk sesame ginger sauce ingredients in a bowl and pour into a skillet. Heat sauce over medium-high heat. Once sauce starts to bubble, add tofu and toss to coat. Cook for about about 1 minute, or until sauce has soaked into tofu. Transfer to a bowl and set aside.

To make the bean sprouts, heat oil in a skillet over medium-high heat. Add bean sprouts and cook for 2 minutes. Add mushroom seasoning and hoisin sauce; toss to coat and transfer to a bowl.

Slice the baguettes in half lengthwise, almost all the way through, and open; toast until just heated or leave untoasted. Fill baguettes with bean sprouts, tofu, and pickles; garnish with cilantro, green onion, nuts, and fresh chili to taste. Drizzle with some of the pickling brine from the carrot daikon pickles for extra flavor.

VARIATION: For air fryer, bake tofu at 350°F (180°C) for 15 to 20 minutes.

LEMON ZUCCHINI PASTA WITH THAI BASIL PESTO

Yield: 4 to 6 servings

Poor zucchini doesn't get the accolades it deserves, which is a shame because it's pretty amazeballs. This is a quick and easy meal perfect for Meatless Monday. If you really want to do some showing off, add some Oyster Bacon (p. 78) or Tofu Bacon Bits (p. 170). Not really necessary, but the more the merrier as they say!

8 ounces (250g) dried short pasta or
   gluten-free pasta (penne, fussili)
1 tablespoon extra-virgin olive oil
2 zucchinis, cut in half lengthwise, then
   sliced into half-moon ¼-inch discs
Salt and freshly cracked black pepper
2 to 3 garlic cloves, minced
½ cup (140g) Thai Basil Pesto (p. 31)
   or store-bought pesto (vegan and/or
   gluten-free)

Zest of 1 lemon
¼ cup (60ml) lemon juice
¼ cup (25g) roughly chopped walnuts
   (see **NOTE**)
Freshly cracked black pepper

GARNISH
2 tablespoons freshly grated vegan
   Parmesan or Mac Parm (p. 23)
8 lemon wedges

Cook penne according to package instructions. Save ½ cup (120ml) of the pasta water before draining; set both aside (see **CHEF'S TIP**).

Heat oil in a large pot over medium-high heat. Add zucchini and season with salt and pepper to taste. Add garlic and sauté for 4 to 5 minutes, or until zucchini is tender. Stir in Thai Basil Pesto. Add cooked pasta and slowly add a little pasta water, 1 tablespoon at a time, to loosen the sauce. Only add as much pasta water as you need. Add lemon zest, lemon juice, and walnuts; toss to combine. Season with pepper to taste. Sprinkle with vegan Parmesan and serve with lemon wedges.

CHEF'S TIP: The pasta water lends flavor, while the starch content adds a silky richness that thickens the sauce and helps it cling to the pasta.

NOTE: If you have time, toast the nuts first. Place on a baking sheet lined with parchment paper and toast at 350°F (180°C) for 8 to 10 minutes, stirring halfway through.

ICE
COLD
Coconut
$5⁰⁰
each

CHAPTER 8

THIS CHEESE IS NUTS!

Cheese is adored and craved the world over; no other food can bring on the smiles and is perhaps why we say "cheese" when taking photos. There's something about cheese people can't say no to and is one of the reasons why many assume they "could never go vegan."

The farmers markets on O'ahu are attracting artisan cheesemakers who are ditching dairy to produce some true plant-based winners. Keep in mind plant-based cheeses are healthier and more environmentally friendly than traditional varieties, and most importantly no animals are harmed in the process. I totally respect people who get all experimental and make plant-based cheese by growing cultures and sprouting grains for rejuvelac. However, if you're just starting out, there's no need to turn mad scientist just yet. Let's start at the beginning and learn the basics of vegan cheesemaking first. This is a collection of my favorite dairy-free cheeses—simple to sophisticated, with varieties that were unimaginable in the earlier days of vegan cheesemaking. The plant-kingdom provides many options for experimentation, allowing you to whip up a batch in the comfort of your own kitchen. When all is said and done, there is absolutely no reason why you can't be vegan and have your cheese, too!

FUN IDEA: Celebrate the simple pleasures in life and throw a wine and vegan cheese-tasting party! Have your guests each prep a bottle of vegan wine and send them one of the cheese recipes in this book (in advance) to make and take. Start building your cheese platter as guests arrive with their home-made delights. Garnish with crackers, nuts, fresh and dried fruit. Save the wine corks to decorate with or collect in a nice, large vase as memories of good times had. Make sure you recycle the wine bottles or use as makeshift vases perfect for slender flowers and lily stems.

CASHEW BRIE

Yield: 2 (2 x 4-inch) cheese rounds

Don't let a lack of unaffordable vegan culture starters hold you back from creating your own homemade cashew brie. This has all the brie vibe; sharp, creamy, and a firm rind. Even the most critical cheese snobs will say it's pretty impressive. There is nothing complicated about this process. It takes a few days to develop the cultured rind so you will need to flip the cheese every few hours, but it's totally worth the small effort! Making your own plant-based cheese is a nice way to learn something new and impress your cheese-loving friends.

1½ cups (360ml) water
¼ cup (40g) raw cashews, rinsed, cooked
   in boiling water for 15 minutes, drained
2 tablespoons nutritional yeast
2 tablespoons tapioca starch
1 tablespoon apple cider vinegar
1 teaspoon salt
1 teaspoon kappa carrageenan powder

1 teaspoon onion powder
½ teaspoon garlic powder
½ teaspoon white miso paste

YOU WILL ALSO NEED
Two (2 x 4-inch) ramekins or containers
Baking sheet lined with parchment paper
Extra tapioca starch for dusting

Blend all ingredients until smooth and creamy. Transfer to a saucepan and bring to a boil over medium-high heat, stirring constantly for 2 to 3 minutes, or until mixture starts to bubble. Remove from heat and divide cheese mixture into two ramekins. Cool to room temperature and refrigerate overnight, or for at least 6 to 8 hours to set.

Carefully unmold the cheeses from ramekins using a spatula and place onto a lined baking sheet. Scrape the cheese from the sides of the ramekin and smooth onto the cheese rounds. They will be soft, almost like a cream cheese. Dust cheese rounds on the top and sides with tapioca starch to give it the "brie" look. Dry in "warm" setting in oven, about 170°F (80°C) for 2 hours. Flip brie, dust other side with tapioca starch and return to oven for another 2 hours. Continue flipping brie and drying in the warm setting of your oven until a nice rind or outer crust has developed, about 6 to 8 hours. Taste the brie as you go. You'll notice a matured or aged flavor starts to develop the longer you dry it out. Once you're happy with how the brie is looking and tasting you can serve it warm or chilled. Store in an airtight container in the refrigerator for 4 to 5 days.

NOTE: Kappa carrageenan powder is made from seaweed and used as a thickening or gelling agent, specifically in vegan cheese, yielding a texture and consistency similar to that of dairy cheeses. Use agar powder if you prefer, but the end result of the cheese will differ substantially.

{ THIS CHEESE IS NUTS! }

CHEF'S TIP: If you really want to develop that rind even further, place cashew brie on a plate lined with parchment paper and dry in the refrigerator, uncovered, for 1 to 3 days, flipping twice a day.

CASHEW MOCKARELLA

Yield: 3 mozzarella balls

Cashew mockarella takes plant-based cooking to a whole new level of amazing! Enjoy it in grilled cheese sandwiches, pizza, lasagna, quesadillas; the possibilities are truly endless. Drizzle your gorgeous mozz with a little extra-virgin olive oil or Vegan Honey (p. 38), sprinkle with freshly cracked pepper, and serve with Sun-Dried Tomato (p. 56). The Caprese Tartare on p. 164 is a knockout! And don't forget that bubbles go with everything.

BRINE
2 cups (480ml) chilled filtered water
1½ teaspoons salt
6 to 8 ice cubes

CASHEW MOCKARELLA
¼ cup (40g) raw cashews, rinsed, cooked
    for 15 minutes in boiling water, drained
¾ cups (180ml) water

2 tablespoons melted refined coconut oil
    or extra-virgin olive oil
2 tablespoons tapioca flour
1 tablespoon nutritional yeast
2 teaspoons apple cider vinegar
1 teaspoon kappa carrageenan powder or
    agar powder
1 teaspoon lemon juice
¾ teaspoon salt

Combine ingredients for brine in a large airtight container and set aside.

Blend the mockarella ingredients until smooth. Transfer to a saucepan and bring to a boil over medium-high heat for 1 to 2 minutes, or until mixture starts to thicken and come together.

Remove from heat and allow to cool slightly. Dip a large spoon or ice cream scoop into the brine and scoop out 1/3 of the mixture. Drop mockarella ball into the brine and repeat two more times. Chill in the refrigerator for 1 hour to set. Drain mockarella balls on a towel before using. Store in an airtight container in the refrigerator for up to 3 to 5 days.

{ THIS CHEESE IS NUTS! }

CHOCOLATE CHILI CHEESE

Yield: 2 rounds

Hold onto your hats people. Chocolate cheese is a thing! I know you're thinking I've gone completely mad but this was a hit in my cooking classes in Japan and proved to be quite the conversation starter. Check out the recipe video for this recipe on my Lillian Vegan YouTube channel. The perfect treat for that food lover in your life who is always on the hunt for something new to try. Great with fresh pear and crackers. A fair warning though—one either loves it, or one hates it!

1½ cups (360ml) water
¼ cup (40g) raw cashews, rinsed, cooked
   in boiling water for 15 minutes, drained
3 tablespoons vegan Chocolate Sauce
   (p. 228) or Hershey's chocolate syrup
2 tablespoons nutritional yeast
2 tablespoons sugar
2 tablespoons tapioca flour

1 tablespoon
   cocoa powder
1 teaspoon kappa
   carrageenan powder
1 teaspoon salt
¼ teaspoon chili powder

¼ teaspoon crushed red pepper

Blend all ingredients until smooth and creamy. Transfer to a saucepan and bring to a boil over medium-high heat for 2 to 3 minutes, or until mixture starts to bubble. Pour mixture into two 4.5-inch ramekins or bowls. Sprinkle tops with crushed red pepper. Cool to room temperature, cover, and refrigerate for at least 4 hours to allow cheese to set.

Remove chocolate cheese from ramekins and place on a plate. Chill in the refrigerator 1 day, uncovered, before serving. Store in the refrigerator for up to 4 to 5 days.

VARIATION: Sprinkle chocolate cheese with chopped nuts such as pistachios, almonds, or walnuts before drying in the oven if you prefer a nutty top crust. Serve with crackers or fruit such as strawberries and pear slices. Pairs well with a nice Pinot Noir.

CASHEW CHEESE SAUCE AND CHEESE FONDUE

Yield: about 2 cups

Even veggie-haters will be tempted to nosh on plant-based food when it's covered in a super cheesy cashew sauce. Let me count the ways I love thee—baked potatoes, steamed broccoli, nachos—you get the picture. Add a squirt of sriracha and you have a thick creamy nacho sauce, or mix it into soups and stews for an instant white sauce without the unhealthy fats and dairy. It can also be a tempting cheeseless fondue, encouraging even more veggies to magically disappear. Pull out your skewers and neglected fondue pots because I'm bringing back the king of all cheese dips! How did we ever let this retro classic disappear from the modern foodie scene? According to some supreme sources on party etiquette, a lady who drops a dipper in the fondue pot has to kiss every man at the table, while a man has to buy a round of drinks. The extent to which you follow these "rules" is at your discretion.

CASHEW CHEESE SAUCE

2 cups (480ml) water

¼ cup (40g) raw cashews, rinsed, cooked in boiling water for 15 minutes, drained (see **NOTE**)

2 tablespoons nutritional yeast

2 tablespoons tapioca flour

1 tablespoon apple cider vinegar

1½ teaspoons salt

1 teaspoon onion powder

½ teaspoon garlic powder

½ teaspoon white miso paste

Place all the ingredients into a mixer and blend on high until smooth and creamy. Transfer to a saucepan and bring to a boil over medium-high heat for 2 to 3 minutes, or until mixture starts to bubble. Use immediately or store in the refrigerator for up to 1 week.

If you're making a fondue, transfer cheese sauce to a fondue pot and serve with mixed dippers.

CHEF'S TIP: For a more authentic tasting fondue, place 1 smashed garlic clove and ¼ cup (60ml) dry white wine in a saucepan. Bring to a boil over medium-high heat to cook off the alcohol, about 1 minute. Remove garlic clove and discard. Blend Cashew Cheese Sauce ingredients until creamy; add to the wine and bring to a boil. Once mixture starts to bubble transfer to a fondue pot and serve.

{ THIS CHEESE IS NUTS! }

NOTE: I prefer to soak cashews overnight for guaranteed softness, but if you need a quick soak, place cashews into a pot and bring to a boil over medium-high heat. (A splash of lemon juice makes them softer.) Once water starts to bubble, turn heat down to medium and simmer for 15 minutes. Drain and use in any of the cheese recipes that call for raw cashews. This is when a high-speed blender comes in handy to ensure the cashews are blended to a creamy consistency.

SUN-DRIED TOMATO CHEESE WITH FURIKAKE

Yield: 2 (4-inch) cheese rounds

My collection of vegan cheeses is always growing and yours should, too. So much tang and texture to this little round of tastiness. It has a savory-sweet profile with rich intense flavors from the sun-dried tomatoes. A sprinkling of furikake adds the perfect umami note to balance out the flavors of this wonderful cheese. Great in a cheese platter with nuts, grapes, dried fruit, and crackers.

1½ cups (350ml) water
¼ cup (40g) raw cashews, rinsed, soaked
   overnight in water, drained
2 tablespoons nutritional yeast
2 tablespoons tapioca flour
1 tablespoon apple cider vinegar
1 teaspoon salt
1 teaspoon onion powder
½ teaspoon garlic powder
½ teaspoon white miso paste

2 tablespoons chopped sun-dried tomato
   in oil, drained

TOPPING
1 tablespoon Japanese Furikake (p. 24)

YOU WILL ALSO NEED
2 (4-inch) ramekins or bowls
Extra-virgin olive oil cooking spray
Baking sheet lined with parchment paper

Place all the ingredients into a mixer and blend on high until smooth and creamy. Transfer to a saucepan, add sun-dried tomato and bring to a boil over medium-high heat, stirring constantly, for 2 to 3 minutes, or until mixture starts to bubble. Remove from heat.

Spray ramekins with cooking spray. Divide cheese mixture into ramekins and sprinkle tops with Japanese Furikake. Cool to room temperature and chill in the refrigerator overnight, or for at least 6 to 8 hours to set.

{ THIS CHEESE IS NUTS! }

Carefully remove cheese from ramekins using a spatula and place onto a baking sheet lined with parchment paper. Dry in "warm" setting in oven, about 170°F (80°C) for 2 hours. Flip cheese and return to oven for another 2 hours. Continue flipping cheese and drying in the warm setting of your oven until a nice rind or outer crust has developed, about 6 to 8 hours. Taste the cheese as you go. You'll notice a matured or aged flavor starts to develop the longer you dry the cheese. Once you're happy with how the cheese is looking and tasting you can serve it warm or chilled. Store in an airtight container in the refrigerator for up to 4 to 5 days.

CAPRESE TARTARE

Yield: 4 servings

Here's a healthy spin on the beloved Italian summer classic using roasted eggplant, bell peppers, and plant-based mozzarella. This Caprese wanna-be makes an elegant pūpū or light supper to kick off the evening. Layer your Caprese in the classic style, or go right ahead and chop it up transforming it into a Caprese tartare you can enjoy with tortilla chips or crostini. Either way, it's the best of summer and fabulously vegan!

1 large red bell pepper
1 large eggplant, sliced into ½-inch disks
Extra-virgin olive oil cooking spray

Salt and freshly crack black pepper

1 batch Cashew Mockarella (p. 158)

GARNISH
Balsamic Glaze to taste (p. 125)
Extra-virgin olive oil to taste
4 to 5 basil leaves, torn

Preheat oven to 425°F. Place whole bell pepper and eggplant slices on a baking sheet lined with parchment paper. Spray eggplant with olive oil and season with salt and freshly cracked pepper on both sides. Bake eggplant for 15 to 20 minutes, or until tender, flipping halfway through.

Remove eggplant from oven and cool on a plate. Continue baking bell pepper for 30 to 40 minutes in total, or until skin is black and blistered. Remove from oven and cool. Peel the skin and discard seeds and membrane. Cut into 4 to 5 pieces.

Layer eggplant, bell peppers and sliced mockarella on a plate or chop ingredients together to form a tartare. Drizzle with Balsamic Glaze and extra-virgin olive oil. Garnish with basil.

{ THIS CHEESE IS NUTS! }

PISTACHIO MAC-CRUSTED CHEESE

Yield: 2 (4-inch) cheese rounds

Thankfully, we've entered a new era when giving up dairy just means we get to try all the healthier versions of the things we thought you could never live without. Encrusted with earthy Pistachio Mac Parm (and that salty kick), you'll create the most delectable nut cheese sure to please any crowd. Luxury cheese at home is only a few steps away. Get on it!

1 batch Cashew Brie mixture (p. 156)
  (follow instructions up until filling the

two ramekins with the cheese mixture)
½ cup (45g) Pistachio Mac Parm (p. 23)

Once you've made the Cashew Brie from p. 156 allow to set in the refrigerator, covered, overnight.

Place pistachio Mac Parm in a bowl. Carefully remove cheese from ramekins using a spatula and place into the bowl of Mac Parm, one at time, dredging cheese on all sides evenly. Repeat with remaining cheese round adding more Mac Parm, if needed. Mold cheese into a log or desired shape.

Place onto a baking sheet lined with parchment paper and dry in "warm" setting in oven, about 170°F (80°C) for 6 to 8 hours, flipping every 2 hours. Taste the cheese as you go. Once you're happy with how the cheese is looking and tasting, it's ready to serve warm or chilled. Enjoy with fresh or dried fruit, nuts, crackers, or bread.

TOFETA PLATTER

Yield: 3 to 4 servings

I'm pretty sure the vegan gods sent us tofu so we could make Tofeta. This recipe captures that tangy feta vibe in all the right ways; zippy, briny, and mildly fermented with a firm touch and slightly grainy feel that's easy to crumble. Arigato, Lady Miso! Marinate it, bottle it in oil, or bake it to a golden protein-packed nugget you can enjoy in so many ways. If you're skeptical about the whole vegan cheese scene, I urge you to try this. Make your friends a Tofeta platter and bring on the vino!

TOFETA
1 (14oz/400g) block extra-firm tofu, pressed and patted dry with a towel, cut into ½-inch cubes

MARINADE
½ cup (120ml) apple cider vinegar
½ cup (120ml) water
¼ cup (60ml) lemon juice
1 tablespoon extra-virgin olive oil

1 tablespoon nutritional flakes
1 tablespoon white miso
½ teaspoon dried basil
½ teaspoon garlic powder
½ teaspoon dried oregano
½ teaspoon salt
¼ teaspoon dried dill
¼ teaspoon lemon extract or ½ teaspoon lemon zest
¼ teaspoon cracked black pepper

Place cubed tofu in a large zip lock bag. In a separate bowl, whisk together marinade ingredients and pour into the bag with the tofu. Swish bag around to make sure the marinade is distributed evenly over the tofu. Seal zip lock bag and place in the refrigerator to marinade for at least 2 to 3 days, flipping zip-lock bag twice a day. Flavors intensify the longer you leave it to marinade. Transfer to an airtight container (do not drain), and store in the refrigerator for up to 1 week. Drain before using.

TOFETA IN OIL

Once Tofeta has marinated for 2 to 3 days, drain liquid and discard. Place Tofeta into mason jars and fill with extra-virgin olive oil. Add fresh or dried herbs, black or red peppercorns, or garlic cloves for an extra-fancy version. Store in the refrigerator for up to 3 weeks. Great as gifts! You can also bottle Baked Tofeta in oil.

BAKED TOFETA

Once Tofeta has marinated for 2 to 3 days, drain liquid and discard. Arrange Tofeta on a baking sheet lined with parchment paper and bake in the oven at 400°F (200°C) for 25 to 30 minutes, or until slightly browned. For air fryer, bake at 350°F (180C) for 15 to 20 minutes. Serve drizzled with Vegan Honey (p. 38) or crumble over salads and pasta dishes.

CHEESY VEGGIE GREATIN

Yield: 4 to 6 servings

Forget the classic flour-butter-milk roux gratin. This is luxurious and indulgent without the dairy fat. We're substituting all with the healthier vegan version using a creamy Cashew Cheese Sauce and tender veggies combined to make a delicious GREAT-in experience fit for any special occasion. Kids will love this, I kid you not!

4 to 6 cups steamed or boiled mixed
   vegetables (see **CHEF'S TIP**)
1 batch Cashew Cheese Sauce (p. 160)
2 tablespoons chopped fresh parsley
½ cup (110g) shredded vegan cheese

Preheat oven to 400°F (200°C).

Combine vegetables, Cashew Cheese Sauce, and parsley in a large bowl and toss gently to coat. Pour into an oven dish. (I use an 11-inch dish.) Sprinkle with vegan cheese and bake 25 to 30 minutes, or until golden brown.

CHEF'S TIP: Try this recipe with any type of cooked veggie: carrots, asparagus, Brussels sprouts, cauliflower, beans, pumpkin, or sweet potato, peas, corn. Anything goes!

BAKED MAC AND CHEESE WITH TOFU BACON BITS

Yield: 4 to 6 servings

Cashew Cheese Sauce is the answer to any kitchen dilemma. It's versatile, keiki-friendly, and tastes great on everything from veggies to mac and cheese. The beauty of a mac and cheese is that it can take on so many different forms. Clean out your refrigerator adding any leftovers you have—cooked broccoli, asparagus, Brussels sprouts, mushrooms, or liven it up with some smoked paprika and jalapeño slices. This is America's favorite comfort food in all its ooey gooey glory.

BACON SEASONING

2 tablespoons nutritional yeast
2 tablespoons soy sauce or gluten-free liquid aminos
1 tablespoon blackstrap molasses
1 tablespoon maple syrup
2 teaspoons onion powder
2 teaspoons smoked paprika
1 teaspoon garlic powder
½ teaspoon liquid smoke
½ teaspoon pepper
Pinch of salt

1 block (14oz/400g) extra-firm tofu, drained, pressed and patted dry with a towel

MAC AND CHEESE

2 cups macaroni pasta, cooked according to package instructions, drained
1 batch Cashew Cheese Sauce (p. 160)
Freshly cracked black pepper
1 cup (220g) shredded vegan cheese
2 tablespoons chopped fresh parsley

Preheat oven to 375°F (190°C) and line a baking sheet with parchment paper.

Mix together bacon seasoning in a bowl. Crumble in tofu and toss gently to coat. Spread evenly on baking sheet and bake for 25 to 30 minutes, or until browned, stirring halfway through. Remove from oven and set aside. Reduce oven heat to 350°F (180°C).

Combine macaroni, tofu bacon (add as much as you like and store the rest in the refrigerator), and Cashew Cheese Sauce; season with pepper to taste. Pour into an oven dish. Top with shredded vegan cheese and parsley. Bake for 25 to 30 minutes, or until bubbling and golden brown on the top.

{ THIS CHEESE IS NUTS! }

The people
who make
screw-top
wine bottles...?

They're the

BAKED TOFETA PASTA

Yield: 4 servings

Baked Tofeta is already amazing, and when you add the words pasta and tomato you know it's going to be a tempting combo to resist. What I love about this recipe is most of the magic happens in the oven and is pretty much hands-off with the Tofeta and tomatoes essentially creating the sauce to coat the pasta. Drizzle with a little Hot Honey (p. 38) should you be so daring (cheese and honey is a match made in heaven), and prepare yourself for a rippa meal!

SAUCE

1 batch Tofeta (p. 166)
1 pint (300g) cherry tomatoes
¼ cup (60ml) extra-virgin olive oil
3 to 4 cloves garlic, thinly sliced
¼ teaspoon crushed red pepper
Salt and freshly cracked black pepper

7 ounces (200g) dried short pasta or
   gluten-free pasta (penne, fussili)
4 cups (5oz/150g) baby spinach leaves
10 basil leaves, torn

GARNISH

2 tablespoons extra-virgin olive oil (If you
   made Garlic Confit p. 32 you can use
   the garlic-infused oil and a few of the
   roasted cloves to garnish)
Freshly cracked black pepper

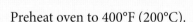

Preheat oven to 400°F (200°C).

Place Tofeta, tomatoes, oil, garlic, and crushed red pepper in an oven dish; toss well to combine and season with salt and pepper to taste. Bake for 40 to 50 minutes, or until tomatoes are roasted and Tofeta is golden brown.

Thirty minutes into baking, cook pasta according to package instructions and drain.

Remove Tofeta and tomato mixture from oven and mash gently with a fork, leaving it slightly chunky. Toss in cooked pasta, spinach, and basil leaves. Drizzle with olive oil and sprinkle with more pepper to taste.

SUGAR Cane
JUICE

SMOOTHIE FLAVORS
PAPAYA DRAGON PINEAPPLE
FRUIT
GINGER LIME COCONUT
GUAVA BANANA
MANGO STRAWBERRY LILIKOI
TANGERINE (PASSION FRUIT)
ACAI.

SMOOTHIES → $5⁰⁰   Sugar Cane Juice →

SWEETENED WITH
CANE J

CHAPTER 9

FOR THE CURIOUS COOK

This is the age of innovation for vegan food, but before I even try to sell you on this chapter, peruse the extraordinary recipes made possible with plants. I will admit, processed plant-based meats are not my thing, but I don't mind soy curls as they contain only one ingredient, non-GMO soybeans. Soy curls are such a great substitute for chicken, and Dave will attest the Chik'n Nuggets on p. 179 are difficult to tell apart from the real "McCoy."

Here's the deal. I don't judge when it comes to how people choose to fuel their bodies. If you're in the first stages of following a plant-based diet, you may be craving comfort food so it's important to have options like meat alternatives to help keep you focused on your plant-based journey. I'm confident the recipes in this section will entice people to give vegan food a try. It's highly likely you'll get a child to eat a Bluffalo Drumstick (p. 183) before they agree to a green salad. Whatever it takes to get people to eat outside of the box, I'm all in.

If you are a curious cook, you'll have a ball testing out these recipes. Expect to spend more time in the kitchen waiting for mixtures to set or dry out. It's inevitable. Keep in mind Rome wasn't built in a day! The splendid joy of seeing unique food come to life right before your very eyes is wholly rewarding. This chapter is literally mind-blowing and will change the way you perceive food. Enjoy making the impossible possible.

CHIK'N HEKKA

Yield: 4 to 6 servings

This one pot noodle dish is Hawai'i's version of Japanese sukiyaki (similar to chicken long rice), consisting of chicken, vegetables, and noodles cooked in a saucy broth. The cellophane noodles turn translucent when cooked and soak up the broth in just minutes. Locals like to serve this with rice. I usually throw in a bunch of baby spinach leaves and enjoy it on its own. If you're not feeling the soy curls, swap it for some Smoky Tofu Supam (p. 185) or lay a few pieces of Supam on top for that extra tasty Island feel. Now that's a hekka of a dish!

¼ cup (5g) sliced dried shiitake
1 cup (240ml) boiling water
1 cup (40g) soy curls
Boiling water to cover
1 tablespoon sesame oil
1 onion, sliced
1 carrot, julienned
Pinch of salt
1 (2-inch) piece ginger, julienned
4 to 5 garlic cloves, minced
2 cups (480ml) vegetable broth
1 can (8z/220g) bamboo shoots, rinsed
  and drained
¼ cup (60ml) mirin

¼ cup (60ml) soy sauce
1 tablespoon sugar
2 teaspoons mushroom seasoning
5 ounces (140g) dried cellophane noodles
  (see **NOTE**)

GARNISH
1 cup (50g) green onion, cut into 1-inch
  pieces
10 to 15 Thai basil leaves or a small bunch
  of watercress, cut into 1-inch pieces or
  1 cup (30g) baby spinach leaves, roughly
  torn
1 tablespoon toasted white sesame seeds

In a small bowl, soak shiitake in boiling water for 30 minutes. Do not drain! In a separate small bowl, place soy curls and enough boiling water to cover. Soak for 15 minutes and drain; set aside.

Heat sesame oil in a large pot over medium-high heat. Add onion, carrot, and a pinch of salt; sauté for 3 minutes. Add ginger and garlic; sauté for another 2 minutes. Add the shiitake with the soaking water, soaked soy curls, vegetable broth, and bamboo shoots. Bring to a boil, then reduce heat to medium; cover pot, and simmer for 5 minutes. Remove lid and add remaining ingredients and cellophane noodles. Cook for 6 to 8 minutes, or until noodles are cooked through and liquid is absorbed. Remove from heat and add green onion and Thai basil. Toss to combine and sprinkle with sesame seeds.

{ FOR THE CURIOUS COOK }

NOTE: Cellophane noodles are sold under many different names. Look for rice noodles (the term we use most in Hawai'i), bean thread noodles, glass noodles, or mung bean noodles. Always check labels and ingredients if you're following a gluten-free diet!

CHIK'N NUGGETS

Yield: 16 nuggets

It may not be refined, classy eating, but many of us likely grew up in a nugget household, making this one of America's favorite treats. Talk about a kid-pleaser! Is there any better finger food at a party than a nugget done right? My inspiration for this came when I was working on the buffalo drumstick recipe and realized it was the perfect nugget mix. These bite-size nibbles can be dipped in batter and breaded if you prefer a crumbed version. The best doggone nuggets on this side of the Islands, and another childhood favorite hit by the magic vegan wand!

1 batch Bluffalo Drumsticks mixture
(p. 183)

BATTER
1 cup (60g) plant-based milk
½ cup (70g) all-purpose flour or
gluten-free flour
1½ teaspoons salt
1 teaspoon onion powder
1 teaspoon smoked paprika
½ teaspoon garlic powder
¼ teaspoon white pepper

Vegetable oil or other neutral oil for frying

DARK SAUCE
½ cup (120g) BBQ sauce
¼ cup (60ml) plant-based milk
2 teaspoons whole grain mustard
Salt and freshly cracked black pepper

SPICY MUSTARD SAUCE
½ cup (120g) yellow mustard
2 tablespoons chipotle in adobo sauce
(sauce only)
Freshly cracked black pepper to taste

Follow instructions for Bluffalo Drumsticks mixture then chill in the refrigerator for 1 hour to set. Divide the mixture into 16 and shape into nuggets.

Whisk together batter ingredients in a large bowl, then dip the nuggets in the batter. Heat two inches of oil to 365°F in a large pot. Fry nuggets on each side for about 2 to 3 minutes, or until golden brown. Drain on paper towels. Whisk together sauce ingredients in separate bowls and serve with nuggets.

VARIATION: Bake in an oven (400°F/200°C) for 20 to 25 minutes or air fryer (350°F/180°C) for 15 to 20 minutes. Spraying lightly with cooking spray before baking will add a nice golden color to the nuggets.

CRISPY OYSTER CHIK'N

Yield: 4 to 6 servings

You don't have to give up your beloved wings if you're craving chicken. These meaty double-battered oyster mushrooms are awesome! Are you starting to get how valuable mushrooms are to the plant-based world? Incredible how a bunch of mere morsels can turn into something that looks like it came straight out of the infamous red and white striped bucket. Game-day pūpū done!

SWEET AND SPICY SAUCE

2 tablespoons barbecue sauce
2 tablespoons maple syrup
2 tablespoons rice vinegar
1 tablespoon toasted white sesame seeds
¼ tablespoon hot sauce

BUTTERMILK

1 cup (240ml) plant-based milk
1 tablespoon apple cider vinegar
½ tablespoon Vegan Chicken-less
    Seasoning Salt (see Glossary, p. 245) or
    mushroom seasoning

½ pound (250g) oyster mushrooms,
    bottom stem removed, pulled apart into
    2-inch pieces

DRY INGREDIENTS

1 cup (240g) all-purpose flour or
    gluten-free flour
2 tablespoons Chicken-less Seasoning Salt
    or mushroom seasoning
1 tablespoon Italian Seasoning
1 tablespoon smoked paprika
1 teaspoon cracked black pepper
½ teaspoon white pepper

Extra-virgin olive oil cooking spray

Preheat oven to 400°F (200°C) and line a baking sheet with parchment paper.

Whisk together sweet and spicy ingredients in a small bowl and refrigerate until ready to use.

For buttermilk, place milk in a large bowl; add vinegar, stir and set aside for 5 minutes to thicken. Mix in Chicken-less seasoning salt; add mushrooms to buttermilk and toss to coat. Set aside for 15 minutes to marinate.

Mix together dry ingredients in a large bowl. Use a slotted spoon to scoop up mushrooms and place in the dry ingredients bowl; toss well to coat. Shake off excess flour from each mushroom piece, return to the buttermilk for a "double coating," then dredge one more time in the dry ingredients. Shake off excess flour and arrange on lined baking sheet. Bake for 20 to 25 minutes, or until golden brown. Toss with sweet and spicy sauce or skip the sauce and serve sprinkled with a little salt.

VARIATION: For air fryer, bake at 350°F (190°C) for 15 minutes.

BLUFFALO "DRUMSTICKS"

Yield: 8 "drumsticks"

The look on my friends' faces when I served them a batch of these "drumsticks" is priceless. Forget about trying to impress your friends. Give this recipe a shot and surprise yourself! I've pulled out all my vegan hacks for this one! You will have to spend some time on this recipe, but it'll be worth the effort. Great with a side of Corn Ribs (p. 67), Tofu Egg and Corn Macaroni Salad (p. 131), and some Pickles (p. 134).

4 cups (120g) soy curls
½ cup (120ml) boiling water

SEASONING
2 tablespoons nutritional yeast
2 teaspoons mushroom seasoning
2 teaspoons onion powder
1 teaspoon garlic powder
½ teaspoon liquid smoke

7 ounces (200g) silken tofu
½ cup (80g) mung bean starch or chickpea
   flour (also known as garbanzo flour)
¼ cup (60ml) plant-based milk

"BONE" OF THE "DRUMSTICK"
1 long burdock root, washed and
   scrubbed, cut into 8 (3-inch) pieces (you
   can also use carrot or celery sticks or
   sugarcane to mimic the bone)

TOFU SKIN: (SEE CHEF'S TIP)
4 cups (1 liter) unsweetened soy milk

BUFFALO SAUCE
½ cup (110g) Frank's hot sauce
2 tablespoons vegan butter
1 tablespoon white wine vinegar
½ teaspoon soy sauce or gluten-free liquid
   aminos

Place soy curls in a bowl, pour over boiling water, and set aside for 10 minutes to rehydrate. Squeeze out excess liquid and pull soy curls apart using your fingers to resemble shredded chicken. Add seasoning ingredients and use your hands to mix it into the soy curls.

In a small bowl, whisk together tofu, bean flour, and milk to form a paste, leaving the mixture slightly lumpy. Add paste to soy curls; mix to combine and chill in the refrigerator for 1 hour to set.

Divide mixture into 8. Place a piece of plastic wrap (big enough to wrap a drumstick in) on your work surface. Scoop one portion of the soy curl mixture onto the center of the plastic wrap. Place a piece of burdock root halfway from the center onto the soy curl mixture. You want the burdock root to act as the "bone" of the "drumstick." Fold over the plastic wrap and mold the mixture

around the bone into the shape of a drumstick. Repeat until all 8 "drumsticks" are done. Place in the refrigerator for 1 hour to set.

Preheat oven to 400°F (200°C) and line a baking tray with parchment paper.

For the skin, heat soy milk in a medium-sized skillet to 175°F (80°C). If you don't stir the soy milk, a layer of skin will appear on the surface, taking about 5 to 6 minutes to develop each skin layer. Use a long chopstick to detach the tofu skin from the side of the skillet; gently lift up and away from the soy milk. Wrap the tofu skin around the "drumstick" and place on lined baking tray. Repeat with remaining "drumsticks." Bake for 20 to 25 minutes, or until golden brown. Transfer to a large bowl.

Heat buffalo sauce ingredients in a skillet over medium heat until butter starts to melt, about 2 minutes. Pour sauce over the "drumsticks" and toss gently to coat. Serve "drumsticks" hot or chilled.

VARIATION: For air fryer, bake "drumsticks" at 375°F (190°C) for 15 to 20 minutes.

CHEF'S TIP: Making the tofu skin can be time consuming. Alternatively, dip the "drumsticks" in batter and dredge in gluten-free panko if you want to skip making the tofu skin. Fry or bake as you like. Or you can use store-bought *Yuba*, dried bean curd sheet (see Glossary, p. 245). Fill a large shallow bowl with water and soak *Yuba* sheets according to package instructions Lift the soaked *Yuba* sheet and wrap around the "drumstick" as best you can. Fry or bake as you like.

SMOKY TOFU SUPAM

Yield: 12 slices

All the goodness of Spam minus the can. Hawai'i's most beloved food is getting a plant-based makeover in the form of tofu, and it rocks! This quintessential staple shows up in a lot of Island faves including musubi and Hawaiian fried rice. Spam consumption here is no joke. It is said about 6 million cans of this salty, nonperishable meat are sold each year in the Aloha state alone! So how does a vegan, gluten-free, oil-free tofu version stand a chance with stats like that? Try it and you decide. Life is all about options.

1 block (14oz/400g) extra-firm tofu, pressed, drained, patted dry with a towel, cut into 12 slices

MARINADE
2 tablespoons maple syrup or agave syrup or 1 tablespoon blackstrap molasses
2 tablespoons soy sauce or gluten-free liquid aminos
1 tablespoon mirin

1 teaspoon beet powder, (optional, for color)
1 teaspoon garlic powder
1 teaspoon liquid smoke
1 teaspoon mushroom seasoning
1 teaspoon onion powder
1 teaspoon smoked paprika
¼ teaspoon ground ginger
¼ teaspoon salt

Place tofu in a shallow container or zip-lock bag. Whisk together marinade ingredients and pour over tofu. Flip tofu to make sure both sides are coated. Cover container (or seal zip-lock bag) and marinate in the refrigerator for 1 hour, flipping once.

Preheat oven to 350°F (180°C). Arrange tofu slices on a baking sheet with parchment paper. Bake for 15 minutes, flip tofu, and bake another 15 to 20 minutes, or until golden brown. Remove from oven and cool to room temperature. Chill Supam for at least 1 hour to firm up and develop a nice texture.

CHEF'S TIP: Cube the tofu instead of slicing if you plan on using the Supam for fried rice or other stir-fries. Add Supam to the Tofu Egg and Corn Macaroni Salad on (p. 131) for an Island twist.

{ FOR THE CURIOUS COOK }

KALUA PORKY PLATE
WITH SPICY PINEAPPLE

Yield: 4 servings

If you have ever been to Hawai'i, chances are you have had a Hawaiian plate lunch and remember it fondly for its big scoop of white rice, creamy mac salad, and kalua pork. To recreate this Island staple, use the magical king oyster mushroom shredded into what can only be described as the real deal. Mildly flavored with only a little 'alaea salt (Hawaiian red salt) and liquid smoke, this vegan version of pulled pork is as close to the real thing as you're ever going to get. Add a side of Island-Style Potato Salad (p. 132) and Tofu Egg and Corn Macaroni Salad (p. 131), then "grind bro!"

KALUA "PORK"
1 pack (10oz/270g) king oyster mushrooms, about 4 to 5 mushrooms
1 tablespoon vegetable oil or other neutral oil
½ to 1 teaspoon 'alaea salt (Hawaiian red salt)

½ teaspoon liquid smoke

GARNISH
4 cups cooked rice
1 batch Spicy Pineapple (p. 219)
3 tablespoons sliced green onion

Preheat oven to 400°F (200°C). Shred mushrooms using a fork to resemble pulled pork. Place in an oven dish and mix in oil, 'alaea salt, and liquid smoke. Bake for 20 to 25 minutes, or until "pork" is tender.

Serve Kalua "Pork" with rice and pineapple. Garnish with green onion.

CHEF'S TIP: For extra flavor, drizzle the rice or the Kalua "Pork" with the leftover juices from the pineapple.

CHEF'S TIP: Top crostini with Kalua Porky for a simple and tasty pūpū.

TIRAM MERAH
PINK OYSTER MUSHROOM
PLEUROTUS DJAMOR

PORKY BEAN CROQUETTES

Yield: 12 croquettes

Pick up any Japanese bento in Hawai'i and you will most likely be met with some kind of croquette, or "korok-ke" as it is pronounced in Japan. A classic style is made with mashed potatoes mixed with sautéed ground beef and onion, shaped into ovals, breaded, and deep-fried. Now let's talk pork and beans. Since moving to Hawai'i, I see the love for this combination to be very deep. While testing the moxtail recipe on page 192, I tried adding beans to the mix and quickly realized it wasn't working. Luckily, I was left with a "porky bean" mixture that was screaming to be a croquette. Just goes to show, mishaps in the kitchen can be culinary blessings in disguise.

2 (20oz/565g) cans young green jackfruit, rinsed and drained

BROTH
½ cup (120ml) water
2 tablespoons nutritional yeast
1 tablespoon mushroom seasoning
2 teaspoons garlic powder
1 teaspoon onion powder
½ teaspoon liquid smoke

1 can (16oz/450g) black-eyed peas, rinsed and drained
1 can (16oz/450g) butter beans, rinsed and drained

½ cup (40g) chickpea flour or mung bean flour

BATTER
1 cup (60g) plant-based milk
½ cup (70g) all-purpose flour or gluten-free flour
2 cups (100g) panko or gluten-free breadcrumbs

Vegetable oil or other neutral oil for frying

GARNISH
BBQ Sauce (p. 199) or Tangy Chipotle Mayo (p. 76)

Place jackfruit in a bowl and use your fingers to squeeze out the seeds and remove hard center pieces. Shred jackfruit by pulling the flesh apart so it starts to resemble pulled pork. Whisk broth ingredients in a pot. Add jackfruit and bring to a simmer over medium-high heat. Cover with a lid and simmer for 4 to 5 minutes, or until liquid is completely absorbed into the jackfruit. Remove from heat; set aside. (See Moxtail Stew photos on p. 195.)

Mash black-eyed peas and butter beans in a large bowl using a potato masher, leaving the mixture slightly chunky. Mix in the jackfruit and bean flour. Divide mixture into 12 and shape into croquettes as you like, round or oval; chill in the refrigerator for 1 hour until firm.

{ FOR THE CURIOUS COOK }

Mix together milk and flour in a large bowl. In a separate bowl, add panko. Coat the croquettes in the batter, then dredge in panko. Heat two inches of oil to 365°F in a large pot. Fry croquettes on each side for about 2 to 3 minutes, or until golden brown. Drain on paper towels and serve with sauce of choice.

VARIATION: For air fryer, bake at (350°F/180°C) for 15 to 20 minutes. (Spraying lightly with cooking spray will add a nice golden color when baking.) For oven, bake at (400°F/200°C) for 20 to 25 minutes.

KING OYSTER "RIBS"

Yield: 4 servings

Vegans in the house will rejoice for these sticky, smoky, off-the-bone BBQ "ribs!" I just cannot get enough of these toothsome fungi. The meaty, mighty 'shrooms release moisture when you set a heavy cast iron skillet over them as they cook, making the earthy flavors highly concentrated. Whether you're vegan or not, I strongly recommend you try these—even the staunchest meat-eater will be impressed!

10 king oyster mushrooms
1 tablespoon toasted sesame oil
2 tablespoons Old Bay seasoning
1 teaspoon mushroom seasoning
2 tablespoons vegetable oil or other
   neutral oil

SAUCE
½ cup (120g) barbecue sauce
¼ cup (60g) hoisin sauce
2 tablespoons sriracha

GARNISH
3 tablespoons chopped fresh parsley

Cut the cap off the mushrooms and slice off slivers from the stems so that the mushrooms are about all the same rectangular size to mimic baby ribs. (Use the caps and other pieces in the Moxtail Stew on p. 192 or the Japanese Dashi Rice recipe on p. 210.)

Preheat oven to 350°F (180°C).

Place mushrooms in a bowl and drizzle with sesame oil (to help seasoning stick); toss to coat. Add Old Bay and mushroom seasoning; rub into mushrooms using your hands. Heat vegetable oil in a skillet over medium-high heat. Add mushrooms, then put a cast iron skillet on top of the mushrooms applying a little pressure to sear mushrooms and lightly char the edges. Cook for 2 to 3 minutes then remove cast-iron skillet. Flip mushrooms, then place the cast-iron skillet back on top again. Continue flipping until mushrooms are lightly charred on all sides. Transfer mushrooms to an oven dish.

Mix together sauce ingredients in a small bowl. Pour sauce over mushrooms; toss gently making sure all sides are coated well. Cover with aluminum foil and bake for 50 to 60 minutes, or until mushrooms are tender. Remove from oven and garnish with parsley.

MOXTAIL STEW

Yield: 4 to 6 servings

Pam's Lemon Chicken was such a hit in my first cookbook, I asked George for another favorite recipe from his late wife's collection. His daughter Lauren writes, "Oxtail was always a family favorite made by my mother and Popo, and they never followed a recipe. To learn how to make oxtail stew you had to watch it being made; the number of shakes of spices and herbs evolved over years of trial and error. Even though I stopped eating meat over twenty years ago, I still make oxtail for my family. It's worth it every time to see my dad close his eyes, smile, and do a happy dance in his seat, remembering my mom and Sunday family dinners at Popo's." Thanks for the challenge you two! This was a time consuming recipe for me to recreate that cut into a lot of my pool time.

2 (20oz/565g) cans young green jackfruit,
    rinsed and drained

MOXTAIL SEASONING

½ cup (120ml) water
2 tablespoons nutritional yeast
2 teaspoons beet powder (for color)
2 teaspoons mushroom seasoning
2 teaspoons onion powder
2 teaspoons soy sauce or gluten-free
    liquid aminos
1 teaspoon garlic powder
½ teaspoon liquid smoke

½ cup (80g) chickpea flour or mung bean
    starch (plus another 2 tablespoons when
    rolling the Moxtail)
7 ounces (200g) soft tofu (also known as
    silken tofu)
¼ cup (60ml) non-dairy milk

"BONE"

1 burdock root, washed, scrubbed, cut
    into 10 (1-inch) pieces (you can also use
    celery, carrots, or sugarcane to mimic
    the bone)

2 to 3 tablespoons Cavender's Seasoning
    (p. 196) or seasoning of choice
¼ cup (60ml) extra-virgin olive oil

STEW

2 tablespoons extra-virgin olive oil
2 large carrots, chopped
1 large onion, chopped
1 stick celery, chopped
Pinch of salt
2 cups (100g) mushrooms, sliced
3 to 4 cloves garlic, thinly sliced
2 tablespoons fresh rosemary leaves or
    2 teaspoons dried rosemary
4 potatoes, cut into 1-inch pieces
4 cups (1 liter) vegetable broth
1 can (15oz/400g) fire-roasted tomatoes
¼ cup (60ml) red wine
3 bay leaves
3 star anise
3 tablespoons tomato paste
2 tablespoons smoked paprika
2 tablespoons soy sauce
1 tablespoon blackstrap molasses or
    maple syrup

1 tablespoon Italian Seasoning
1 tablespoon mushroom seasoning
1 tablespoon onion powder
1 teaspoon cracked black pepper
1 teaspoon garlic powder

1 pack spinach, thawed, drained, and
    excess liquid wrung out (optional)
Freshly cracked black pepper

GARNISH
2 tablespoons chopped fresh parley

Place jackfruit in a bowl; use your fingers to squeeze out the seeds and remove hard center pieces. Shred jackfruit by pulling the flesh apart so it starts to resemble pulled pork; set aside.

Whisk together moxtail seasoning in a small pot. Add jackfruit and bring to a simmer over medium-high heat. Once liquid starts to bubble, reduce heat to medium, cover with a lid, and simmer for 4 to 5 minutes, or until liquid is completely absorbed into the jackfruit. Remove from heat and cool to room temperature.

Whisk together bean flour, tofu, and milk in a small bowl; gently fold into jackfruit mixture without over mixing. (You want the tofu mixture to appear as the "fatty" part of the moxtail.)

Place a 24-inch piece of large plastic wrap on your work surface. Sprinkle 1 tablespoon bean flour along the center of plastic wrap horizontally. Spoon jackfruit mixture over the bean flour along the center in a cylindrical shape, about 16-inches long. Sprinkle another 1 tablespoon bean flour on top of the jackfruit mixture without mixing it in. Carefully roll the mixture up into a cylinder shape forming the "moxtail," sealing both sides with the plastic wrap. Place in the refrigerator for at least 4 hours, or overnight to set. Remove plastic from moxtail and cut into 10 pieces. Place "bone" (burdock root) into center of each piece. You may need to mold the moxtail back into shape once you place the "bone" in. (Keep in mind the "bone" is not edible and only there for the visual effect.)

Before browning the moxtail, sprinkle each piece with Cavender's Seasoning (or seasoning of choice) and gently rub onto all sides. Heat oil in a skillet over medium-high heat, add moxtail, and cook on all sides until golden brown, about 5 to 6 minutes. Turn and flip to ensure all sides, including edges, are nicely browned. Transfer to a plate and set aside. (The moxtail tastes great on its own. Try one before popping it into the stew and see what you think.)

To prepare stew, heat oil in a large pot over medium-high heat. Add carrot, onion, celery, and a pinch of salt. Cook for 5 to 6 minutes, or until onion is translucent. Stir in mushrooms and

rosemary; cook for another 2 minutes. Add remaining ingredients and bring to a simmer. Once stew starts to bubble, turn heat down to medium, cover partially with a lid and cook for 10 minutes. Stir in spinach, season with pepper to taste, and adjust seasonings as you like. Gently place moxtails in stew and cook for another 5 minutes, or until vegetables are tender and moxtails are heated through. Remove bay leaves and star anise before serving hot.

CAVENDER'S SEASONING

Yield: about ½ cup

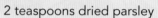

1 tablespoon dried basil
1 tablespoon garlic powder
1 tablespoon dried oregano
1 tablespoon salt
2 teaspoons dried dill
2 teaspoons marjoram

2 teaspoons dried parsley
2 teaspoons pepper
2 teaspoons dried rosemary
1 teaspoon ground cinnamon
1 teaspoon ground nutmeg
1 teaspoon dried thyme

Mix together all ingredients and store in an airtight container for up to 6 months.

NOTE: George says when his late wife, Pamela, discovered Cavender's seasoning, she starting using it in everything, but you can use any type of seasoning you like to flavor your stew.

{ FOR THE CURIOUS COOK }

GEORGE'S VEGNOG

Yield: 4 to 6 servings

Having a neighbor who is a total wine connoisseur (in his own right) that knocks on your door during the festive season with a glass of vegan nog is quite special. George explains in his ever-so-gentlemanly voice, "it's fun" trying out plant-based recipes. Eggnog is synonymous with the holidays and no vegan should have to go without this warm-spiced creamy dreamy beverage. Serve your nog spiked, if desired, or keep it kid-friendly and enjoy this cozy drink with your celebrations.

3 cups (720ml) water
1 cinnamon stick
½ cup (100g) uncooked basmati rice
3 cups (720ml) plant-based milk (George's family prefers coconut milk)
¼ cup (50g) sugar
2 tablespoons tahini
1½ teaspoons vanilla extract
¼ teaspoon ground cardamom
¼ teaspoon salt

Splash of cognac, bourbon, or rum (optional)

GARNISH
1 cinnamon stick for each cup
Fresh grated nutmeg

Place water and cinnamon stick in a small pot and bring to a boil over medium-high heat. Add rice and reduce heat to medium-low. Cook for 25 to 30 minutes, or until rice is tender and creamy. Remove from heat, discard cinnamon, and transfer to a blender. Add remaining ingredients and blend until smooth and creamy. Pour mixture into a saucepan and heat before serving hot. Garnish with cinnamon stick, nutmeg, and alcohol, if using. Serve warm or chilled. Store Vegnog in an airtight container in the refrigerator for up to 1 week.

CONPOY DRIED "SCALLOP"

Yield: about 1 cup

Conpoy, dried scallop, is a Cantonese product made from the abductor muscles of scallops used to flavor soups, condiments (XO Sauce often contains dried scallops), or enjoyed on their own. Think of them as a scallop jerky. Hawaiʻi residents love king oyster mushrooms which are available year-round, making them wonderful tidbits to experiment with. The stems actually look like scallops when cut into discs with the same texture and mouth feel. When marinated and dried they become highly concentrated and savory just like a scallop. Enjoy the conpoy as a delicacy on its own. In Japan, people pay big bucks for these. We're talking beyond umami!

BROTH

1 cup (240ml) water
2 tablespoons sugar
1 tablespoon miso paste
1 tablespoon mushroom seasoning
1 teaspoon apple cider vinegar
1 teaspoon onion powder

½ teaspoon liquid smoke
⅛ teaspoon white pepper

"SCALLOPS"

4 king oyster mushrooms, sliced into
   ¾-inch disks

Whisk together broth ingredients in a pot. Add "scallops" and bring to a simmer on medium-high heat. Once liquid starts to bubble, turn heat down to medium and cover with a lid. Cook for 20 to 25 minutes, or until most of the liquid has evaporated; remove from heat and cool to room temperature.

Preheat oven to "warm" setting, about 170°F (80°C), or the lowest setting on your oven and line a baking sheet with parchment paper. Arrange "scallops" on the baking sheet and dry (or dehydrate, see variation) in your oven for 6 to 8 hours, flipping every 2 hours, until you're happy with the texture. Store in an airtight container in the refrigerator for up to 1 month.

VARIATION: If you have a dehydrator, set the temperature at 125°F (50°C) and dehydrate the "scallops" for 4 to 5 hours.

BBQ MUSHROOM "STEAK" WITH CAULIFLOWER MASH

Yield: 4 servings

I remember when the portobello reigned supreme as the mushroom "steak." Today, vital wheat gluten has taken seitan steaks to whole new level. Unfortunately, that won't work for the gluten-free crowd. Enter the oyster mushroom! An oversized cluster with petal-like leaves that shrivel up and char around the edges when cooked. Undeniably meaty in texture and loaded with umami, it crispens up when pan-fried and develops a deep brown crust with a ton of textural variety in every heavenly bite. Once you grill these fungi miracles to char-perfection, they'll be smoky and savory with a "steak-y" attitude you'll want to serve at any dinner.

CAULIFLOWER MASH

1 pound (500g) cauliflower florets

¼ cup (60ml) plant-based milk

2 tablespoons vegan butter or extra-virgin olive oil

1 teaspoon onion powder

1 teaspoon chopped fresh rosemary leaves

½ teaspoon garlic powder

Salt and freshly cracked black pepper

QUICK BBQ SAUCE

⅓ cup (80g) ketchup

2 tablespoons apple cider vinegar

1 tablespoon maple syrup

1 tablespoon blackstrap molasses

1 tablespoon soy sauce or gluten-free molasses

2 teaspoons smoked paprika

1 teaspoon liquid smoke

1 teaspoon onion powder

½ teaspoon garlic powder

½ teaspoon salt

¼ teaspoon chili powder

Freshly cracked black pepper

MUSHROOM "STEAKS"

1 pound (500g) oyster mushrooms (about 2 clusters of mushrooms)

2 tablespoons vegetable oil or other neutral oil with a low smoking point

Salt and freshly cracked black pepper

YOU WILL ALSO NEED

Cast-iron skillet to use as a weight over the mushrooms

Place cauliflower in a steamer over a large pot of boiling water; steam for 15 minutes, or until tender (alternatively, boil cauliflower in salted water for 10 to 15 minutes). Remove from heat and drain. Place cauliflower in a blender or food processor. Add remaining ingredients and blend until smooth and creamy. Adjust seasoning as you like.

For BBQ sauce, whisk together all ingredients in a small bowl and set aside.

While cauliflower is cooking, prepare mushroom "steaks." Trim the bottom of the mushroom cluster to remove the tough stems while keeping the cluster intact. Heat oil in a skillet over medium-high heat. Add mushrooms and place the cast-iron skillet on top. Cook for 3 to 4 minutes until it starts to sizzle. Remove cast-iron skillet and allow some of the liquid in the pan to evaporate, about 1 minute. Season with salt and pepper to taste then flip the mushrooms. Season the other side with a little salt and pepper to taste and cook for another 2 minutes. Brush "steaks" with BBQ sauce and flip over again. Cook another 2 minutes until a nice char develops on the bottom side. Brush tops with BBQ sauce and flip again. Cook the other side until charred and crispy, brushing with sauce and flipping the mushrooms until you're happy with how they look. The whole process should only take 10 to 12 minutes in total. Serve with cauliflower mash.

PULLED MUSHROOM "PORK" TACOS WITH TERIYAKI SAUCE

Yield: 8 tacos

The taco is a beautiful thing. Bloggers, instafluencers, and taco worshippers don't sweep social with their endless creations for nothing. In a food group of its own, the Mexican fave can be eaten on the go or fancied up like a classy restaurant menu. Crispy, savory pulled mushrooms are the trend of the foodie scene highlighting the mighty mushroom once again. Stick with a BBQ sauce if teriyaki is not your thing. Either way you'll be chomping into one of the best tasting dishes ever!

PULLED "PORK"
1 package (10oz/270g) king oyster
   mushrooms, 4 to 5 mushrooms
1 tablespoon sesame oil or oil of choice
½ teaspoon mushroom seasoning or salt
2 cloves garlic, minced
1 teaspoon minced ginger

TERIYAKI SAUCE
½ cup (120ml) mirin
½ cup (120ml) sake
½ cup (120ml) soy sauce
¼ cup (60ml) sugar

8 taco shells or gluten-free tortillas, heated

SUGGESTED GARNISHES
Kale Slaw Potato Salad (p. 130)
Tofu Egg and Corn Macaroni Salad
   (p. 131)
Crispy Baked Tofu and Watercress Salad
   (p. 53)
Green Avocado Pickles or Mixed Pickles
   (p. 134)
XO Sauce (p. 36)
Shredded lettuce or mixed greens
Salsa
Shredded vegan cheese

Preheat oven to 400°F (200°C). Shred mushrooms using a fork to resemble pulled pork and place in an oven dish. Mix in remaining pulled "pork" ingredients and bake for 30 minutes.

While pulled "pork" is baking, whisk together teriyaki sauce ingredients in a saucepan. Bring to a simmer over medium heat to thicken slightly, about 4 to 5 minutes. Remove from heat and set aside.

Once pulled "pork" has baked for 30 minutes, remove from oven and add Teriyaki Sauce to taste. (Chill any leftover sauce for later use.) Return mixture to oven for another 8 to 10 minutes, or until mushrooms are crispy and brown on the edges. Build your taco with pulled "pork" and suggested garnishes as you like.

VARIATION: Serve in sandwiches, burritos, wraps, or on top of rice or noodles. Substitute Teriyaki Sauce for BBQ sauce, if you prefer.

MUSHROOM JERKY

Yield: about 1 cup

This is undeniably a most creative spin on jerky, not to mention one of my favorite pool snacks. I'm talking sensory overload! It has visual appeal, tastes great, and will have your home filled with the most irresistible smell of jerky! The biggest question is what to jerky. Chinatown in Honolulu sells an eclectic assortment of dried mushrooms, Lion's Mane being one of them. King oysters, cremini, shiitake, and portobello all make interesting versions you can take anywhere to chew on. Dang exciting!

JERKY FLAVORING

1½ cups (360ml) water

3 tablespoons maple syrup or sugar

2 tablespoons soy sauce or gluten-free liquid aminos

1 tablespoon miso paste

2 teaspoons mushroom seasoning

1 teaspoon apple cider vinegar

1 teaspoon beet powder

1 teaspoon liquid smoke

1 teaspoon onion powder

½ teaspoon garlic powder

½ teaspoon black pepper

2 cups (40g) sliced dried shiitake mushrooms or dried mushroom of choice (I used shiitake and Chinese Lion's Mane)

Whisk together jerky flavoring ingredients in a pot. Add dried shiitake and bring to a simmer on medium-high heat. Once liquid starts to bubble, turn heat down to medium and cover with a lid. Cook for 20 to 25 minutes, or until broth has thickened and most of the liquid has evaporated; remove from heat and cool to room temperature.

Preheat oven to "warm" setting, about 170°F (80°C), or the lowest setting on your oven. Arrange the shiitake slices on a baking tray lined with parchment paper. Dry in your oven for 5 to 6 hours, or until you're happy with the texture of the jerky. Store in an airtight container in the refrigerator for up to 1 month.

VARIATION: If you have a dehydrator, set the temperature at 125°F (50°C) and dehydrate the mushrooms for 4 to 5 hours.

WHOLE DRIED SHIITAKE

DRIED LION'S MANE

SLICED DRIED SHIITAKE

EGGPLANT UNAGI DON

Yield: 4 servings

Unagi is Japanese for freshwater eel. It's commonly grilled over charcoal and served over a bed of warm white rice with a generous drizzle of sweet and savory caramelized unagi sauce. People assume they'll never have sushi again once they go vegan, but it's simply not true. Eggplant is the perfect faux eel both in its appearance and tender texture allowing it to soak up that delightful glaze, giving you a very realistic unagi experience.

4 long Japanese eggplants
2 sheets nori, cut in half

¼ cup (60ml) sake

UNAGI SAUCE
½ cup (120ml) soy sauce or gluten-free
   liquid aminos
½ cup (120ml) mirin
⅓ cup (80g) sugar

GARNISH
Sushi Rice (p. 207)
3 tablespoons thinly sliced green onion
1 tablespoon toasted white sesame seeds

Preheat oven to 400°F (200°C) and line a baking sheet with parchment paper.

Poke holes in the eggplant using a fork to keep it from exploding and to help the skin release after roasting. Place on baking sheet and bake for 45 to 50 minutes, or until skins are blistered and eggplant feels soft inside; cool to room temperature.

Peel away the skin and cut the stems off. Make an incision down the center of each eggplant without cutting all the way to the bottom. Carefully open up eggplant to make one flat piece. Remove any clusters of seeds. Gently press using a paper towel to remove any excess liquid. Trim the nori to fit on the eggplant unagi and place on the seed side.

Whisk together unagi sauce ingredients in a saucepan and bring to boil over medium-high heat. Reduce heat to medium and cook until the sauce is reduced to a glaze and evenly coats the back of a spoon, about 3 to 5 minutes. Fill bowls with sushi rice and drizzle with half of the sauce. Top rice with eggplant unagi, nori side down, and drizzle with remaining sauce. Garnish with green onion and sesame.

VARIATION: For air fryer, bake eggplant at 350°F (180°C) for 30 to 40 minutes.

SUSHI RICE

Yield: about 6 cups cooked rice

SUSHI VINEGAR
2 tablespoons rice vinegar
2 tablespoons sugar
2 teaspoons salt

SUSHI RICE
2 cups (400g) Japanese short grain white
   rice, rinsed and drained
2¼ cups (540ml) water

Combine Sushi Vinegar ingredients in a small bowl and set aside while the rice is cooking to allow sugar to melt.

For Sushi Rice, combine the rice with the water in a pot, cover, and let stand 1 hour. Bring to a boil over medium-high heat and simmer until water level equals rice level; about 5 minutes. Reduce heat to low and simmer for 15 minutes. Turn heat off and allow to steam for another 15 minutes. Transfer to a large bowl, drizzle the sushi vinegar over the hot rice and gently fold to combine; cool to room temperature before using.

KING OYSTER "CALAMARI"

Yield: 4 to 6 servings

I served this to my neighbors at one of my taste-testing gatherings, and the reaction I got assured me I was on to something amazingly delicious. Alternatively, you can cut the oyster mushrooms lengthwise to create long "calamari" tentacles, using the whole mushroom and therefor creating more yield. But if you really want to surprise your guests, stick with the rings—it will blow their minds! Crispy, with a nice bite, yet not as rubbery as squid. Furikake adds a subtle Hawaiian/Japanese touch to the batter with the nori bringing that taste of the ocean. This is an insane dish your pescatarian friends will go mad for!

5 king oyster mushrooms, caps removed
   (reserve caps for other use)
1 tablespoon cornstarch

BATTER
½ cup (70g) all-purpose flour or gluten
   free flour
¼ cup (60ml) plant-based milk
2 tablespoons Japanese Furikake (p. 24)
1 teaspoon onion powder
1 teaspoon salt

2 cups (120g) gluten-free panko or bread-
   crumbs

Vegetable oil or other neutral oil for frying

GARNISH
Lemon Dipping Sauce (p. 209)
8 lemon wedges
3 tablespoons chopped fresh parsley

Slice oyster mushrooms into ¼-inch thick disks. Use an apple corer or small cookie cutter to remove the center of the disk creating a calamari-shaped ring. (Use the center pieces in stews or stir-fries.) Toss "calamari" rings in cornstarch to help batter cling.

Mix together batter ingredients in a large bowl. Place panko in a separate bowl. Dip "calamari" in batter, then dredge in panko. Heat two inches of oil to 365°F in a large pot. Fry "calamari" on each side, about 2 to 3 minutes, or until golden brown; drain on paper towels. Serve with Lemon Dipping Sauce, lemon wedges, and garnish with parsley.

{ FOR THE CURIOUS COOK }

LEMON DIPPING SAUCE

Yield: about 1 cup

½ cup (115g) vegan mayonnaise
¼ cup (60ml) plant-based milk
3 tablespoons lemon juice
2 cloves garlic, minced

1 tablespoon chopped fresh basil
1 tablespoon whole grain mustard
Zest of 1 lemon
Salt and freshly cracked black pepper

Whisk together all ingredients in a small bowl. Season with salt and pepper to taste. Chill in the refrigerator until ready to use.

ORANGE TERIYAKI "SCALLOPS" WITH JAPANESE DASHI RICE

Yield: 4 servings

There is no denying that king oyster mushroom stems have all the components of a scallop in terms of texture and aesthetics and are a perfectly plump, nice seafood substitute. Spoil your friends at a dinner party with "scallop" sushi or serve them over dashi rice for a homey meal with the family. Keep it hush and you'll find most people will have a hard time realizing they aren't real bivalves.

ORANGE TERIYAKI SAUCE
¼ cup (60ml) orange juice
¼ cup (60ml) mirin
¼ cup (60ml) sake
¼ cup (60ml) soy sauce or gluten-free
  liquid aminos
2 tablespoons sugar

4 king oyster mushrooms, caps removed,
  sliced into 1-inch disks (save caps for
  soup or stew)
3 tablespoons vegan butter or oil of
  choice
Salt and freshly cracked black pepper

GARNISH
2 tablespoons chopped fresh parsley
2 tablespoons garlic chips
1 teaspoon toasted white sesame seeds

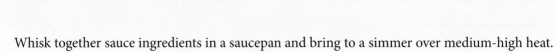

Whisk together sauce ingredients in a saucepan and bring to a simmer over medium-high heat. Cook for 4 to 5 minutes, or until sauce starts to thicken. Remove from heat and set aside.

Score each of the "scallops" (mushroom disks) with bisecting lines to create a diamond pattern. Heat butter in a large skillet over medium-high heat. Add the "scallops," scored side down, and cook for 2 to 3 minutes, or until golden brown on the bottom. Flip mushrooms over and season with salt and pepper to taste. Turn heat down to medium and cook for another 2 to 3 minutes, or until tender. Add orange teriyaki sauce and toss gently to coat; remove from heat. Sprinkle with parsley, garlic chips, and sesame seeds. Serve with Japanese Dashi Rice (p. 211).

JAPANESE DASHI RICE
Yield: about 6 cups cooked rice

2 cups (370g) sushi rice, rinsed and drained
2¼ cups (540ml) water
¼ cup (5g) roughly chopped dried shiitake
1 (2-inch) piece dried kombu (Japanese kelp)

SEASONING

2 tablespoons soy sauce or gluten-free liquid
   aminos
1 tablespoon mirin or sugar
1 tablespoon sake

OPTIONAL ADD-IN

1 (6 x 3-inch) piece aburaage fried tofu,
   chopped (usually comes in a pack of 5)

Combine the rice, water, shiitake, and kombu
in a small pot; soak for 1 hour. Add seasoning
ingredients and aburaage fried tofu, if using.
Cover and bring to a boil over medium-high
heat. Reduce heat to medium and continue to
simmer until water level equals rice level; about
5 minutes. Reduce heat to low and cook another
15 minutes. Turn heat off and allow to steam for
another 15 minutes. Mix gently before serving
hot.

POI

Yield: will vary depending on the size of the taro root.

Poi is the traditional staple food of Hawai'i made from kalo, the root of the taro plant. Traditionally, the taro root was cooked in an imu for several hours, then pounded on a large flat board called papa ku'i a'i, using a heavy stone or pōhaku ku'i 'ai. The taro was then pounded into a smooth, sticky paste known as pa'i 'ai (poi without added water). Poi is created by adding water to the pa'i 'ai. The consistency to which it is pounded is described by how many fingers it takes to dip and carry the poi to the mouth; one-finger, two-finger, or three-finger poi. Fresh poi is referred to as "sweet poi," whereas poi that has fermented for several days is often called "sour poi" resulting in very unique sour flavors. Thank you to Robert K. for the photos.

2 taro roots, scrubbed under cold water
  (not peeled)

Water to cover

Use a vegetable brush to scrub the taro root. Do not peel. Place taro in a large pot and fill with water to cover. Bring to a boil over medium-high heat. Reduce heat to medium and simmer for 20 to 25 minutes, or until taro is tender.

Drain and rinse under cold water. Peel the taro and cut into small pieces. Place half the mixture into a food processor and blend, adding a tablespoon of water at a time until thick enough to stick to one finger. Adding more water will yield two-finger poi or three-finger poi.

Use immediately or transfer the mixture to a bowl and pour a thin layer of cold water on top of the poi. Cover with a towel and let poi sit for 2 to 4 days at room temperature to ferment and become "sour poi."

CHEF'S TIP: If you're new to poi, add a little sugar, salt, or coconut milk for flavor.

CHAPTER 10

LIFE'S LITTLE LUXURIES

If you do indulge, "moderation not deprivation" is my mantra. Dessert is often used as the reward to get picky eaters (ie. kids) to finish their meal. Knowing if they get down the unappealing stuff first, there'll be that sweet light at the end of the tunnel, making dinner less of the enemy. Having a normal relationship with sweets is key to controlling undeniable cravings that can backfire when you deprive yourself of something you love. "Life's Little Luxuries" should be treated as such—a luxury. I don't eat Baked Vegan Cheesecake (p. 238) every day the same way I don't buy "luxury" tableware every day. (It's no lie. I love plates.) Treating yourself to sweet food is not completely terrible in my opinion, just savor the moment when you do. Get familiar with healthier options for sweets like vegan chocolate chips. They contain only two ingredients—cane sugar and cocoa butter. Use unsweetened chocolate and you'll be cutting out the sugar all together. The beautiful Chocolate Bark (p. 230) is filled with healthy nuts and seeds nestled atop of a layer of antioxidant rich chocolate making this a sweet I think you can enjoy often. Chocolate-Covered Strawberries (p. 223) are another example of how sweets can be healthy. I mean, they're strawberries! Don't wait for someone to fill you a bubble bath and pour you a glass of champagne before you experience the true delight of a juicy strawberry encased in chocolate. You can have these guilt-free pleasures any time of day and feel good about yourself. I mean, why have just dates when you can fill them with Chocolate Sauce (p. 228) and homemade Nutty Butter (p. 26)? Plant-based desserts have evolved into a whole new beautiful world of their own and one to be reckoned with.

HAUPIA AND MEYER LEMON CURD

Yield: 6 servings

Haupia is a traditional Hawaiian coconut pudding dessert often found at local potlucks or lūʻau. Next time you're feeling a tropical itch, try this! Hau is the Hawaiian word for "cool" and pia means "arrowroot," although these days cornstarch is widely used as the thickening or binding agent instead of arrowroot. The blissful layer of tangy Meyer lemon curd has just the right amount of tart and sweet to riff with the haupia. The glossy lemon finish in dazzling yellow is the color of sunlight and a good example of how stunning plant-based food can be.

HAUPIA
¾ cup (180ml) water
⅓ cup (70g) sugar
¼ cup (30g) cornstarch
1 can (14oz/400ml) coconut milk

LEMON CURD
½ cup (120ml) plant-based milk

⅓ cup (80g) sugar
¼ cup (60ml) Meyer lemon juice
1 tablespoon cornstarch
2 teaspoons lemon zest
⅛ teaspoon turmeric (for color)

GARNISH
2 tablespoons toasted coconut flakes

Whisk together water, sugar, and cornstarch in a small bowl and set aside. Pour coconut milk into a saucepan and bring to a simmer over medium heat. Whisk in the cornstarch mixture and cook for about 2 to 3 minutes, or until mixture thickens and sugar has completely dissolved. Pour into 6 small dessert bowls and chill in the refrigerator for 30 minutes to set.

Whisk together lemon curd ingredients in a saucepan and bring to a simmer over medium heat, whisking constantly until curd thickens and sugar is completely dissolved, about 5 minutes. Remove from heat and pour a thin layer over haupia. Chill in the refrigerator to set, about 1 hour. Garnish with toasted coconut.

DALGONA WHIPPED COFFEE

Yield: 2 servings

Dalgona coffee, or "whipped coffee," can be traced back to South Korea where it gets its name from a popular street toffee it resembles. India, Pakistan, Greece, and Macau also have similar versions in their countries and cultures. The viral trend first gained prominence during the Covid-19 pandemic when social media influencers started posting videos of their fluffy drinks, which led to it being dubbed the "quarantine coffee." This light and frothy layer of foam is delicious, but very strong. Depending on how much of a caffeine rush you want, I suggest you sip at your own discretion. Be generous with the Kahlua if it's after 5!

MOCKTAIL VERSION

2 tablespoons instant coffee
2 tablespoons sugar
2 tablespoons boiling water
⅛ teaspoon cinnamon (optional)
2 cups (480ml) plant-based milk

Combine the coffee, sugar, water, and cinnamon in a bowl. Whip using a mixer on high speed for about 2 minutes. Mixture should become light and fluffy. Fill two glasses with ice and milk. Spoon whipped coffee mixture on top and serve.

COCKTAIL VERSION

Add Kahlua and/or Hawaiian dark rum to each glass of milk. Mix well before topping with whipped coffee.

VARIATION: Spoon it over George's Vegnog (p. 197) for a holiday pick-me-up.

{ LIFE'S LITTLE LUXURIES }

CUSTARD WITH SPICY PINEAPPLE

Yield: 4 servings

I'm a sucker for creamy desserts; thankfully vegans don't have to miss out on custard. The art of custard making can be quite fiddly and can undergo undesirable texture changes if it's overcooked, resulting in scrambled eggs or the mix splitting. This egg-free goodness, undetectably vegan, is stress-free to make and does not compromise on flavor. Paired with delicious chili water-infused pineapple (pineapple for your information is not a single fruit, but a group of berries that have fused together), you have yourself a beautiful Island dessert ready for any lūʻau.

CUSTARD
2 cups (480ml) plant-based milk
¼ cup (30g) cornstarch
¼ cup (60g) sugar
2 tablespoons lemon juice
1 teaspoon vanilla extract
⅛ teaspoon turmeric (for color)
Pinch of salt

SPICY PINEAPPLE
1 pound (500g) diced fresh pineapple

2 tablespoons maple syrup or agave syrup
1 tablespoon lemon juice
Pinch of salt
1 teaspoon brandy or rum (optional)
¼ teaspoon crushed red pepper

GARNISH
3 tablespoons Crunchy Granola (p. 226)
(optional)
1 tablespoon chopped macadamia nuts

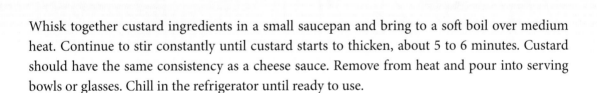

Whisk together custard ingredients in a small saucepan and bring to a soft boil over medium heat. Continue to stir constantly until custard starts to thicken, about 5 to 6 minutes. Custard should have the same consistency as a cheese sauce. Remove from heat and pour into serving bowls or glasses. Chill in the refrigerator until ready to use.

Combine pineapple, maple or agave syrup, lemon juice, and a pinch of salt in a saucepan and bring to a soft boil over medium heat. Cook 7 to 8 minutes, or until liquid evaporates and mixture thickens. Add brandy or rum, if using, and crushed red pepper. Cook another 30 seconds and remove from heat.

Serve pineapple warm or chilled. Top custard with granola, if using, and pineapple. Sprinkle with macadamia nuts and serve.

TIP: Try the Spicy Pineapple over the Haupia and Lemon Curd Cups (p. 216).

BERRY CHIA PUDDING

Yield: 4 servings

When chia started to make its way onto the food scene, you better believe I jumped on that train. Like flax-seed, it has a mild, nutty flavor and expands when combined with a liquid to form a thick gel-like, creamy texture similar to tapioca. Rumor has it, chia seeds are said to have been used by Mayan and Aztec cultures for supernatural powers. In fact, chia is the Mayan word for "strength." It delivers a massive amount of nutrients, is loaded with fiber, protein, omega-3 fatty acids, and according to some studies, may help with chronic inflammation as well as bone health. This pudding is great at breakfast leaving you satiated and energized for the day, or as a healthy dessert option.

1 cup (240ml) plant-based milk
1 cup (250g) frozen berry mix (black-berries, blueberries, raspberries, and strawberries)
½ cup (40g) chia seeds
¼ cup (60ml) maple syrup or agave syrup
1 teaspoon vanilla extract

½ teaspoon salt

SUGGESTED TOPPINGS
Crunchy Granola (p. 226)
Fresh chopped fruit
Nuts and seeds

Mix together all the ingredients in a bowl and divide into 4 mason jars or bowls. (Leave berries whole as shown in picture, or blend and mix through for a deep purple pudding.) Chill overnight in the refrigerator to set, or for at least 8 hours. Serve with suggested toppings of choice.

NOTE: Just one tablespoon of chia seeds mixed with 3 tablespoons of water becomes a gel after 5 minutes you can use as a simple, natural, egg replacer in any recipe for muffins, cookies, and cakes, just as you would a regular egg.

AVOCADO CHOCOLATE MOUSSE

Yield: 2 servings

What is it about chocolate mousse that is so romantic and considered a special indulgence, rather than a regular event? Long gone are the days of high maintenance chocolate mousse recipes where a slight slip in the series of executed steps can turn your sweet bowl into a complete flop. This raw dessert requires only a few ingredients and a blender; even the most hapless and inexperienced cooks can whip it up with absolute success. The avocado adds healthy fats, fiber, vitamins, and all the qualities that make mousse fabulous—creaminess, richness, and a buttery texture—leaving only a faint hint that it's there. This healthy twist will take you completely by surprise!

1 cup (250g) mashed ripe avocado (about 2 avocados)
½ cup (50g) cocoa powder
½ cup (120ml) plant-based milk
¼ cup (60ml) maple syrup or agave syrup
1 teaspoon vanilla extract
¼ teaspoon salt

SUGGESTED TOPPINGS
Chocolate shavings, chopped nuts, or fresh berries

Mix ingredients in a blender until soft and creamy. Divide into 2 bowls and chill in the refrigerator for 1 hour to set. Serve with suggested toppings of choice.

CHOCOLATE COVERED STRAWBERRIES

Yield: about 15 strawberries

Let's just all agree that everything tastes better dipped in chocolate. Despite being one of the easiest and cheapest desserts to make, chocolate covered strawberries are indulgent, classy, and very romantic. We've all seen movies scenes and know how fun these naughty bites can be. Once you choose your choc between sweet, semi-sweet, or dark, the process is simple—melt, dip, and coat. Don't stop at strawberries! Create your own edible arrangements with chocolate covered apples, blackberries, blueberries, kiwi, pears, pineapple, dried fruit (orange and mango work well, even candied ginger), pretzels, nuts, cookies—the options are endless!

1 pack (about 12 to 15) strawberries
100g vegan chocolate, melted

SUGGESTED SPRINKLES
Chopped nuts or dried fruit
Crushed freeze-dried strawberries
Toasted coconut
Crushed muesli
Vegan sprinkles

Dip strawberries into melted chocolate and cover in your favorite sprinkles. Place on a baking sheet lined with parchment paper and chill in the refrigerator to set before serving.

MERMAID AÇAI BOWL

Yield: 2 servings

This powerhouse of antioxidants is called a superfood for a reason. Açai contains iron and healthy omega fats, is rich in minerals, full of fiber to help detox, and happens to taste like a tropical cross between blackberries and unsweetened chocolate. The purple berries found on palm trees in the Amazon are relatively new to the Western world. Hawai'i has embraced this health craze with a passion, turning it into one of paradise's favorite foods. Vendors all over the Islands serve açai bowls and blue spirulina sorbet-textured blends made with frozen banana and topped with a variety of fruits, nuts, and toasted coconut. Top with Crunchy Granola (p. 226) packed with good-for-you ingredients and enjoy it in a quiet moment on your lānai. Life is good.

MERMAID SMOOTHIE
1 frozen banana (about 120g)
¾ cup (100g) frozen pineapple
½ teaspoon blue spirulina

AÇAI SMOOTHIE
2 frozen bananas (about 240g)
1 packet (3.53oz/100g) frozen
   unsweetened açai purée
½ cup (60g) frozen berry mix

¼ cup (60ml) plant-based milk

SUGGESTED TOPPINGS
Crunchy Granola (p. 226)
Toasted nuts
Fresh or dried fruit
Ground chia and flaxseed
Maple syrup
Vegan Honey (p. 38)

Blend smoothies separately in a mixer until smooth. Divide into two bowls. Garnish with suggested toppings of choice.

CHEF'S TIP: Add liquid sweeteners if you prefer your smoothie blend on the sweeter side, or mix in some peanut or nut butter for a creamier version.

CRUNCHY GRANOLA

Yield: about 2 cups

Let's face it, we all love cereal deep down inside and you always have a stash in your cabinet. Homemade granola is sweet and crunchy like cereal, but made of oats, nuts, seeds, and has a good balance of fats and carbs that will keep you full and energized for hours. Make your own toasty indulgence from ingredients you can trust. Dessert in a cereal always wins the race!

1 cup (100g) old-fashioned rolled oats
½ cup (25g) mixed raw nuts and seeds,
  roughly chopped (almonds, pecans,
  walnuts, cashews)
2 tablespoons coconut flakes
1 tablespoon ground flax or chia

seeds (or a combination of both)
1 teaspoon ground cinnamon
¼ teaspoon ground nutmeg
½ teaspoon salt
¼ cup (60ml) melted refined coconut oil
  (microwave for 15 seconds if coconut oil
  is hard)
2 tablespoons maple syrup
½ teaspoon vanilla extract

¼ cup (30g) diced dried fruit (cranberries,
  mango, raisins, cherries, kiwi)

Preheat oven to 275°F (135°C). Line a baking sheet with parchment paper.

Mix oats, nuts, coconut flakes, flax or chia, cinnamon, nutmeg, and a pinch of salt in a large bowl. Add coconut oil, maple syrup, and vanilla; mix until well-combined. Spread mixture onto lined baking sheet and bake for 30 minutes.

Remove from oven and add dried fruit; mix to combine. Return to oven and bake another 20 to 30 minutes, or until granola is crispy. Remove from oven and cool to room temperature. Store in an air-tight container for up to 2 weeks.

LEMON BERRY OATMEAL BARS

Yield: 8 bars

Now we're speaking my language with this crisp fruity bar bursting with berries and hearty oats. Your morning bowl of oatmeal just got a makeover! This is a guilt-free pleasure you can indulge in that will surely brighten your day. Perfect as a pre- or post-workout snack, on-the-go breakfast, or treat for dessert with an inviting crumble in every bite. Caring for your health has never been so delicious!

OAT BASE AND TOPPING

1 cup (120g) oat flour
1 cup (100g) old-fashioned rolled oats
¼ cup (50g) sugar
1 teaspoon baking powder
1 teaspoon ground cinnamon
¼ teaspoon salt
Zest of 1 Meyer lemon

⅓ cup (80g) melted refined coconut oil (microwave for 15 seconds if coconut oil is hard)

BLUEBERRY FILLING

2 cups (250g) fresh or frozen mixed berries (blackberries, blueberries, strawberries, raspberries)
2 tablespoons Meyer lemon juice
2 tablespoons sugar
1 tablespoon cornstarch

Preheat oven to 350°F (180°C) and line a line a 9 x 5-inch loaf pan with parchment paper allowing 1-inch of overhang on each side for easy removal.

Mix together the flour, oats, sugar, cinnamon, baking powder, and salt in a large bowl. Mix in lemon zest and coconut oil. Pour half of the mixture into the loaf pan and press down using your hands or the bottom of a measuring cup.

Mix together blueberry filling in a bowl. Pour mixture over the oat base and spread evenly. Sprinkle the reserved oat mixture over the top of the blueberry layer. Bake for 40 minutes. Remove from oven and cool to room temperature. Lift out of pan and slice into 8 bars.

STUFFED DATES

Yield: 12 dates

Next time you want to make something a little special that requires no effort at all, make these. All you have to do is stuff them! Dates are perfect for stuffing since you're left with a gap after you pit them. You can enjoy these as an after-dinner treat or served as an appetizer. The perfect way to start or end a meal!

12 dates

SUGGESTED FILLINGS
Baked Tofeta (p. 173)
Cashew Brie

Nutty Butter (p. 26)
Mac Nut Parm (p. 23)

Chocolate Sauce (recipe below)
Vegan Honey (p. 38)

Use your fingers to carefully open up the dates and remove the pit. Stuff with any of the suggested fillings and drizzle with Chocolate Sauce or Vegan Honey.

CHOCOLATE SAUCE

Yield: about 1½ cups

This rich and silky chocolate sauce has just the right amount of sweetness, and the fact that it's a cinch to make means you can whip up a batch anytime. Dip your strawberries in a bit of chocolate heaven, stir it into your milk or coffee, or douse your desserts. Be forewarned, it vanishes quickly, so make sure you have ample supply at all times.

1 cup (240ml) plant-based milk
½ cup (100g) sugar
¼ cup (60ml) melted refined coconut oil

¼ cup (25g) cocoa powder
¼ teaspoon salt
¼ teaspoon vanilla extract

Heat milk, sugar, and coconut oil in a saucepan over medium-low heat and bring to a low simmer. Stir in cocoa powder and salt. Cook for 2 minutes, or until cocoa powder has melted and there are no lumps remaining. Remove from heat and stir in vanilla extract. Pour into an airtight container and store in the refrigerator for up to 2 weeks.

CHOCOLATE BARK

Yield: 6 to 8 servings

In case you were wondering why chocolate is a food we crave on so many levels, here's what I found. Cacao means "food of the gods" in Greek. Chocolate creates a unique chemical signature that switches on the feel-good neurotransmitters in the brain (mainly dopamine), which is released when you experience anything you enjoy, elevating your mood instantly. It is the Swiss army knife of the sexy food world, sometimes referred to as the "love supplement." No need to fact-check that statement. Just assume it's true.

9 ounces (250g) sweetened or
    unsweetened vegan chocolate chips

**SUGGESTED TOPPINGS (YOU'LL NEED
    ABOUT ½ CUP IN TOTAL)**
Toasted coconut
Edible dried roses

Chopped or slivered roasted nuts
Toasted seeds
Dried fruits
Hawaiian sea salt

Edible glitter dust (you can find vegan and
    gluten-free ones online)
Chili powder or crushed red pepper

Place chocolate chips in a bowl and melt over a pot of simmering hot water, stirring constantly with a spatula, about 1 to 2 minutes. Once chocolate has melted, spoon onto a baking tray lined with parchment paper and smooth out until about ¼-inch thick. Sprinkle over desired toppings and refrigerate until set, about 1 hour. Break chocolate bark into pieces and store in an airtight container in the refrigerator for up to 2 weeks, or freeze for up to 3 months.

VARIATION: You can make your own chocolate by mixing together ½ cup (120ml) virgin coconut oil, ½ cup (50g) cocoa powder, and ¼ cup (70ml) maple syrup and following the instructions above. This mixture can start to melt quickly so you will need to serve it chilled.

PB&J COOKIE SANDWICH

Yield: about 16 cookies

There is no debate when it comes to the universal love of peanut butter and jelly sandwiches. We even overlook the fact that peanut butter sticks to the roof of your mouth making it uncomfortable to eat until you shove your finger in to detach what you can before continuing on in solitary bliss. While testing the recipe for the soft and chewy peanut butter cookie, I had an epiphany. The berry chia jam (jelly) in my first book turned out to be just the right filling for this cookie sandwich. If this doesn't guarantee to pique your taste buds, try other peanut butter flavors from p. 26 to whet your appetite.

1 cup (270g) creamy or crunchy peanut
   butter (see **CHEF'S TIP**)
1 cup (200g) sugar
1 cup (120ml) non-dairy milk
2 teaspoons vanilla essence

2 cups (250g) all-purpose flour or
   gluten-free flour
1 teaspoon baking soda
½ teaspoon salt
Berry Chia Jelly (p. 233)

Preheat oven to 350°F (180°C) and line a baking sheet with parchment paper.

Using a spatula, mix together the peanut butter, sugar, non-dairy milk, and vanilla in a large bowl until creamy, about 1 minute. Combine flour, baking soda, and salt in a separate bowl and add to peanut butter mixture; mix until dough is well combined. Roll dough into 16 balls and place on the lined baking sheet. Flatten each ball with the back of a fork in a crisscross pattern. Bake for 13 minutes. Remove from oven and cool to room temperature. Store in the refrigerator for up to 2 weeks or freeze for up to 2 months. Make a cookie sandwich with Berry Chia Jelly in the center and serve.

{ LIFE'S LITTLE LUXURIES }

BERRY CHIA JELLY

Yield: about 2 cups

3 tablespoons water
2 tablespoons chia seeds
2 cups (200g) fresh or frozen berry mix
  (blackberries, blueberries, raspberries,
  and strawberries)
2 tablespoons lemon juice
¼ cup (50g) sugar
Pinch of salt

Mix together the water and chia seeds in a small bowl; set aside for 5 minutes to thicken. In a small saucepan, combine the berries, lemon juice, sugar, and a pinch of salt. Bring to a boil over medium-high heat. Once it starts to bubble, reduce heat to medium and gently mash the big pieces of fruit using the back of a fork; cook for another 5 minutes. Stir in the chia seed mixture.

Remove from the heat and cover; let jelly sit for 10 minutes. Store in an airtight container in the refrigerator for up to 2 weeks.

CHEF'S TIP: Try using the homemade chocolate or Spicy Nutty Butter on p. 26 for a unique twist.

IMPOSSIBLE SNICKY BITES

Yield: 18 squares

If chocolate and caramel are what dreams are made of, then you're in for a treat with this clever no-bake recipe. There are three easy steps with chilling periods, so don't let the instructions scare you away. There's a layer of oat and cashew nougat filling, creamy caramel made with dates, and crunchy peanuts covered in choc full of cocoa whoa. You may never buy another candy bar again once you try these wicked bites—eerily like the store-bought version, and not impossible to veganize!

NOUGAT
½ cup (80g) raw cashews
¾ cup (60g) old-fashioned rolled oats
½ cup (120g) smooth peanut butter
3 tablespoons maple syrup or agave syrup

CARAMEL COATED PEANUTS
10 pitted Medjool dates

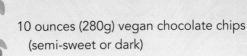

⅓ cup (80g) vegan butter
⅓ cup (80g) sugar
1 teaspoon vanilla essence
¾ cup (90g) dry roasted peanuts (salted or unsalted)

10 ounces (280g) vegan chocolate chips (semi-sweet or dark)

Line a 9 x 5-inch loaf pan with parchment paper. (Spraying the pan with cooking spray helps the parchment paper stick to it.)

Combine the cashews and oats in a mixer. Blend until a fine mixture is achieved. Transfer to a bowl; mix in the peanut butter and maple syrup. It should feel like a sticky dough. Spoon the "nougat" into the loaf pan, then use a spatula to spread and press down evenly.

For the caramel coated peanuts, combine the dates, butter, and sugar in a saucepan. Bring to a simmer on medium high until sugar starts to melt, about 2 to 3 minutes. Transfer to a mixer; add vanilla essence, and blend until smooth. Transfer to a bowl and add peanuts; mix well to combine. Spread mixture over the nougat and place in the freezer for 1 to 2 hours to set. Cut into 18 bite-size squares.

Place chocolate chips in a bowl and melt over a pot of simmering hot water, stirring constantly, about 1 to 2 minutes. Dip nougat squares into melted chocolate using a toothpick and arrange on a baking sheet lined with parchment paper. Place in the refrigerator for 30 minutes to set before serving.

ROCKY BEACH ROAD

Yield: 18 squares

I remember growing up in Sydney and sharing bags of Rocky Road chocolates with my mom. Shop, drink coffee, and ambush the chocolatier near Sydney Tower. Tart dried cherries with little pockets of soft marshmallow in every sweet nutty bite. Tweaked the recipe to give you an Island version with some dried Hawaiian fruit and the option to sprinkle a little Hawaiian sea salt and chili pepper over the top. If this doesn't fix that sweet tooth and get you in the chocky mood, we need to talk!

10 ounces (280g) semi-sweet vegan chocolate chips
1 cup (100g) mini vegan and gluten-free marshmallows (see Glossary, p. 245)
¾ cup (100g) peanuts, roughly chopped (or almonds, cashews, peanuts, pecans, walnuts, or seeds)
½ cup (60g) diced dried Hawaiian fruit mix (papaya, mango, pineapple, coconut, cherry)

Line a 9 x 5-inch loaf pan with parchment paper allowing 1-inch of overhang on each side for easy removal and set aside.

Melt chocolate chips over a pot of simmering hot water, stirring constantly until smooth and glossy, about 1 to 2 minutes. Remove from heat and add remaining ingredients. Pour into loaf pan and smooth out using a spatula. Chill in the refrigerator for 1 to 2 hours to set.

Cut into 3 pieces lengthwise, then cut into 6 pieces the other way to make 18 squares. Store in an airtight container in the refrigerator for up to 2 weeks, or freeze for up to 3 months.

CHEF'S TIP: Wrap the squares in colorful cupcake liners when gifting.

PUMPKIN PIE SLICE

Yield: 8 slices

When it comes to this Thanksgiving classic, I think I just may have cracked the pumpkin pie code. My dessert standards are high, and what I'm trying to say is I can rest easy at night knowing I've delivered a recipe even the slight snobs at the table won't be able to resist. It's a cheesecake meets pumpkin pie kind-of-affair with a crispy pecan oat crust you just know is going to be good. It's the perfect ending to any holiday feast. Live well and bake often!

CRUST
⅓ cup (30g) pecans
⅓ cup (30g) old-fashioned rolled oats
½ teaspoon nutritional yeast
2 tablespoons sugar
2 tablespoons melted refined coconut oil (microwave for 15 seconds if coconut oil is hard)

FILLING
1 can (15oz/425g) pumpkin purée

1 cup (160g) raw cashews, rinsed, cooked in boiling water for 15 minutes, drained
1 cup (250g) canned coconut cream (see **NOTE**)
⅓ cup (80g) sugar
2 tablespoons cornstarch
1 tablespoon nutritional yeast
1 teaspoon ground cinnamon
1 teaspoon ground ginger
1 teaspoon salt
½ teaspoon ground nutmeg
⅛ teaspoon ground cloves

Preheat oven to 350°F (180°C) and line a 9 x 5-inch loaf pan with parchment paper allowing 1-inch of overhang on each side.

Pulse the pecans, oats, nutritional yeast, and sugar in a food processor until crumbly. Pour in the coconut oil and pulse again until well-combined. Press into the bottom of the loaf pan and bake for 15 minutes. Remove from oven and reduce heat to 325°F (160°C).

Blend the filling ingredients in a mixer until smooth. Pour the filling evenly over crust. Bake for 50 minutes. (The center until should appear slightly jiggly and will continue to set as it cools.) Remove from oven and cool on a wire rack. Chill in the refrigerator for at least 5 hours or over-night. Lift out of pan and cut into triangles or bars.

NOTE: Can must be chilled for at least 24 hours in the refrigerator so the layer of cream at the top of the can solidifies and separates from the liquid making it easy to scoop out. Reserve liquid for another use such as in soups.

BAKED VEGAN CHEESECAKE WITH MACADAMIA NUT CRUST

Yield: 1 (9 x 5-inch) loaf pan, about 8 slices

What's not to love about cheesecake? I can't think of anything more soothing to the soul, satisfying, and sociable than having a piece of cheesecake. It's rich, not too sweet, and contains none of the world's most loved ingredients—cheese. Whaat, you ask? No cheese?! I'm a huge fan of "cheese" cake, and after going on a recipe adventure to create the perfect vegan version, I can honestly say this is my favorite dessert hands down. Test it out and see for yourself why people go crazy for plant-based cheesecake. Regardless of your apprehensions, it tastes like cheesecake, looks like cheesecake, and will have you feeling like a pastry chef of note once you pull it off. Don't wait for National Cheesecake Day on July 30. Bring it on now!

CRUST
⅓ cup (40g) macadamia nuts
⅓ cup (30g) old-fashioned rolled oats
2 tablespoons sugar
½ teaspoon nutritional yeast
2 tablespoons melted refined coconut oil
   (microwave for 15 seconds if coconut oil
   is hard)

1 (8-ounce/227g) container vegan cream
   cheese
½ cup (170g) maple syrup or agave syrup
3 tablespoons lemon juice
2 tablespoons cornstarch or arrowroot
1 tablespoon nutritional yeast
2 teaspoons vanilla extract
¼ teaspoon salt

FILLING
1 cup (160g) raw cashews, rinsed, soaked
   overnight, drained
1 cup (240g) canned coconut cream (see
   NOTE)

GARNISH
¼ cup fresh pomegranate seeds or fresh
   berries
2 tablespoons chopped roasted
   macadamia nuts

Preheat oven to 350°F (180°C) and line a 9 x 5-inch loaf pan with parchment paper allowing 1-inch of overhang on each side for easy removal.

Pulse the nuts, oats, sugar, and nutritional yeast in a food processor until crumbly. Pour in the coconut oil and pulse again until well-combined. Press into the bottom of the pan using your hands or the bottom of a measuring cup. Bake for 15 minutes. Remove from oven and reduce heat to 325°F (160°C).

Blend the filling ingredients until smooth and creamy. Pour the filling evenly over crust. Bake for 50 to 55 minutes until the center appears slightly jiggly when you shake it. (Filling will continue to set as it cools.) Cool to room temperature and chill in the refrigerator for at least 5 hours or overnight.

Lift out of pan and slice into 8 triangles or bars. Sprinkle with pomegranate seeds and macadamia nuts.

NOTE: Can must be chilled for at least 24 hours in the refrigerator so the layer of cream at the top of the can solidifies and separates from the liquid making it easy to scoop out. Reserve liquid for another use such as in soups.

GLOSSARY AND SUBSTITUTIONS

(If not indicated, there is no suitable substitution)

Aburaage: A thinly sliced deep-fried tofu pouch that forms an air pocket when fried. Often stuffed with a sweet rice filling to make inari sushi. Available at Nijiya.

Açai: A dark berry of the açai palm tree rich in antioxidants, used often in açai bowls or smoothies. Substitute blackberries, blueberries, or strawberries. Available at Costco.

Agave syrup: A natural sweetener used as a substitute for sugar in food and beverages. Substitute coconut syrup, maple syrup, or sugar. Available at Down To Earth.

'Alaea salt: Also known as Hawaiian red sea salt, 'alaea is an unrefined sea salt that has been mixed with an iron oxide-rich volcanic clay called 'alaea, giving it its characteristic brick red color. Available in most supermarkets in Hawai'i or online.

'Ahi: Hawaiian name for yellowfin or bigeye tuna. Vegan substitute: roasted red bell peppers.

All-purpose flour: Also known as refined flour or plain flour, is commonly used in baking. Substitute gluten-free flour.

Apple cider vinegar: A liquid made by fermenting the sugar in apples. Substitute white vinegar or white wine vinegar.

Artichoke hearts: A thistle plant with a bud containing the heart, or meaty core, of the artichoke, surrounded by rows of spiny petals. Used as a vegan substitute for fish or seafood in recipes. Substitute hearts of palm.

Bacon bits: Vegan versions made from tofu or TVP (textured vegetable protein) deliver a meaty bacon taste and crispy texture

used as a topping in salads or in any recipe calling for crumbled bacon.

Baguette: A long, thin loaf of French bread. Substitute ciabatta.

Bang bang sauce: A sweet and spicy creamy sauce usually containing mayonnaise, sweet chili sauce, and hot sauce.

Balsamic vinegar: A deep brown vinegar made from fermented wine grapes barrel-aged for many years. With bold, tart, and complex flavors it can be used in marinades, salad dressings, and sauces.

Balsamic glaze: A reduction of balsamic vinegar and a sweetener that has been cooked down to form a thick syrup. Balsamic glaze can be drizzled over fruit such as strawberries, or tossed with vegetables such as roasted Brussels sprouts.

Blackstrap molasses: Molasses is the thick, brown syrup left over after the crystals have been removed. It comes in three varieties—light molasses produced by the first boiling is light and sweet and can be used in baking; dark molasses produced by the second boiling is, as its name suggests, darker and thicker in flavor and color; and blackstrap molasses produced by the third boiling has the thickest consistency, is darkest in color and slightly bitter. Substitute maple syrup.

Broth: Broth is a savory liquid made of water in which a particular food such as bonito, chicken, or kombu (example kombu broth) are simmered to flavor dishes such as rice, or to serve as a foundation for a soup; whereas "stock" involves simmering a variety of vegetables and spices in water used to form the basis for many dishes.

Brown rice: A whole-grain rice with the inedible outer hull removed. Substitute white rice or other grains such as farro.

Burdock root: A crisp, earthy-flavored root often used in Japanese cuisine or to make herbal tea and Chinese medicines. Available at Nijiya.

Canned coconut milk: Rich, creamy liquid extracted by squeezing the grated meat of a coconut. Commonly sold in cans. When full-fat canned coconut milk is chilled, the cream separates from the liquid forming a solid white layer at the top of the can used for making whipped coconut cream and in desserts.

Canned fire-roasted tomato: Tomatoes charred over a flame with blackened flecks on the skins before they're diced and canned. Substitute regular canned tomato.

Cellophane noodles: Sold under many different names; rice noodles (the term we use mostly in Hawai'i), bean thread noodles, glass noodles, or mung bean noodles. Most commonly used for stir-fries, soups, salads, or in spring rolls.

Chia seeds: A "superfood" of tiny, oval, brown, black, or white seeds from a plant in the mint family. Eaten raw or used in puddings, blended into smoothies, or mixed with water to use as a thickening agent or egg replacement in baking. Substitute flax seeds.

Chili oil: Chili-infused oil made with various chili peppers and oils.

Cilantro: Spanish word for "coriander leaves," is a pungent flat-leaf herb also known as coriander or Chinese parsley. Substitute parsley.

Chickpeas: Also known as garbanzo beans; have a nutty, creamy taste widely used in vegan recipes and as the base for hummus, falafel, and veggie burgers, or plant-based fish patties. Substitute cannellini beans, navy beans, or white northern beans.

Chocolate syrup: A sweet, chocolate-flavored condiment made with cocoa powder, salt, sugar, and water. Hershey's Chocolate Syrup is vegan and available in most supermarkets.

Choy sum: A leafy green vegetable that is like a mix between bok choy and rapini. Often used in stir-fries.

Cocoa powder: Made from the cacao bean, an unsweetened chocolate-flavored powder used commonly in desserts and beverages. Substitute vegan chocolate powder.

Coconut aminos: A gluten-free alternative for soy sauce made from the aged sap of coconut blossoms and salt. Substitute liquid aminos or tamari. Available at Down To Earth.

Coconut milk: Sold in cartons in the non-dairy milk section in supermarkets. Substitute 1 cup water beaten with 1 to 3 tablespoons coconut milk powder depending on how thick you want it. Do not use coconut milk when a recipe calls for canned coconut milk.

Conpoy: Dried scallop; a Cantonese product made from the abductor muscles of scallops used to flavor soups or condiments.

Coriander: The dried fruit (not seeds) of the Coriandrum sativum plant, belonging to the parsley family. Used whole or ground to season curries, or to flavor pickling liquid.

Dates: A sweet, chewy fruit of the palm tree that when dried can be eaten as a snack. Also used in raw vegan pie crusts, crushed or processed with nuts.

Deep-fried tofu: Vacuum-packed blocks of deep-fried tofu. Substitute baked tofu. Aloha deep-fried tofu is available at Nijiya.

Dengaku sauce: A sweet and savory Japanese sauce made from miso, fermented soybean paste, mirin, sake, and sugar.

Yellow mustard: Made from finely crushed mustard seeds and "verjuice," an acidic juice made from unripe grapes. Robust and pungent in flavor with an intensified heat often used in vinaigrettes and sauces. Substitute whole grain mustard. Avoid mustard made with white wine as the wine is often not vegan.

Dill seeds: Technically not a seed, but an annual herb in the celery family often used for pickling. Substitute celery seed or coriander seed.

Edamame: Whole, immature soybeans that are soft and edible. Lightly boiled and salted edamame are a classic Japanese snack.

Extra-virgin olive oil: Made from pure, cold-pressed olives, whereas olive oil is a blend of both cold-pressed and processed oils.

Feta: A salty goat cheese. Substitute Tofeta.

Furikake Seasoning: Japanese condiment made from dried seaweed flakes, sesame seeds, sugar, salt, and other seasonings.

Garam masala: An aromatic blend of spices often used in Indian cooking. Substitute curry powder.

Garbanzo beans: See chickpeas.

Garbanzo flour: Also known as besan, chickpea flour, or gram flour; a popular ingredient for gluten-free baking. Substitute gluten-free flour. Available at Down To Earth.

Gochujang: A sweet, savory, and spicy fermented chili paste which is an essential ingredient in Korean cuisine. Substitute sriracha or Thai chili paste. Available at Palama Supermarket.

Green jackfruit: Unripe jackfruit; a relative of the fig and breadfruit family. With a stringy consistency similar to that of chicken or pork, it is used widely as a plant-based alternative to shredded meat. Substitute hearts of palm.

Green tea: A popular beverage made from camellia sinensis leaves and buds that are steamed, pan-fried, then dried out. Green tea leaves do not undergo the same withering and oxidation process used to make darker teas.

Haupia: Hawaiian coconut pudding.

Hawaiian Chili Pepper Water: A combination of a condiment and hot sauce made with water and vinegar infused with chili.

Hawaiian sea salt: Course, black, red, or white crystals made from evaporated seawater. Substitute Himalayan pink salt or Kosher salt.

Hoisin sauce: A fermented soybean paste with other flavors or spices used as a glaze, dipping sauce, or in stir-fries. Sweet, tangy, spicy and with an umami taste often used in Asian cooking.

Ichimi togarashi: Japanese chili pepper seasoning. Substitute chili powder. Available at Nijiya.

Italian seasoning: A blend of dried Italian-inspired herbs such as basil, oregano, rosemary, sage, and thyme.

Japanese eggplant: Long and narrow eggplants with a tender skin. Substitute regular eggplant.

Jarred sliced jalapeño: Sold often in jars, sweet and spicy pickled jalapeño peppers used in tacos, burgers, and dips such as guacamole. Substitute fresh jalapeño peppers.

Kabocha: Kabocha squash, or "Japanese pumpkin," is a sweet winter squash variety with a slightly bumpy dark green skin that is edible. Substitute pumpkin or butternut squash.

Kala namak: Himalayan black salt high in sulfur which gives food an "eggy" taste. Available at India Market.

Kappa carrageenan powder: Made from an edible seaweed and used as a binder, emulsifying stabilizer, thickening, and gelling agent in food.

King oyster mushroom: Also known as king trumpet mushroom; the largest of the oyster mushroom family, meaty in texture, and full of umami flavor.

Kombu dashi powder: Kelp granules often used in soup broths and stocks. A soup stock powder essential in Japanese dishes. Available at Nijiya.

Lemon extract: Made by extracting oil from ripe lemons, not the juice. Bold and pure in flavor, often used in baking and frosting. Substitute lemon zest.

Lemon pepper seasoning: A zesty sharp seasoning made from granulated lemon zest and cracked peppercorns. Substitute lemon zest and black pepper.

Li Hing powder: Made from dried, salted plums often sprinkled on tropical fresh or dried fruits such as mango, papaya, and pineapple. Sweet, salty, tart, and tangy in flavor, also used to rim glasses for cocktails. Available at Down To Earth.

Liquid aminos: A naturally vegan and gluten-free alternative to soy sauce. Liquid aminos are not fermented and contain no alcohol. Substitute coconut aminos or tamari. Bragg's Liquid Aminos are available in bottles and spray bottles at Down To Earth.

Liquid smoke: Made by condensing the smoke from hickory or mesquite wood chips burned at high temperatures resulting in a concentrated liquid. Used in a variety of dishes to contribute a smoky taste and aroma without cooking in the smoker.

Lūʻau: Hawaiian name for feast that usually includes prepared foods in an imu, or underground oven.

Lomi: Lomi lomi is taken from the method of preparation used for fish. Literally meaning "to massage" in Hawaiian.

Macadamia nuts: Round, oily nuts with a creamy, slightly crunchy texture. Harvested from trees and grown locally on the Big Island. Substitute pine nuts.

Maui onion: A sweet, mild onion, originally grown in the Kula district of Maui. Substitute sweet onion.

Meyer lemon: A cross between a lemon and a mandarin orange with a high volume of juice and slightly sweet in taste. Substitute regular lemon.

Mirin: Sweet Japanese rice wine.

Miso: A soybean paste made by salting and fermenting soybeans and rice. Often used in Japanese dishes such as miso soup.

Mousse: A sweet or savory dish, lighter and fluffier than pudding, with the consistency of a dense foam.

Mushroom seasoning: Dehydrated ground mushroom powder stirred into broths or added to sauces to give a savory umami flavor. Substitute kombu dashi powder. Available at Don Quijote.

Mustard seeds: Small round seeds of various mustard plants often used in pickling liquid. Available at Down To Earth.

Musubi: A ball of rice covered with nori to which a topping of meat or salted/fermented vegetables are added, differing from sushi in that the rice is not vinegared.

Nacho sauce: A creamy cheese sauce often drizzled over tortilla chips or used as a dip.

Natto: A traditional Japanese food made from soybeans that have been fermented. Often served at breakfast mixed with Japanese mustard, soy sauce, and green onion. Available at most Asian supermarkets.

Nori: Paper-thin sheets of seasoned, dried seaweed often used for sushi and musubi.

Nutritional yeast: Sometimes referred to as "nooch"; a deactivated yeast packed with B vitamins, including B12, sold in the form of flakes, granules, or powder. Nutty and cheesy in taste, it's often used as an alternative to Parmesan cheese that can be sprinkled over pasta, popcorn, or salads; added to sauces, cheese dishes, and soups, or any dish to enhance flavor. Substitute Vegan Parmesan cheese.

Okra: Also known as gumbo or ladies' fingers, has a long, slender, tube-like shape. Okra is a green seed pod with small edible seeds inside that becomes very slimy and sticky when cooked.

Oyster mushrooms: A common, cultivated mushroom with an oversized cluster of petal-like leaves that shrivel up and char around the edges when cooked. Meaty in texture and packed with umami flavors.

Papaya seed powder: Ground papaya seeds zesty in flavor used as a seasoning in salad dressings, smoothies, juices, desserts, or teas. Substitute Li Hing powder.

Panko: A crispy, flaked Japanese breadcrumb available in small, medium, or large flakes; used for crunchy deep-fried coatings.

Parmesan: An Italian hard cheese served grated on pasta

and salads or added to soups and sauce recipes. Violife 100% "just like Parmesan" is available at Whole Foods.

Plant-based milk: Consumed as an alternative to dairy-free milk made from plant-based ingredients such as almonds, cashews, coconuts, oats, and soybeans.

Poi: A paste made from steamed, pounded taro, pale purple in color with a delicate flavor and creamy mouth feel. Available at Whole Foods.

Poke: Hawaiian word for slice, poke is a traditional Hawaiian dish made of raw fish, Hawaiian salt, seaweed, and chilies.

Pulled jackfruit: Vegan alternative for pulled pork using jackfruit.

Raw cashews: Uncooked cashew nuts used to make vegan cheeses and desserts such as raw cheesecake.

Rolled oats: A lightly processed whole grain made from oat groats that have been de-husked and steamed before being rolled into flat flakes.

Sake: A slightly sweet Japanese rice wine used in Japanese cuisine.

Sangria: A mixed alcoholic drink from Spain made with red or white wine and often contains fresh fruit.

Short grain white rice: Short grain Japanese rice is chewy and sticky when cooked, perfect for sushi rice.

Shredded vegan cheese: Pizza cheese; pre-shredded and available in most supermarkets.

Sichuan peppercorn: A very fragrant spice from the Sichuan province of China, strong and pungent in flavor with slightly woody and lemony undertones. When bitten into, can give a unique tingly and numbing sensation to the mouth.

Slurry: A mixture of cornstarch and water used as a thickener in sauces or soups.

Soy curls: Dehydrated strips of soy protein that take on the texture of chicken and are used as a meat alternative. Substitute seitan strips.

Soy sauce: Also known as shoyu, the commonly-used Japanese name; a dark, salty liquid made from fermented soybeans, flour, salt, and water. A staple in most Asian cuisines. Substitute liquid aminos or tamari.

Smoked paprika: Made from smoke-dried chilies ground to a powder. Substitute sweet, mild, or hot paprika.

Spam: A salty mix of pork, water, salt, starch, sugar, and sodium nitrate packed in square-shaped tins.

Spicy chili crisp: Sold in jars, a crispy infused chili oil condiment made by simmering chili peppers, garlic, onion, and seasonings in oil.

Sriracha: A chili sauce made from a smooth paste of chili peppers, distilled vinegar, garlic, sugar, and salt. Substitute Sambal Oelek.

Stock: See broth.

Sushi: A Japanese dish of vinegar-flavored rice served with raw or cooked seafood, vegetables, and other morsels.

Sushi rice: Steamed white, short grain Japanese rice flavored with sushi vinegar.

Sushi vinegar: A mixture of rice vinegar, sake, salt, and sugar used to flavor rice for sushi.

Tapioca flour: A gluten-free starch extracted from the roots of the cassava plant. Often used in gluten-free baking and as a thickening agent in soups, sauces, and vegan cheeses. Substitute arrowroot flour. Available at Down To Earth.

Taro: A nutritious, starchy tuber used for making poi that can also be boiled or steamed and used in many traditional Hawaiian dishes.

Teriyaki sauce: A sweet and savory marinade or sauce generally made from soy sauce, sugar, sake, and mirin, sometimes flavored with garlic and ginger. Substitute BBQ sauce.

Thai basil: A member of the mint family, Thai basil has a stronger flavor than regular basil with slightly peppery notes and hints of anise and licorice.

Toasted coconut: Toasted coconut flakes used as a garnish or topping.

Toasted sesame seeds: Black or white sesame seeds toasted to enhance their nutty flavor and crunchy texture used as a garnish or topping. Essential ingredient in Japanese furikake seasoning.

Tofu: Japanese for soybean curd, used chiefly in Asian and vegan cooking.

Tofu scramble: A scrambled egg alternative using tofu and seasoned with kala namak (black salt) to give an "eggy" flavor.

Vegan butter: A vegan substitute for regular butter that is sold in many forms: tubs, sticks, olive oil-based, coconut-based.

Vegan cheese: Dairy-free cheese made from plant-based ingredients.

Vegan Chicken-less Seasoning Salt: Made from a blend of sea salt, onion powder, garlic powder, turmeric, celery seed, ginger powder, and black pepper. This seasoning conjures the flavor of chicken without actually containing chicken. Available online.

Vegan marshmallows: A soft, chewy confection usually made with sugar and gelatin. This product is gluten-free, dairy-free, kosher-friendly and 100% vegan with no gelatin, cornstarch, or artificial colors and flavorings. Available at Down To Earth.

Vegan mayonnaise: Dairy-free mayonnaise made from plant-based ingredients.

Vegetable stock powder: A seasoning made with dried herbs and spices used to flavor soups, stocks, and stews. Substitute kombu dashi powder or mushroom powder. VEGETA brand available online.

Wasabi: Pungent green Japanese horseradish condiment often mixed with soy sauce as a dipping sauce for sushi.

Worcestershire sauce: A fermented liquid condiment savory and sweet with a distinct tang from the vinegar. Flavored with anchovies, molasses, tamarind, onion, garlic, and other seasonings.

XO Sauce: A condiment made with dried seafood, chili, garlic, spices, and oil. Commonly used in Chinese cooking.

Yuba: A food product made from boiling soy milk in an open shallow pan until a film, or skin forms on the liquid surface. The film is collected and dried into sheets known as tofu skin. Available in Chinatown, Downtown.

Zest: Outer part of the peel of a citrus fruit used as a flavoring in baking or salad dressings.

INDEX

A

aburaage, 240
    Japanese Dashi Rice, 211
    Japanese Nabe, 105
açai
    Mermaid Açai Bowl, 225
agave syrup, 15, 26
    Baked Vegan Cheesecake with Macadamia Nut Crust, 238
    Bang Bang Broccoli, 42
    Berry Chia Pudding, 220
    Cashew Cream Cheese, 72
    Chocolate Mousse, 222
    Custard with Spicy Pineapple, 219
    Impossible Snicky Bites, 235
    Nutty Butter, 26
    Oil-Free Tofu Mayo, 28
    Paradise Salad, 120
    Peanut Butter Oat Bites, 66
    Peanut Dipping Sauce, 149
    Smoky Tofu Supam, 185
'ahi, 81
    Lomi Bell Pepper "'Ahi" Avocado, 124
'alaea
    Soup to Go, 116
almonds, 6, 8, 13, 22, 23
    Choose Your Mac Parm, 22
    Crunchy Granola, 226
    Nutty Butter, 26
    Peanut Butter Oat Bites, 66
    Rocky Beach Road, 236
Almost Borscht Roasted Beet Soup, 93
apple cider vinegar, 9
    Bang Bang Broccoli, 42
    BBQ Mushroom "Steak" with Cauliflower Mash, 199
    Cashew Brie, 156
    Cashew Cheese Sauce and Cheese Fondue, 160
    Cashew Cream Cheese, 72
    Cashew Mockarella, 158
    Cauliflower Steak with Cheese Peppercorn Sauce, 142
    Conpoy Dried "Scallop", 198
    Corn Okra Fritters, 76
    Crispy Oyster Chik'n, 180
    Mushroom Jerky, 204
    Oil-Free Tofu Mayo, 28
    Sun-Dried Tomato Cheese with Furikake, 162
    Tofeta Platter, 166
    Tofu Egg and Corn Macaroni Salad, 131
    Worcestershire Sauce, 34
apple juice
    Vegan Honey, 38

artichoke hearts
    Phishcakes with Sweet Chili Sauce, 48
avocado, 81, 119
    Avocado Chocolate Mousse, 222
    Green Avocado Pickles, 134, 202
    Lomi Bell Pepper "'Ahi" Avocado, 124
    Watermelon Chuna Poke Bowl, 87
avocado oil
    Island-Style Potato Salad, 132
    Tea Leaf Salad, 128

B

Bacon Seasoning, 170
Bahn Mi with Sesame Ginger Tofu, 150
Baked Mac and Cheese with Tofu Bacon Bits, 170
Baked Okinawan Sweet Potato with Garlic Herb Butter, 141
Baked Tofeta, 167
Baked Tofeta Pasta, 173
Baked Vegan Cheesecake with Macadamia Nut Crust, 238
Balsamic Glaze, 9, 125
    Caprese Tartare, 164
    Creamy Charred Brussels Sprouts Soup, 96
    Grilled Watermelon and Tofeta Salad with Balsamic Glaze, 125
    Stuffed Mini Peppers, 47
balsamic vinegar, 9, 122
    Balsamic Glaze, 125
    Spinach and Orange Quinoa Salad, 122
bamboo shoots
    Chik'n Hekka, 176
banana
    Mermaid Açai Bowl, 225
Bang Bang Broccoli, 42
basil
    Baked Tofeta Pasta, 173
    Caprese Tartare, 164
    Cavender's Seasoning, 196
    Lemon Dipping Sauce, 209
    Paradise Salad, 120
    Pea, Basil, and Mint Soup, 107
    Soup to Go, 116
    Sun-Dried Tomato and Sun-Dried Tomato Cashew Butter, 56
    Tofeta Platter, 166
BBQ Mushroom "Steak" with Cauliflower Mash, 199
beans, 3, 13
    black beans, 8
        Sweet Potato and Black Bean Soup, 115
    black-eyed peas
        Porky Bean Croquettes, 188

butter beans
    Almost Borscht Roasted Beet Soup, 93
    Creamy Charred Brussels Sprouts Soup, 96
    Pea, Basil and Mint Soup, 107
    Porky Bean Croquettes, 188
garbanzo beans, 8, 48
    Chuna Sandie, 73
    Roasted Corn Chowder, 111
    Roasted Eggplant and Chickpea Soup, 112
Japanese Curry Broth for Soups, Stews, and Noodles, 103
long beans
    Paradise Salad, 120
soybeans, 4, 175
white beans, 4
bean sprouts
    Bahn Mi with Sesame Ginger Tofu, 150
Beetiful Poke, 84
beets, 4, 15
    Almost Borscht Roasted Beet Soup, 93
    Beetiful Poke, 84
    Beet These Arancini, 44
    Chuna Sandie, 73
Beet These Arancini, 44
bell pepper, 17
    Caprese Tartare, 164
    Chinese Stir-Fry, 145
    Lomi Bell Pepper "'Ahi" Avocado, 124
    Soup to Go, 116
Berry Chia Jelly, 233
Berry Chia Pudding, 220
black olives
    Lemony Cream of Broccoli, 106
    Roasted Eggplant and Chickpea Soup, 112
blueberries, 4
    Berry Chia Jelly, 233
    Berry Chia Pudding, 220
    Lemon Berry Oatmeal Bars, 227
Bluffalo "Drumsticks", 183
bok choy
    Bok Choy Noodles with Creamy XO Sauce, 139
    Japanese Nabe, 105
broccoli, 13
    Bang Bang Broccoli, 42
    broccoli sprouts
        Chuna Sandie, 73
        Crispy Tofu Pockets with Dashi Sauce, 146
    Chinese Stir-Fry, 145
    Kale Slaw Potato Salad, 130
    Lemony Cream of Broccoli, 106
    Soup to Go, 116
Brussels sprouts
    Charred Brussels with Cranberries and XO Sauce, 140
    Creamy Charred Brussels Sprouts Soup, 96
burdock root
    Bluffalo "Drumsticks", 183

Japanese Nabe, 105
Moxtail Stew, 192

C
cabbage
    napa cabbage
        Japanese Nabe, 105
    red cabbage
        Kale Slaw Potato Salad, 130
    Soup to Go, 116
cakes, 3
    cheesecake
        Baked Vegan Cheesecake with Macadamia Nut Crust, 238
Candied Ginger, 59
Candied Hurricane Crispy Tofu, 65
Candied Hurricane Glaze Done 3 Ways, 62
Candied Hurricane Popcorn with Pecans, 62
Candied Hurricane Sweet Potato, 64
capers
    Carrot Smoked "Salmon" and Cashew Cream Cheese, 71
Caprese Tartare, 164
carrots, 4
    Almost Borscht Roasted Beet Soup, 93
    Bahn Mi with Sesame Ginger Tofu, 150
    Bluffalo "Drumsticks", 183
    Carrot Smoked "Salmon" and Cashew Cream Cheese, 71
    Chik'n Hekka, 176
    Japanese Nabe, 105
    Kale Slaw Potato Salad, 130
    Moxtail Stew, 192
    Roasted Eggplant and Chickpea Soup, 112
    Soup to Go, 116
    Tea Leaf Salad, 128
    Tofu Egg and Corn Macaroni Salad, 131
Carrot Smoked "Salmon" and Cashew Cream Cheese, 71
Cashew Brie, 156
Cashew Cheese of Mushroom Soup, 94
Cashew Cheese Sauce and Cheese Fondue, 160
Cashew Cream Cheese, 72
Cashew Mockarella, 158
cashews, 8
    Baked Vegan Cheesecake with Macadamia Nut Crust, 238
    Cashew Brie, 156
    Cashew Cheese Sauce and Cheese Fondue, 160
    Cashew Cream Cheese, 72
    Cashew Mockarella, 158
    Cauliflower Steak with Cheese Peppercorn Sauce, 142
    Chinese Stir-Fry, 145
    Chocolate Chili Cheese, 159
    Choose Your Mac Parm, 23
    Crunchy Granola, 226
    Impossible Snicky Bites, 235
    Japanese Curry Broth for Soups, Stews, and Noodles, 103
    Peanut Butter Oat Bites, 66

Pumpkin Pie Slice, 237
Rocky Beach Road, 236
Sun-Dried Tomato Cheese with Furikake, 162
Thai Basil Pesto, 31
cauliflower, 4
    BBQ Mushroom "Steak" with Cauliflower Mash, 199
    Cauliflower Steak with Cheese Peppercorn Sauce, 142
    Rich Cauliflower Potage, 108
    Soup to Go, 116
Cauliflower Steak with Cheese Peppercorn Sauce, 142
Cavender's Seasoning, 196
celery
    Bluffalo "Drumsticks", 183
    Chuna Sandie, 73
    Lobsta Roll, 74
    Moxtail Stew, 192
    Soup to Go, 116
Charred Brussels with Cranberries and XO Sauce, 140
Cheesy Veggie Greatin, 169
cherries
    Crunchy Granola, 226
    Spinach and Orange Quinoa Salad, 122
chia seeds, 8, 13
    Berry Chia Jelly, 233
    Berry Chia Pudding, 220
    Crunchy Granola, 226
Chik'n Hekka, 176
Chik'n Nuggets, 179
chili peppers
    Bahn Mi with Sesame Ginger Tofu, 150
    Hawaiian Chili Pepper Water, 33
    Island-Style Potato Salad, 132
    Paradise Salad, 120
Chinese Stir-Fry, 145
chipotle
    Chik'n Nuggets, 179
    Corn Okra Fritters, 76
    Stuffed Mini Peppers, 47
chocolate, 9, 215
    Avocado Chocolate Mousse, 222
    Chocolate Bark, 230
    Chocolate Chili Cheese, 159
    chocolate chips, 8, 215
        Chocolate Bark, 230
        Impossible Snicky Bites, 235
        Peanut Butter Oat Bites, 66
        Rocky Beach Road, 236
    Chocolate Covered Strawberries, 223
    Chocolate Sauce, 215, 228
        Chocolate Chili Cheese, 159
        Nutty Butter, 26
        Stuffed Dates, 228
    chocolate syrup, 159
    Nutty Butter, 26
Chocolate Bark, 230

Chocolate Chili Cheese, 159
Chocolate Covered Strawberries, 223
Chocolate Sauce, 228
Choose Your Mac Parm, 23
Choy Sum with Dengaku Sauce, 54
Chuna Sandie, 73
cilantro
    Bahn Mi with Sesame Ginger Tofu, 150
    Chuna Sandie, 73
    Corn Okra Fritters, 76
    Curry Kabocha Soup, 99
    Da Hawaiian Taro Spinach Soup, 101
    Island-Style Potato Salad, 132
    Phishcakes with Sweet Chili Sauce, 48
    Roasted Eggplant and Chickpea Soup, 112
    Soup to Go, 116
    Sweet Potato and Black Bean Soup, 115
    Tea Leaf Salad, 129
cocoa powder
    Avocado Chocolate Mousse, 222
    Chocolate Chili Cheese, 159
    Chocolate Sauce, 228
coconut, 2
    Chocolate Bark, 230
    Chocolate Covered Strawberries, 223
    coconut aminos, 5, 9
    coconut cream
        Baked Vegan Cheesecake with Macadamia Nut Crust, 238
        Cashew Cream Cheese, 72
        Pumpkin Pie Slice, 237
    coconut flakes
        Crunchy Granola, 226
        Peanut Butter Oat Bites, 66
    coconut milk
        Curry Kabocha Soup, 99
        Da Hawaiian Taro Spinach Soup, 101
        George's Vegnog, 197
        Haupia and Meyer Lemon Curd, 216
    coconut oil, 26
        Baked Vegan Cheesecake with Macadamia Nut Crust, 238
        Cashew Mockarella, 158
        Chocolate Sauce, 228
        Crunchy Granola, 226
        Lemon Berry Oatmeal Bars, 227
        Pumpkin Pie Slice, 237
    coconut sugar, 15
    Rocky Beach Road, 236
Conpoy Dried "Scallop", 198
cookies
    PB&J Cookie Sandwich, 232
corn
    Corn Okra Fritters, 76
    Corn Ribs, 67

Roasted Corn Chowder, 111
Soup to Go, 116
Tofu Egg and Corn Macaroni Salad, 131
cornmeal
Corn Okra Fritters, 76
Corn Okra Fritters, 76
Corn Ribs, 67
cranberries
Charred Brussels with Cranberries and XO Sauce, 140
Crunchy Granola, 226
Kale Slaw Potato Salad, 130
Peanut Butter Oat Bites, 66
Spinach and Orange Quinoa Salad, 122
cream cheese
Baked Vegan Cheesecake with Macadamia Nut Crust, 238
Carrot Smoked "Salmon" and Cashew Cream Cheese, 71
Cashew Cream Cheese, 72
Creamy Charred Brussels Sprouts Soup, 96
Crispy Baked Tofu, 53, 65, 85, 145, 202
Crispy Oyster Chik'n, 180
Crispy Tofu Pockets with Dashi Sauce, 146
Crispy Tofu Watercress Poke, 85
Crunchy Granola, 226
Crunchy Warm Cheese and Spinach Romaine Salad, 127
cucumber
Chuna Sandie, 73
Cucumber Sukemono, 89
Watermelon Chuna Poke Bowl, 87
Lobsta Roll, 74
Tofu Egg and Corn Macaroni Salad, 131
Cucumber Sukemono, 89
curry
Curry Kabocha Soup, 99
curry powder, 9
Curry Kabocha Soup, 99
Japanese Curry Broth for Soups, Stews, and Noodles, 103
Soup to Go, 116
Japanese Curry Broth for Soups, Stews, and Noodles, 103
Curry Kabocha Soup, 99
Custard with Spicy Pineapple, 219

D
Da Hawaiian Taro Spinach Soup, 101
daikon
Bahn Mi with Sesame Ginger Tofu, 150
Japanese Nabe, 105
Dalgona Whipped Coffee, 218
Darry & Lee's Sangria, 57
dates, 4, 215
Impossible Snicky Bites, 235
Peanut Butter Oat Bites, 66
Stuffed Dates, 228
Worcestershire Sauce, 34
Dave's Hydro Gin, 58
Dengaku Sauce, 53, 54

Dijon mustard, 11
dried fruit, 8
Chocolate Bark, 230
Chocolate Covered Strawberries, 223
Crunchy Granola, 226
Mermaid Açai Bowl, 225
Peanut Butter Oat Bites, 66
Pistachio Mac-Crusted Cheese, 165

E
edamame, 13
Island-Style Potato Salad, 132
XO Edamame, 37
eggplant
Caprese Tartare, 164
Japanese eggplant
Eggplant Unagi Don, 206
Roasted Eggplant and Chickpea Soup, 112
Eggplant Unagi Don, 206

F
furikake
Furikake Mac Parm, 23
Furikake Mayo, 28
Japanese Furikake, 24
Candied Hurricane Popcorn with Pecans, 62
King Oyster "Calamari", 208
Sun-Dried Tomato Cheese with Furikake, 162
Tofu Egg and Corn Macaroni Salad, 131
Furikake Mayo, 28

G
garam masala
Curry Kabocha Soup, 99
Japanese Curry Broth for Soups, Stews, and Noodles, 103
Soup to Go, 116
garbanzo flour
Bluffalo "Drumsticks", 183
Oyster Bacon Chickpea Frittata, 78
garlic, 4, 9, 81
Almost Borscht Roasted Beet Soup, 93
Baked Tofeta Pasta, 173
Cashew Cheese of Mushroom Soup, 94
Cauliflower Steak with Cheese Peppercorn Sauce, 142
Chik'n Hekka, 176
Chinese Stir-Fry, 145
Corn Okra Fritters, 76
Curry Kabocha Soup, 99
Da Hawaiian Taro Spinach Soup, 101
Garlic Confit, 32
Garlic Herb Butter, 141
Baked Okinawan Sweet Potato with Garlic Herb Butter, 141
garlic powder, 9
Baked Mac and Cheese with Tofu Bacon Bits, 170

Bang Bang Broccoli, 42
BBQ Mushroom "Steak" with Cauliflower Mash, 199
Beet These Arancini, 44
Bluffalo "Drumsticks", 183
Carrot Smoked "Salmon" and Cashew Cream Cheese, 71
Cashew Brie, 156
Cashew Cheese Sauce and Cheese Fondue, 160
Cauliflower Steak with Cheese Peppercorn Sauce, 142
Cavender's Seasoning, 196
Chik'n Nuggets, 179
Japanese Curry Broth for Soups, Stews, and Noodles, 103
Moxtail Stew, 194
Mushroom Jerky, 204
Oil-Free Tofu Mayo, 28
Oyster Bacon Chickpea Frittata, 78
Porky Bean Croquettes, 188
Smoky Tofu Supam, 185
Sun-Dried Tomato Cheese with Furikake, 162
Tofeta Platter, 166
Tofu Egg and Corn Macaroni Salad, 131
Worcestershire Sauce, 34
Hawaiian Chili Pepper Water, 33
Island-Style Potato Salad, 132
Lemon Dipping Sauce, 209
Lemony Cream of Broccoli, 106
Lemon Zucchini Pasta with Thai Basil Pesto, 153
Lobsta Roll, 74
Moxtail Stew, 192
Mushroom Walnut Pâté, 55
Orange Teriyaki "Scallops" with Japanese Dashi Rice, 210
Paradise Salad, 120
Peanut Dipping Sauce, 149
Phishcakes with Sweet Chili Sauce, 48
Pickle Mayo, 28
Pulled Mushroom "Pork" Tacos with Teriyaki Sauce, 202
Spicy Chili Crisp, 25
Spicy Mayo, 28
Spinach and Orange Quinoa Salad, 122
Stuffed Mini Peppers, 47
Sweet Potato and Black Bean Soup, 115
Tater Stacks, 50
Tea Leaf Salad, 128
Thai Basil Pesto, 31
Vegan "Scallop" Roll, 69
XO Sauce, 36
Garlic Confit, 32
Garlic Herb Butter, 141
George's Vegnog, 197
ginger, 9, 58
    Bahn Mi with Sesame Ginger Tofu, 150
    Candied Ginger, 59
    Chik'n Hekka, 176
    Chinese Stir-Fry, 145
    Curry Kabocha Soup, 99
    Da Hawaiian Taro Spinach Soup, 101

Dave's Hydro Gin, 58
Hawaiian Chili Pepper Water, 33
Japanese Curry Broth for Soups, Stews, and Noodles, 103
Japanese Nabe with Kombu Dashi Broth, 104
Paradise Salad, 120
Peanut Dipping Sauce, 149
Pineapple Ginger Honey, 38
Poke Dressing, 82
Pulled Mushroom "Pork" Tacos with Teriyaki Sauce, 202
Pumpkin Pie Slice, 237
Sesame Ginger Sauce, 150
Smoky Tofu Supam, 185
Spicy Chili Crisp, 25
Tea Leaf Salad, 128
Worcestershire Sauce, 34
XO Sauce, 36
gochujang
    Paradise Salad, 120
Green Avocado Pickles, 134
green onion, 81
    Bahn Mi with Sesame Ginger Tofu, 150
    Bang Bang Broccoli, 42
    Bok Choy Noodles with Creamy XO Sauce, 139
    Chik'n Hekka, 176
    Chinese Stir-Fry, 145
    Corn Okra Fritters, 76
    Eggplant Unagi Don, 206
    Island-Style Potato Salad, 132
    Japanese Nabe, 105
    Kalua Porky Plate with Spicy Pineapple, 187
    Miso Yaki Grilled Tofu, 51
    Oyster Bacon Chickpea Frittata, 78
    Phishcakes with Sweet Chili Sauce, 48
    Poke Dressing, 82
    Soup to Go, 116
    Stuffed Mini Peppers, 47
    Tea Leaf Salad, 128
    Watermelon Chuna Poke Bowl, 87
    XO Sauce, 36
Grilled Watermelon and Tofeta Salad with Balsamic Glaze, 125

H
Haupia and Meyer Lemon Curd, 216
Hawaiian chili pepper
    Hawaiian Chili Pepper Water, 33
        Island-Style Potato Salad, 132
    Poke Dressing, 82
Hawaiian Chili Pepper Water, 33
hearts of palm, 9
    Phishcakes with Sweet Chili Sauce, 48
hoisin sauce
    Bahn Mi with Sesame Ginger Tofu, 150
    King Oyster "Ribs", 191
Hot Honey, 38
Hurricane Glaze, 62

I

Impossible Snicky Bites, 235
Island-Style Potato Salad, 132

J

jackfruit, x
    Moxtail Stew, 192
    Porky Bean Croquettes, 188
jalapeños, 8, 81
    Cashew Cheese of Mushroom Soup, 94
    Chuna Sandie, 73
    Corn Okra Fritters, 76
    Miso Yaki Grilled Tofu, 51
    Roasted Corn Chowder, 111
    Sweet Potato and Black Bean Soup, 115
    Tea Leaf Salad, 129
Japanese Curry Broth for Soups, Stews, and Noodles, 103
Japanese Dashi Rice, 211
Japanese Furikake, 24
Japanese Nabe, 105
Japanese Nabe with Kombu Dashi Broth, 104
Japanese sweet potato, 64

K

kabocha
    Curry Kabocha Soup, 99
    Roasted Kabocha Poke, 83
    Thai Basil Pesto, 31
kala namak, 6, 9
    Oyster Bacon Chickpea Frittata, 78
    Tofu Egg and Corn Macaroni Salad, 131
kale, 4, 13
    Kale Slaw Potato Salad, 130
    Mac Parm Kale Chips, 68
    Soup to Go, 116
Kale Slaw Potato Salad, 130
Kalua Porky Plate with Chili Water Pineapple, 187
kappa carrageenan powder
    Cashew Brie, 156
    Cashew Mockarella, 158
    Chocolate Chili Cheese, 159
King Oyster "Calamari", 208
King Oyster "Ribs", 191
kombu, 14, 15
    Japanese Dashi Rice, 211
    Japanese Nabe with Kombu Dashi Broth, 104
    Kombu Dashi Broth, 104
        Japanese Nabe, 105
    kombu dashi powder, 9
        Carrot Smoked "Salmon" and Cashew Cream Cheese, 71
        Chuna Sandie, 73
        Japanese Furikake, 24
        Kombu Dashi Broth, 104
        Lobsta Roll, 74

        Soup to Go, 116
Kombu Dashi Broth, 104

L

Lemon Berry Oatmeal Bars, 227
Lemon Dipping Sauce, 209
Lemony Cream of Broccoli, 106
Lemon Zucchini Pasta with Thai Basil Pesto, 153
li hing powder
    Japanese Curry Broth for Soups, Stews, and Noodles, 103
limu, 81
    Island-Style Potato Salad, 132
    Poke Dressing, 82
liquid smoke
    Baked Mac and Cheese with Tofu Bacon Bits, 170
    BBQ Mushroom "Steak" with Cauliflower Mash, 199
    Bluffalo "Drumsticks", 183
    Carrot Smoked "Salmon" and Cashew Cream Cheese, 71
    Conpoy Dried "Scallop", 198
    Corn Ribs, 67
    Kalua Porky Plate with Spicy Pineapple, 187
    Moxtail Stew, 192
    Mushroom Jerky, 204
    Porky Bean Croquettes, 188
    Smoky Tofu Supam, 185
Lobsta Roll, 74
Lomi Bell Pepper "'Ahi" Avocado, 124

M

macadamia nuts
    Baked Vegan Cheesecake with Macadamia Nut Crust, 238
    Beetiful Poke, 84
    Choose Your Mac Parm, 23
    Custard with Spicy Pineapple, 219
    Island-Style Potato Salad, 132
    Nutty Butter, 26
    Peanut Butter Oat Bites, 66
    Poke Dressing, 82
    Roasted Kabocha Poke, 83
macaroni
    Baked Mac and Cheese with Tofu Bacon Bits, 170
    Tofu Egg and Corn Macaroni Salad, 131
Mac Parm Kale Chips, 68
mango
    Crunchy Granola, 226
    Paradise Salad, 120
    Rocky Beach Road, 236
maple syrup, 6, 9, 15, 26
    Avocado Chocolate Mousse, 222
    Baked Mac and Cheese with Tofu Bacon Bits, 170
    Baked Vegan Cheesecake with Macadamia Nut Crust, 238
    Bang Bang Broccoli, 42
    BBQ Mushroom "Steak" with Cauliflower Mash, 199
    Berry Chia Pudding, 220
    Cashew Cream Cheese, 72

Crispy Oyster Chik'n, 180
Crunchy Granola, 226
Custard with Spicy Pineapple, 219
Impossible Snicky Bites, 235
Mermaid Açai Bowl, 225
Moxtail Stew, 192
Mushroom Jerky, 204
Nutty Butter, 26
Oyster Bacon Chickpea Frittata, 79
Peanut Butter Oat Bites, 66
Peanut Dipping Sauce, 149
Smoky Tofu Supam, 185
Spinach and Orange Quinoa Salad, 122
Mermaid Açai Bowl, 225
mirin, 9, 51
Bahn Mi with Sesame Ginger Tofu, 150
Chik'n Hekka, 176
Choy Sum with Dengaku Sauce, 54
Crispy Tofu Pockets with Dashi Sauce, 146
Eggplant Unagi Don, 206
Japanese Dashi Rice, 211
Japanese Nabe with Kombu Dashi Broth, 104
Orange Teriyaki "Scallops" with Japanese Dashi Rice, 210
Pulled Mushroom "Pork" Tacos with Teriyaki Sauce, 202
Smoky Tofu Supam, 185
miso, 15
Conpoy Dried "Scallop", 198
miso paste, 9
Carrot Smoked "Salmon" and Cashew Cream Cheese, 71
Cashew Brie, 156
Cashew Cheese Sauce and Cheese Fondue, 160
Choy Sum with Dengaku Sauce, 54
Mushroom Jerky, 204
Phishcakes with Sweet Chili Sauce, 48
Sun-Dried Tomato Cheese with Furikake, 162
Miso Yaki Grilled Tofu, 51
Tea Leaf Salad, 128
Tofeta Platter, 166
Miso Yaki Grilled Tofu, 51
molasses, 9, 15
Bahn Mi with Sesame Ginger Tofu, 150
blackstrap molasses, 9, 13
Baked Mac and Cheese with Tofu Bacon Bits, 170
BBQ Mushroom "Steak" with Cauliflower Mash, 199
Chinese Stir-Fry, 145
Japanese Curry Broth for Soups, Stews, and Noodles, 103
Moxtail Stew, 192
Smoky Tofu Supam, 185
XO Sauce, 36
Worcestershire Sauce, 34
Moxtail Stew, 192
Mushroom Jerky, 204
mushrooms, 15
Cashew Cheese of Mushroom Soup, 94
cremini mushrooms

Mushroom Walnut Pâté, 55
Japanese Nabe with Kombu Dashi Broth, 105
king oyster mushrooms
Conpoy Dried "Scallop", 198
Kalua Porky Plate with Spicy Pineapple, 187
King Oyster "Calamari", 208
King Oyster "Ribs", 191
Orange Teriyaki "Scallops" with Japanese Dashi Rice, 210
Pulled Mushroom "Pork" Tacos with Teriyaki Sauce, 202
Vegan "Scallop" Roll, 69
Moxtail Stew, 192
oyster mushrooms
BBQ Mushroom "Steak" with Cauliflower Mash, 199
Crispy Oyster Chik'n, 180
Oyster Bacon Chickpea Frittata, 78
pink oyster mushrooms
Lobsta Roll, 74
shiitake mushrooms
Chik'n Hekka, 176
Japanese Dashi Rice, 211
Japanese Nabe, 105
Japanese Nabe with Kombu Dashi Broth, 104
Kombu Dashi Broth, 104
Mushroom Jerky, 204
Soup to Go, 116
XO Sauce, 36
Soup to Go, 116
mushroom seasoning, 9, 15, 24, 25, 36, 44, 47, 55, 69, 71, 73, 74, 89, 94, 101, 103, 104, 112, 116, 128, 139, 145, 146, 176, 180, 183, 185, 188, 191, 192, 198, 204
Mushroom seasoning, 14
Mushroom Walnut Pâté, 55
mustard, 11
Chik'n Nuggets, 179
Chuna Sandie, 73
hot mustard
Cucumber Sukemono, 89
Kale Slaw Potato Salad, 130
Lemon Dipping Sauce, 209
mustard powder
Worcestershire Sauce, 34
mustard seeds
A Wonderful World of Pickles, 134
Paradise Salad, 120
Spinach and Orange Quinoa Salad, 122
yellow mustard
Chik'n Nuggets, 179
Oil-Free Tofu Mayo, 28
Phishcakes with Sweet Chili Sauce, 48

N
noodles, 8
Bok Choy Noodles with Creamy XO Sauce, 139
cellophane noodles

Chik'n Hekka, 176
Soup to Go, 116
Japanese Curry Broth for Soups, Stews, and Noodles, 103
macaroni
Baked Mac and Cheese with Tofu Bacon Bits, 170
Tofu Egg and Corn Macaroni Salad, 131
rice noodles
Japanese Nabe, 105
nori, 8
Crispy Tofu Pockets with Dashi Sauce, 146
Cucumber Sukemono, 89
Eggplant Unagi Don, 206
Japanese Furikake, 24
Phishcakes with Sweet Chili Sauce, 48
Watermelon Chuna Poke Bowl, 87
nutritional yeast, 9, 15, 17
Baked Mac and Cheese with Tofu Bacon Bits, 170
Baked Vegan Cheesecake with Macadamia Nut Crust, 238
Beet These Arancini, 44
Bluffalo "Drumsticks", 183
Cashew Brie, 156
Cashew Cheese Sauce and Cheese Fondue, 160
Cashew Mockarella, 158
Cauliflower Steak with Cheese Peppercorn Sauce, 142
Chocolate Chili Cheese, 159
Choose Your Mac Parm, 23
Creamy Charred Brussels Sprouts Soup, 96
Garlic Herb Butter, 141
Japanese Curry Broth for Soups, Stews, and Noodles, 103
Lemony Cream of Broccoli, 106
Moxtail Stew, 192
Oil-Free Tofu Mayo, 28
Oyster Bacon Chickpea Frittata, 78
Porky Bean Croquettes, 188
Pumpkin Pie Slice, 237
Rich Cauliflower Potage, 108
Roasted Corn Chowder, 111
Stuffed Mini Peppers, 47
Sun-Dried Tomato Cheese with Furikake, 162
Thai Basil Pesto, 31
Tofu Egg and Corn Macaroni Salad, 131
nuts, 3, 5, 8, 13, 155, 215
Almost Borscht Roasted Beet Soup, 93
Avocado Chocolate Mousse, 222
Bahn Mi with Sesame Ginger Tofu, 150
Berry Chia Pudding, 220
cashews, 8
Baked Vegan Cheesecake with Macadamia Nut Crust, 238
Cashew Brie, 156
Cashew Cheese Sauce and Cheese Fondue, 160
Cashew Cream Cheese, 72
Cashew Mockarella, 158
Cauliflower Steak with Cheese Peppercorn Sauce, 142
Chinese Stir-Fry, 145

Chocolate Chili Cheese, 159
Choose Your Mac Parm, 23
Crunchy Granola, 226
Impossible Snicky Bites, 235
Japanese Curry Broth for Soups, Stews, and Noodles, 103
Peanut Butter Oat Bites, 66
Pumpkin Pie Slice, 237
Rocky Beach Road, 236
Sun-Dried Tomato Cheese with Furikake, 162
Thai Basil Pesto, 31
Charred Brussels with Cranberries and XO Sauce, 140
Chocolate Bark, 230
Chocolate Covered Strawberries, 223
Choose Your Mac Parm, 23
coconuts, 2
Crunchy Granola, 226
hazelnuts
Nutty Butter, 26
Peanut Butter Oat Bites, 66
'inamona
Poke Dressing, 82
macadamia nuts
Baked Vegan Cheesecake with Macadamia Nut Crust, 238
Beetiful Poke, 84
Choose Your Mac Parm, 23
Custard with Spicy Pineapple, 219
Island-Style Potato Salad, 132
Nutty Butter, 26
Peanut Butter Oat Bites, 66
Poke Dressing, 82
Roasted Kabocha Poke, 83
Mermaid Açai Bowl, 225
Peanut Butter Oat Bites, 66
peanuts
Impossible Snicky Bites, 235
Nutty Butter, 26
Paradise Salad, 120
Peanut Butter Oat Bites, 66
Rocky Beach Road, 236
pecans
Candied Hurricane Popcorn with Pecans, 62
Crunchy Granola, 226
Glazed Pecan Mac Parm, 23
Pumpkin Pie Slice, 237
Rocky Beach Road, 236
pine nuts
Pine Nut Mac Parm, 23
Pistachio Mac-Crusted Cheese, 165
Rich Cauliflower Potage, 108
Tea Leaf Salad, 129
walnuts, 13
Chili Walnut Mac Parm, 23
Crunchy Granola, 226
Lemon Zucchini Pasta with Thai Basil Pesto, 153

Mushroom Walnut Pâté, 55
Peanut Butter Oat Bites, 66
Rocky Beach Road, 236
Spinach and Orange Quinoa Salad, 122
Nutty Butter, 26

O

Oil-Free Tofu Mayo, 28
Okra Natto Poke, 86
olives
    black olives
        Lemony Cream of Broccoli, 106
        Roasted Eggplant and Chickpea Soup, 112
onion, 81
    Almost Borscht Roasted Beet Soup, 93
    Cashew Cheese of Mushroom Soup, 94
    Chik'n Hekka, 176
    Chuna Sandie, 73
    Crispy Tofu Pockets with Dashi Sauce, 146
    Curry Kabocha Soup, 99
    Da Hawaiian Taro Spinach Soup, 101
    Lemony Cream of Broccoli, 106
    Lobsta Roll, 74
    Maui onion
        Island-Style Potato Salad, 132
        Poke Dressing, 82
    Moxtail Stew, 192
    Mushroom Walnut Pâté, 55
onion powder, 9, 15
    Baked Mac and Cheese with Tofu Bacon Bits, 170
    Bang Bang Broccoli, 42
    BBQ Mushroom "Steak" with Cauliflower Mash, 199
    Beet These Arancini, 44
    Bluffalo "Drumsticks", 183
    Carrot Smoked "Salmon" and Cashew Cream Cheese, 71
    Cashew Brie, 156
    Cashew Cheese Sauce and Cheese Fondue, 160
    Cashew Cream Cheese, 72
    Cauliflower Steak with Cheese Peppercorn Sauce, 142
    Chik'n Nuggets, 179
    Conpoy Dried "Scallop", 198
    Corn Okra Fritters, 76
    Da Hawaiian Taro Spinach Soup, 101
    Japanese Curry Broth for Soups, Stews, and Noodles, 103
    King Oyster "Calamari", 208
    Moxtail Stew, 192
    Mushroom Jerky, 204
    Oil-Free Tofu Mayo, 28
    Oyster Bacon Chickpea Frittata, 78
    Pea, Basil, and Mint Soup, 107
    Porky Bean Croquettes, 188
    Roasted Corn Chowder, 111
    Smoky Tofu Supam, 185
    Stuffed Mini Peppers, 47
    Sun-Dried Tomato Cheese with Furikake, 162

Tater Stacks, 50
Tofu Egg and Corn Macaroni Salad, 131
Worcestershire Sauce, 34
red onion
    Carrot Smoked "Salmon" and Cashew Cream Cheese, 71
Rich Cauliflower Potage, 108
Roasted Corn Chowder, 111
Roasted Eggplant and Chickpea Soup, 112
Sweet Potato and Black Bean Soup, 115
Tea Leaf Salad, 128
Vegan "Scallop" Roll, 69
oranges
    Spinach and Orange Quinoa Salad, 122
Orange Teriyaki "Scallops" with Japanese Dashi Rice, 210
Oyster Bacon, 78
Oyster Bacon Chickpea Frittata, 78

P

papaya
    green papaya
        Paradise Salad, 120
    Rocky Beach Road, 236
Paradise Salad, 120
PB&J Cookies Sandwich, 232
Pea, Basil, and Mint Soup, 107
peanut butter, 9
    Impossible Snicky Bites, 235
    Nutty Butter, 26
    PB&J Cookie Sandwich, 232
    Peanut Butter Oat Bites, 66
    Peanut Dipping Sauce, 149
Peanut Butter Oat Bites, 66
peas
    Island-Style Potato Salad, 132
    Pea, Basil, and Mint Soup, 107
    Tea Leaf Salad, 129
    Tofu Egg and Corn Macaroni Salad, 131
pecans, 8, 62
peppers
    sweet mini peppers, 47
Phishcakes with Sweet Chili Sauce, 48
pineapple
    Custard with Spicy Pineapple, 219
    Kalua Porky Plate with Spicy Pineapple, 187
    Mermaid Açaí Bowl, 225
    Pineapple Ginger Honey, 38
    Rocky Beach Road, 236
    Twice Frozen Tofu Skewers with Peanut Dipping Sauce, 148
Pineapple Ginger Honey, 38
pine nuts
    Pine Nut Mac Parm, 23
    Rich Cauliflower Potage, 108
Pistachio Mac-Crusted Cheese, 165
Pistachio Mac Parm, 23
poi, 7, 212

poke, 81
    Beetiful Poke, 84
    Crispy Tofu Watercress Poke, 85
    Okra Natto Poke, 86
    Poke Dressing, 82
        Lomi Bell Pepper "'Ahi" Avocado, 124
    Roasted Kabocha Poke, 83
    Watermelon Chuna Poke Bowl, 87
Poke Dressing, 82
pomegranate
    Baked Vegan Cheesecake with Macadamia Nut Crust, 238
Porky Bean Croquettes, 188
potatoes
    Cashew Cheese of Mushroom Soup, 94
    Curry Kabocha Soup, 99
    Island-Style Potato Salad, 132
    Kale Slaw Potato Salad, 130
    Lemony Cream of Broccoli, 106
    Moxtail Stew, 192
    Rich Cauliflower Potage, 108
    Tater Stacks, 50
Pulled Mushroom "Pork" Tacos with Teriyaki Sauce, 202
pumpkin, 4
    Curry Kabocha Soup, 99
    Pumpkin Pie Slice, 237
    pumpkin seeds, 8
        Creamy Charred Brussels Sprouts Soup, 96
        Curry Kabocha Soup, 99
        Peanut Butter Oat Bites, 66
        Roasted Eggplant and Chickpea Soup, 112
        Spinach and Orange Quinoa Salad, 122
        Sweet Potato and Black Bean Soup, 115
    pumpkin spice
        Worcestershire Sauce, 34
Pumpkin Pie Slice, 237

Q

quinoa
    Spinach and Orange Quinoa Salad, 122

R

rice, 8, 81
    basmati rice
        George's Vegnog, 197
    Beet These Arancini, 44
    Japanese Dashi Rice, 211
        King Oyster "Ribs", 191
        Orange Teriyaki "Scallops" with Japanese Dashi Rice, 210
    Japanese Nabe, 105
    Kalua Porky Plate with Spicy Pineapple, 187
    Orange Teriyaki "Scallops" with Japanese Dashi Rice, 210
    Stuffed Mini Peppers, 47
    Sushi Rice, 207
        Eggplant Unagi Don, 206

    Watermelon Chuna Poke Bowl, 87
rice noodles
    Bok Choy Noodles with Creamy XO Sauce, 139
    Japanese Nabe, 105
rice vinegar
    A Wonderful World of Pickles, 134
    Bahn Mi with Sesame Ginger Tofu, 150
    Carrot Smoked "Salmon" and Cashew Cream Cheese, 71
    Chinese Stir-Fry, 145
    Crispy Oyster Chik'n, 180
    Crispy Tofu Pockets with Dashi Sauce, 146
    Hawaiian Chili Pepper Water, 33
    Paradise Salad, 120
    Peanut Dipping Sauce, 149
    Soup to Go, 116
    Sushi Rice, 207
    Tea Leaf Salad, 128
    Wasabi Mayo Dressing, 89
Rich Cauliflower Potage, 108
Roasted Corn Chowder, 111
Roasted Eggplant and Chickpea Soup, 112
Roasted Kabocha Poke, 83
Roasted XO Asparagus, 37
Rocky Beach Road, 236
rosemary
    BBQ Mushroom "Steak" with Cauliflower Mash, 199
    Cauliflower Steak with Cheese Peppercorn Sauce, 142
    Cavender's Seasoning, 196
    Moxtail Stew, 192
    Mushroom Walnut Pâté, 55
    Roasted Beet Soup, 93
    Tater Stacks, 50
rum
    Custard with Spicy Pineapple, 219
    Darry & Lee's Sangria, 57

S

salad dressing
    Creamy Lemon Dressing, 130
    Mango Dressing, 120
    Wasabi Mayo Dressing, 89
sesame oil
    Bahn Mi with Sesame Ginger Tofu, 150
    Candied Hurricane Sweet Potato, 64
    Chik'n Hekka, 176
    Chinese Stir-Fry, 145
    Crispy Tofu Watercress Poke, 85
    King Oyster "Ribs", 191
    Paradise Salad, 120
    Poke Dressing, 82
    Pulled Mushroom "Pork" Tacos with Teriyaki Sauce, 202
    Tea Leaf Salad, 128
    XO Sauce, 36
Sichuan pepper
    Spicy Chili Crisp, 25

Smoky Tofu Supam, 185
Soup to Go, 116
soy curls, 8, 175
    Bluffalo "Drumsticks", 183
    Chik'n Hekka, 176
Spicy Chili Crisp, 25
Spicy Cold XO Tofu, 37
Spicy Pineapple, 219
spinach, 4, 119
    Baked Tofeta Pasta, 173
    Chik'n Hekka, 176
    Chuna Sandie, 73
    Crunchy Warm Cheese and Spinach Romaine Salad, 127
    Da Hawaiian Taro Spinach Soup, 101
    Japanese Nabe, 105
    Moxtail Stew, 194
    Soup to Go, 116
    Spinach and Orange Quinoa Salad, 122
    Tea Leaf Salad, 128
    Vegan "Scallop" Roll, 69
Spinach and Orange Quinoa Salad, 122
sriracha
    Bahn Mi with Sesame Ginger Tofu, 150
    Crispy Baked Tofu, 53
    Hawaiian Chili Pepper Water, 33
    King Oyster "Ribs", 191
    Paradise Salad, 120
    Peanut Dipping Sauce, 149
    Spicy Mayo, 28
    Watermelon Chuna Poke, 87
strawberries, 215
    Berry Chia Jelly, 233
    Berry Chia Pudding, 220
    Chocolate Covered Strawberries, 223
    Lemon Berry Oatmeal Bars, 227
Stuffed Dates, 228
Stuffed Mini Peppers, 47
Sun-Dried Tomato and Sun-Dried Tomato Cashew Butter, 56
Sun-Dried Tomato Cheese with Furikake, 162
sunflower seeds, 26
Sushi Rice, 207
Sweet Chili Sauce, 49
Sweet Potato and Black Bean Soup, 115
sweet potatoes, 2
    Sweet Potato and Black Bean Soup, 115

T
tahini, 13, 81
    Watermelon Chuna Poke, 87
Tangy Chipotle Mayo, 76
taro, 2
    Da Hawaiian Taro Spinach Soup, 101
    Poi, 212
Tater Stacks, 50
Tea Leaf Salad, 128

Thai basil
    Chik'n Hekka, 176
    Crispy Baked Tofu, 53
    Da Hawaiian Taro Spinach Soup, 101
    Lemon Zucchini Pasta with Thai Basil Pesto, 153
    Paradise Salad, 120
    Thai Basil Pesto, 31
Thai Basil Pesto, 31
Tofeta, 125
    Baked Tofeta, 167
        Stuffed Dates, 228
    Baked Tofeta Pasta, 173
    Tofeta in Oil, 166
Tofeta in Oil, 166
Tofeta Platter, 166
tofu, 8, 9, 13, 103
    deep-fried tofu
        Bahn Mi with Sesame Ginger Tofu, 150
        Crispy Tofu Pockets with Dashi Sauce, 146
        Miso Yaki Grilled Tofu, 51
    extra-firm tofu
        Baked Mac and Cheese with Tofu Bacon Bits, 170
        Crispy Baked Tofu, 53
        Crispy Tofu Watercress Poke, 85
        Paradise Salad, 120
        Smoky Tofu Supam, 185
        Tofeta Platter, 166
        Tofu Egg and Corn Macaroni Salad, 131
        Twice Frozen Tofu Skewers with Peanut Dipping Sauce, 148
    fried tofu
        Japanese Dashi Rice, 211
    Japanese Nabe, 105
    silken tofu
        Bluffalo "Drumsticks", 183
        Corn Okra Fritters, 76
        Moxtail Stew, 192
        Oil-Free Tofu Mayo, 28
        Spicy Cold XO Tofu, 37
    Soup to Go, 116
Tofu Bacon Bits, 170
Tofu Egg and Corn Macaroni Salad, 131
tomato
    cherry tomato
        Baked Tofeta Pasta, 173
        Island-Style Potato Salad, 132
        Lomi Bell Pepper "'Ahi" Avocado, 124
        Sun-Dried Tomato and Sun-Dried Tomato Cashew Butter, 56
        Tea Leaf Salad, 128
    Chuna Sandie, 73
    fire-roasted tomato
        Moxtail Stew, 192
        Sweet Potato and Black Bean Soup, 115
    Lobsta Roll, 74

sun-dried tomato
    Creamy Charred Brussels Sprouts Soup, 96
    Sun-Dried Tomato Cheese with Furikake, 162
tomato paste, 9
    Moxtail Stew, 192
tomato sauce
    Curry Kabocha Soup, 99
    Japanese Curry Broth for Soups, Stews, and Noodles, 103
    Roasted Eggplant and Chickpea Soup, 112
tortillas
    Pulled Mushroom "Pork" Tacos with Teriyaki Sauce, 202
Twice Frozen Tofu Skewers with Peanut Dipping Sauce, 148

V

vegan cheese, 1, 3, 6, 8, 9, 155
    Baked Mac and Cheese with Tofu Bacon Bits, 170
    Baked Tofeta Pasta, 173
    Carrot Smoked "Salmon" and Cashew Cream Cheese, 71
    Cashew Brie, 156
    Cashew Cheese of Mushroom Soup, 94
    Cashew Cheese Sauce and Cheese Fondue, 160
    Cashew Cream Cheese, 72
    Cashew Mockarella, 158
    Cauliflower Steak with Cheese Peppercorn Sauce, 142
    Cheesy Veggie Greatin, 169
    Chocolate Chili Cheese, 159
    Chuna Sandie, 73
    Crunchy Warm Cheese and Spinach Romaine Salad, 127
    Oyster Bacon Chickpea Frittata, 78
    Pistachio Mac-Crusted Cheese, 165
    Pulled Mushroom "Pork" Tacos with Teriyaki Sauce, 202
    Sun-Dried Tomato Cheese with Furikake, 162
    Tofeta Platter, 166
    vegan Parmesan cheese
        Crunchy Warm Cheese and Spinach Romaine Salad, 127
        Garlic Herb Butter, 141
Vegan Honey, 38
veganism, 2
vegan mayonnaise, 9
    Bang Bang Broccoli, 42
    Chuna Sandie, 73
    Corn Okra Fritters, 76
    Kale Slaw Potato Salad, 130
    Lemon Dipping Sauce, 209
    Lobsta Roll, 74
    Phishcakes with Sweet Chili Sauce, 48
    Tofu Egg and Corn Macaroni Salad, 131
    Vegan "Scallop" Roll, 69
    Wasabi Mayo Dressing, 89
Vegan "Scallop" Roll, 69
vegetable broth, 91
    Almost Borscht Roasted Beet Soup, 93
    Cashew Cheese of Mushroom Soup, 94
    Chik'n Hekka, 176
    Creamy Charred Brussels Sprouts Soup, 96

Curry Kabocha Soup, 99
Da Hawaiian Taro Spinach Soup, 101
Japanese Curry Broth for Soups, Stews, and Noodles, 103
Moxtail Stew, 192
Pea, Basil, and Mint Soup, 107
Rich Cauliflower Potage, 108
Roaster Eggplant and Chickpea Soup, 112
Spinach and Orange Quinoa Salad, 122
Sweet Potato and Black Bean Soup, 115
vegetable stock powder, 9

W

wakame
    Island-Style Potato Salad, 132
    Japanese Nabe, 105
    Poke Dressing, 82
    Soup to Go, 116
Wasabi Mayo Dressing, 89
Watermelon Chuna Poke, 87
Watermelon Chuna Poke Bowl, 87
Wonderful World of Pickles, A, 134
Worcestershire Sauce, 34

X

XO Edamame, 37
XO Sauce, 36

Z

zucchini
    Lemon Zucchini Pasta with Thai Basil Pesto, 153

ABOUT THE AUTHOR

Lillian Cumic is the author of *Hawai'i A Vegan Paradise* and a vegan chef, cooking instructor, and recipe developer from Sydney, Australia. Lillian lived in Japan for thirty years and worked in the food industry, including as head chef/owner of Cocktail Oz, a vegetarian dining bar. She is the host of *Lillian's Vegan World* with ThinkTech Hawaii promoting the benefits of a vegan lifestyle and plant-based diet. Lillian graced the cover of CRAVE magazine, *MidWeek Hawai'i*, and was featured in the UK's *Vegan Food and Living magazine*.

Creator of Lillian Vegan on YouTube and Facebook, you can follow her journey on Instagram @lillianvegan_chefhawaii. Lillian and her husband, Dave, live in Honolulu with their cat, Lulu.